A CRITICAL

DICTIONARY OF PSYCHOANALYSIS

Charles Rycroft

Second Edition

PENGUIN BOOKS

PENGUIN BOOKS

Published by the Penguin Group
Penguin Books Ltd, 27 Wrights Lane, London w8 5tz, England
Penguin Books USA Inc., 375 Hudson Street, New York, New York 10014, USA
Penguin Books Australia Ltd, Ringwood, Victoria, Australia
Penguin Books Canada Ltd, 10 Alcorn Avenue, Toronto, Ontario, Canada m4v 3b2
Penguin Books (NZ) Ltd, 182–190 Wairau Road, Auckland 10, New Zealand

Penguin Books Ltd, Registered Offices: Harmondsworth, Middlesex, England

First published by Nelson 1968
Published in Penguin Books 1972
Second edition published 1995
3 5 7 9 10 8 6 4

Set in 10/12 pt Monophoto Bembo
Filmset by Datix International Limited, Bungay, Suffolk
Printed in England by Clays Ltd, St Ives plc

...YCHOANALYSIS

Charles Rycroft was born in 1914 and educated at Wellington College and Trinity College, Cambridge, where he took an honours degree in economics and was a research student in modern history. He took his MB at University College Hospital in London and worked as house physician at the Maudsley Hospital. He has had a private practice as a psychoanalyst since 1947, and from 1956 to 1968 he was a part-time Consultant in Psychotherapy at the Tavistock Clinic. In 1973 he became a Fellow of the Royal College of Psychiatrists. His books include *Anxiety and Neurosis* (1968), *Imagination and Reality* (1968), *The Innocence of Dreams* (1979), *Psychoanalysis and Beyond* (1985) and *Viewpoints* (1991). He has reviewed for the *Observer*, *The Times Literary Supplement*, the *New York Review of Books* and elsewhere.

PENGUIN REFERENCE BOOKS

A CRITICAL DICTIONARY OF PSYCHOANALYSIS

CONTENTS

ACKNOWLEDGEMENTS

I should like to express my gratitude to the late James Mitchell for suggesting that I construct this dictionary and for his moral support while I was doing so, and to Peter Ford, copy editor of both the first and second editions, for his labours in creating order out of an exceptionally chaotic manuscript.

CHARLES RYCROFT

AUTHOR'S NOTE

Cross-references are indicated by the use of bold type. The abbreviation *C.O.D.* is used to refer to the *Concise Oxford Dictionary*, *O.E.D.* to the *Oxford English Dictionary*, and *S.O.E.D.* to the *Shorter Oxford English Dictionary*.

INTRODUCTION

Psychoanalysis remains a sufficiently controversial subject for it to be perhaps necessary to state explicitly that this book is not a dictionary of criticisms of psychoanalysis but a critical dictionary of psychoanalysis. Its aim is not to provide ammunition for those who, for whatever reason, wish to demolish psychoanalysis, but to help those who need or wish to inform themselves about it to do so intelligently and critically. To this end its entries consist not merely of formal dictionary definitions of technical terms used in the analytical literature, but also give some account of their origin, of their connection with other terms and concepts used in analytical theory, and of the controversies relating to them that exist among analysts themselves. Extensive use has been made of cross-references which will, it is hoped, enable readers who look up one entry to discover the position it occupies within the total frame of reference of analytical theory.

Since the author is a practising psychoanalyst who was trained in the Freudian school, and since, furthermore, this dictionary has grown out of a notebook in which he recorded his puzzlement and doubts about certain aspects of Freudian theory, the term 'psycho-analysis' refers throughout, unless explicitly qualified, to Freudian psychoanalysis. This is not parochialism on the author's part but conformity to the usage generally current among those profession-ally involved in the field. For them the term 'psychoanalysis' refers specifically to the psychological theories and forms of treatment which derive directly from Freud and which are taught to students who seek training at any of the institutes affiliated to the Inter-national Psycho-Analytical Association. Other schools of thought, such as the Jungian, Adlerian, and existential, all of which are psychoanalytical in the popular sense, have their own distinguishing names and labels, the purpose of which is to ensure that their members are not mistaken for Freudians. Jungian analysts call themselves 'analytical psychologists' and their theory 'analytical psychology', Adlerians are 'individual psychologists', while existentialists talk of 'existential psychoanalysis'. These distinctions are a source of great confusion to the general public, which tends to be more impressed by the resemblances between the various psychotherapeutic schools than by their differences, and it is hoped that the relevant entries in this dictionary will do something to clarify matters.

For rather similar reasons I have included entries explaining the differing functions of psychiatrists, psychotherapists, psychoanalysts, and psychologists. These are words which cause considerable confusion to the laity, who frequently misuse them to the irritation of workers in the field who, like most professional people, dislike being incorrectly designated.

However, despite the fact that this dictionary contains fuller accounts of Freudian concepts than it does of those belonging to other schools, it is far from being exclusively Freudian. Its range is wider than, for instance, Laplanche and Pontalis's *Vocabulaire de la psychanalyse* (which is an introduction to psychoanalytical theory constructed in dictionary form), since it includes:

1. Definitions of psychiatric terms, particularly those used to describe symptoms and make diagnoses. These have been included for two reasons. First, most psychoanalysts are doctors. The disorders they treat and write about are regarded both by society at large and by the medical profession in particular as 'illnesses', and as such they are subject to the same procedures of description in technical language and diagnostic labelling as are physical illnesses. As a result, much of the psychoanalytical literature uses the technical, medical, and psychiatric vocabulary with which its authors and the readers for whom it was originally intended are at home. Secondly, many of these psychiatric terms have of recent years passed into general currency, without, however, retaining their original, precise meanings. As a result readers who are familiar with the journalistic and literary connotations of words such as 'manic', 'depressive', 'schizophrenic', 'compulsive', 'ambivalent' are liable to get confused when they encounter them in the psychoanalytical literature, where they are almost always used to refer to specific clinical phenomena.

Alternatively, and even worse, they may imagine that they are understanding what in fact they are not.

The same consideration applies, of course, to specifically psychoanalytical terms which have passed into general currency. For instance, 'narcissism', a term which was invented by Havelock Ellis to describe a form of sexual perversion, was borrowed by Freud to describe a variety of phenomena concerned with the individual's relation to himself, and has since passed into everyday language as a derogatory term, which the *Concise Oxford Dictionary* defines as: 'n. (psycho-anal.) Tendency to self-worship; absorption in one's own personal perfections.' Anyone reading the technical psychoanalytical literature with this definition in mind will, however, soon be in difficulties, since he will encounter references to narcissistic wounds, traumata, identifications, depletions, supplies which clearly have little if anything to do with self-worship, and will find distinctions being made between primary and secondary narcissism, or between healthy and defensive narcissism, which are obviously entirely unrelated to moral judgements.

2. Definitions of a number of specifically medical terms, which, for the reasons given above, psychoanalysts use without explanation.

3. Definitions of Jungian terms. Since the author suffers from the not uncommon constitutional defect of being incapable of understanding Jung's writings, it seemed fairer to the reader, and to Jung, to take these from E. A. Bennet's *What Jung Really Said* than to vamp them himself. Bennet was a close friend of Jung and his book explains Jung's ideas clearly and simply – indeed so clearly and simply that it leaves the reader wondering why Jung has ever been regarded as mystical or obscure.

4. Definitions and descriptions of the basic existential concepts. These have been included for a number of reasons. First, the writings of Sartre, R. D. Laing, and Rollo May have aroused considerable interest and discussion among both the general public and the psychotherapeutic professions. Secondly, many of the criticisms and doubts about the validity of a number of basic Freudian assumptions which have recently been voiced from within the Freudian fold are essentially existential in nature. I refer here

specifically to the doubts which have been expressed by Szasz, Home, Lomas, myself, and others as to whether the causal-deterministic assumptions of Freudian theory are valid, i.e. whether it is really possible to maintain that human behaviour has causes in the sense that physical phenomena do or that human personality can really be explained as the result of events that happened to it as a child. Thirdly, existential criticisms of Freudian psychoanalysis are, in general, well informed and made by persons who understand the nature of psychotherapeutic relationships and take subjective phenomena and suffering seriously. As a result they constitute a greater challenge than do the criticisms of Eysenck and the behaviour therapists, which derive from a theoretical position – that provided by learning theory – which is concerned to remove the psyche from psychology and attempts to understand human nature by dehumanizing it.

5. Definitions of a number of biological concepts which are necessary for an understanding of Freud's views on instinct and evolution.

6. Definitions of a number of anthropological concepts which are necessary for an understanding of Freud's speculative excursions into this field.

7. I have also included an entry about the maverick psychoanalyst Jacques Lacan.

Having given a brief account of the scope and aims of this dictionary, it is now necessary for me to describe some of the stumbling-blocks and pitfalls which beset the path of those who seek to discover what psychoanalysis is really all about. I must confess to a conviction that there is something daunting about the psychoanalytical literature and that many who venture to explore it get lost and confused – sometimes permanently. There are, I believe, three main reasons for this, which I shall discuss under the headings of linguistics, dissension, and sources.

LINGUISTICS

I have already referred to one of the linguistic stumbling-blocks to gaining entry into the psychoanalytical literature. This is jargon, the existence of a technical language constructed by psychoanalysts for communication among themselves. Some people object on principle to analytical jargon, maintaining that it should be possible to write about human experience without using technical terms, but I doubt whether those who take this view really appreciate how remote from everyday experience some abnormal mental states are. Nor are they taking into account the fact that sciences develop by classifying facts – a procedure which makes it necessary to attach definable labels to the classes so established – and by discovering latent connections (between apparently unconnected facts) which also require exact labels. Diagnostic terms, such as 'obsessional neurosis' and 'schizophrenia', and descriptive terms, such as 'Isakower phenomenon' or 'depersonalization', arise from the need to classify facts, while the technical terms used by psychoanalysis to formulate its theories of infantile development arise from the need for concepts to explain the hidden, developmental connection between childhood and maturity.

The misuse of jargon can, however, create pitfalls for the unwary, and indeed often does. One pitfall is created by the use of abstract explanatory concepts while describing facts, as occurs when analysts use technical terms while describing the data provided them by patients. Ideally case-histories are written in everyday language, theoretical concepts only being used during the ensuing discussion of the data, but all too often this ideal is not even aimed at, and the reader is only allowed to see the reported facts through a theoretical haze. As a result he is given no opportunity to consider the possibility that the facts presented to him might have been explained in some other way.

Another is the ease with which technical jargon can be used to construct theories which are tautologous, which are internally consistent and intellectually satisfying not because they really explain the facts but because the definitions of the technical terms involved interlock beautifully. To my mind, the fascination exerted on some analysts by Freud's cherished conception, the 'psychic apparatus', derives not from the accuracy with which it reflects the workings of the human mind but from the intellectual and aesthetic appeal of an internally consistent theory. Its bits fit together perfectly and would continue to do so even if it were proved to be nonsense.

Yet another pitfall is that created by the use of jargon to conceal ignorance. Learned words, particularly if derived from an ancient tongue, sound impressive and can be used to impress the innocent. Psychiatrists, following a long-established medical tradition, are more often guilty of this form of unconscious deception than are the analysts, the procedure or trick being to translate the patient's complaint into Greek and then assure him that his troubles are due to an illness with an outlandish and exotic name. The patient complains that he has lost his memory, so the physician tells him he is suffering from *amnesia*; the patient is frightened of open spaces and the physician tells him he has *agoraphobia*. And curiously enough both parties to the transaction feel better for it, the physician because he feels he has done something, the patient because his suffering has found a label which renders it less mysterious. Freud himself seems to have been remarkably free from the tendency to be duped by words, and one of the least-sung achievements of psychoanalysis has been to rescue psychiatry from a preoccupation with the art of diagnostic labelling by demonstrating that it is dynamic processes not states of mind that count.

Having circumvented jargon, the reader who is determined to come to grips with psychoanalysis next has to contend, if he is English, with the complications arising from the fact that most of the psychoanalytical literature was originally written, and even more of it originally thought out, in German. Unfortunately ideas cannot be transported bodily from one language to another simply by translating them word by word and the possibility has to be seriously envisaged that something significant happens to an idea or a theory when it is translated into another language. Like immigrants, ideas from a foreign tongue are only assimilated with difficulty, and by the time they have been naturalized they are likely to have changed. Geoffrey Gorer, in an essay entitled 'Cultural Community and Cultural Diversity', pointed out that those four freedoms – freedom of speech, freedom of religion, freedom from want, and freedom from fear – of which we heard so much in the later days of the Second World War, do not in fact make sense in any language other than English, for the simple reason that no other language possesses a word analogous to our 'freedom', which can embrace both 'not being prevented from' and 'being protected from'. Similarly a number of psychoanalytical concepts do not travel well and create difficulties for readers who have to encounter them at second hand.

One of the key concepts of Freudian theory is *Angst*, which all English translators render 'anxiety'. No one has suggested a better translation than this, but unfortunately the range of meanings covered by *Angst* and 'anxiety' are not identical. *Angst* seems to be inextricably involved with ideas of anguish, fear, and pain and not to be all that closely tied to the notion of futurity, while 'anxiety' is, as *Roget's Thesaurus* puts it, one of the 'prospective affections' and can even be used to refer to pleasurable anticipation – 'I'm anxious to see such and such a film.' As a result of this linguistic discrepancy between English and German, anxiety always features in the analytical literature as an unpleasant experience which the individual seeks to avoid or to rid himself of and never as an eager preparedness to embrace the future. It is also used, particularly in the form of 'primary anxiety', to refer to experiences which an English writer would be inclined to describe as fright or terror. One curious and unfortunate consequence of this equation of anxiety with *Angst* has been the dissemination of the idea that anxiety is always a neurotic symptom and that the ideal 'healthy', 'adjusted' person would be 'anxiety-free'. This idea belongs, however, more to popular psychiatric folklore of the American variety than to psychoanalytical theory.

But it is not only single words that cause difficulties. It is also linguistic structure and the habits of thought that are both engendered and reflected by it. Freud's writings are permeated by the idea of opposites in conflict with one another. Until the 1920s he based his theory of neurosis on the assumption that there were two groups of instincts – the sexual (reproductive) and ego (self-preservative) instincts – and maintained that the human predisposition to neurosis derived from the inherent tendency of these two opposed forces to come into conflict with one another. But, one may ask, why did Freud assume that there were two groups of instincts and not three or four, and why did he assume that they were opposed and not complementary to one another? Was it really because the clinical facts compelled him to make these assumptions, or was it perhaps because linguistic habits of thought impelled him to follow Hegel and Marx and to construct a dialectical theory which came naturally to him but which seems alien to those who have been nurtured on the English language and on English empiricism? One's suspicion that the latter explanation is correct, that Freud's preoccupation with opposites was culturally and linguistically predetermined, is increased and indeed confirmed by the fact that when, in the 1920s, Freud proposed an entirely new theory of instincts, this new theory was again one of two groups of instincts, the Life and Death instincts, which were again assumed to be inherently opposed to one another. This new theory was also frankly speculative and, as we now know, totally misguided, since it was based on a misunderstanding of the second law of thermodynamics and on unwarrantable deductions from the fact that organisms are poisoned by their own excreta.

As I mention at several points in the main text of this book, contemporary animal psychology recognizes at least seven instincts (or innate behaviour patterns) and sees no necessity to assume inherent opposition between any two groups of them – though it does, of course, maintain that on specific occasions any two or more may be in conflict with one another.

Another aspect of psychoanalytical theory which is, I suspect, essentially Germanic is its habit of explaining behaviour by reference to hypothetical forces such as 'Sex', 'Aggression', 'Love', and 'Hate', which are conceived to impel the individual by, as it were, pushing him along from behind. These concepts presumably arise in the first instance from the need to generalize experiences of loving, hating, and being aggressive, and in English their gerundive nature (i.e. the fact that they are nouns derived from verbs and refer to processes and actions and not to things) is indicated by the absence of a preceding article. In German, however, abstract nouns are frequently preceded by a definite article and are treated grammatically as things with properties. I have recently read an article by myself translated into German and it includes frequent references to 'the childhood', 'the consciousness', 'the psychoanalysis', 'the cosmology', etc., when I have been using these ideas generally and have not been referring to any particular person's childhood or cosmology. It seems to me that one of the effects of this grammatical reification of abstract nouns must be to encourage belief in the real existence of abstractions and the propensity to invoke them as explanatory agents, as essences or noumena actuating behaviour in a way that is reminiscent of the angels which medieval cosmology invoked to explain the movements of the planets. These angels enabled the problem of how inanimate objects could move to be solved by postulating the existence of living creatures who pushed them along. Rather similarly, Freud assumed that the human ego was a passive entity lacking energy or force of its own and therefore only capable of movement in so far as it was acted upon by forces external to itself, these forces being located either in the Id (Unconscious) or the environment. But the idea that each individual has an 'I', an ego, on which some other unconscious part of himself acts, is itself an artefact of language, which arises as a result of treating 'I' as first a noun and then as a concrete one; the facts of the matter are that we do things, but that on occasion our acts are not those we intended; e.g. we make slips of the tongue, or are forced to realize that our motives were other than we thought.

Another difficulty confronting English readers of the psychoanalytical literature derives from the fact that English differs from German in having in effect two vocabularies, one largely Anglo-Saxon in origin, which is used as the vehicle of ordinary social intercourse, and another largely derived from Latin and Greek, which is used for conceptual thinking. In German the word for referring to oneself is *ich* and that for conceptual thinking about the idea of oneself is *das Ich*, but in English the equivalent terms are 'I' and 'ego'. As a result it is easy for an English reader of the psychoanalytical literature to lose sight of the fact that the ego, which is so often presented to him as though it were an impersonal structure with properties and characteristics and occasionally even a shape, is really nothing other than himself being thought of in conceptual terms.

The classic example of this particular difficulty is provided by the noun 'cathexis' and its companion verbs 'to cathect' and 'to decathect'. These words, which have mystified countless English-speaking students of psychoanalysis, were invented by Freud's English translators for the purpose of rendering his concept *Besetzung*. In German, *Besetzung* is an ordinary, everyday, homely word, related to *setzen*, 'to place or set', and can be used to describe such activities as garrisoning a town, manning a ship, putting money on a horse, stocking a pond with fish – to cite only examples taken from a school dictionary. In psychoanalytical theory, however, it is used to describe one of Freud's most obscure and difficult concepts: the hypothesis that there exists some form of mental energy 'which possesses all the characteristics of a quantity (though we have no means of measuring it), which is capable of increase, diminution, displacement and discharge, and which is spread over the memory traces of ideas somewhat as an electric charge is spread over the surface of a body' – Freud (1894). According to this hypothesis, ideas (i.e. mental images in the mind) are *besetzt*, or invested, with some sort of mental energy, and psychological changes, such as shifts in interest or personal attachments, are accompanied by changes in the *Besetzung* attached to the ideas corresponding to the things or persons involved. This is not an easy concept to grasp, but in German the reader's difficulties must presumably be mitigated by the fact that the word *Besetzung* is a familiar one which inevitably conjures up images which help to explain its meaning in its novel context. In English, on the other hand, the word 'cathexis' evokes no such images and effectively dissociates the theoretical concept from the metaphors which could give it life and meaning. It also fails to remind the reader that there must be a person or agent lurking somewhere inside the machinery who is doing the cathecting and decathecting.

Freud, incidentally, was himself unhappy about the introduction of this neologism into English in 1922, but he must have become reconciled to it, since he later used it himself in German.*

Ego and cathexis are, apparently, not the only instances of psychoanalytical technical terms which sound more impersonal and abstract in English than they do in German. Indeed, according to Brandt (1961), the majority of them have suffered a regrettable sea-change in their passage from German to English, in some instances having lost an essential part of their meaning and in others having lost vital associative overtones. Whether Brandt is right about this I am not qualified to say, but certainly the argument that psychoanalysis is only comprehensible if read in the original German

* See Strachey's footnote on page 63 of the Standard Edition, vol. III.

is a gambit not uncommonly used by continental analysts in controversy with English ones. If he is, it would, however, do much to
explain the curious impression one sometimes gets that psychoanalysis has not got its feet on the ground and is not about people after
all. In the main text of this work I have drawn attention to gross
discrepancies between English and German connotations whenever
I have been aware of them.

Until recently it was almost universally accepted that James
Strachey's translation of Freud, the Standard Edition, was excellent,
but in 1983 Bruno Bettelheim attacked it vigorously, asserting that
Strachey had made Freud sound like a detached Victorian scientist
when in fact he had been a humanist who wrote in the language of
the people. Bettelheim objected particularly to the fact that Strachey
used the word 'mind' to translate the German *Seele*; he should have
translated it 'soul', Freud's atheism notwithstanding. Since Bettelheim's polemic, the desirability and feasibility of a new translation
has been a talking-point among English and American analysts.

DISSENSION

It is a notorious and melancholy fact that psychoanalysts lack the
capacity to agree among themselves and that their professional
organizations exhibit an apparently inherent tendency towards fission. Their disruptive controversies are typically not of the minor,
technical kind which occur in every science and branch of medicine,
but concern fundamental principles, even though they are often
found to involve clashes of personality and temperament when
viewed historically. The original dissensions between Freud, Jung,
and Adler are by now past history and well known and perhaps
even generally understood – on the basis that Freud believed in Eros
and Reason, that Adler believed in power and self-assertion, and
that Jung was a mystic – but the unsuspecting inquirer into contemporary psychoanalysis is likely to be led astray unless he realizes that
radical differences of opinion exist within the Freudian fold itself
and that these are of sufficient seriousness to be reflected in the
structure of psychoanalytical institutions. In Great Britain, for instance, the theoretical differences between sub-schools have necessitated the establishing of conventions (the so-called 'Gentleman's

Agreement') to prevent the British Psycho-Analytical Society ever being taken over by one of the three groups into which it is divided, and parts of its training scheme are run in duplicate. In a number of other countries, the absence of a native genius for compromise has led to complete fission with, usually, one of the resulting fragments resigning or being expelled from the International Psycho-Analytical Association.

This is not the place to discuss the historical and psychological reasons for these dissensions, but several entries in this dictionary are designed to explain the theoretical points at issue. See particularly **classical (analytical) theory**, **classical analytical technique**, **ego psychology**, **Fairbairn's revised psychopathology**, **instinct theory and object theory**, **Kleinian**, **Kohut**, **personology**, **process theory**, and **Winnicottian**. Their existence does, however, make it necessary for me to alert prospective readers of the psycho-analytical literature to a number of hazards of which he might otherwise be unaware.

First, books and papers which appear to be merely contributions to the understanding of some particular psychological problem or illness and which read as though they were expressing a generally accepted point of view, may in fact be highly controversial and propaganda in favour of the author's own theoretical position. It would be invidious to cite examples of this, particularly since demonstrating the ability of a scientific theory to explain specific phenomena is, of course, a legitimate way of advancing it.

Secondly, references to the 'classical' literature and quotations from Freud's own writings which occur in papers written by contemporary analysts are sometimes dictated not by scientific good manners, which demand that an author should acknowledge his sources, but by the writer's need to make covert appeals to authority in order to legitimize the ancestry of his theories or to ward off charges of unorthodoxy. The reasons for anyone wanting, or feeling it necessary, to be devious in this way derive from two sources: the early history of the psychoanalytical movement, which has left it with traumatic, tribal memories of earlier, primal secessions; and the fact that every analyst has been analysed during his years of training by some other analyst senior to himself and nearer to Freud. This feature of psychoanalytical training has led to the development of a mystique analogous to that of the Apostolic Succession, which compels contemporary analysts to trace their lineage back to one or other of the founding fathers. Analysts are in general extremely curious to discover by whom an unfamiliar colleague was analysed and are often inclined to judge his worth by his descent rather than by his own qualities. Future historians of psychoanalysis will no doubt find it necessary to construct pedigrees tracing the analytical lineage of third- and fourth-generation analysts.

Since many people find these aspects of the psychoanalytical literature rather shocking, it should perhaps be mentioned that covert in-fighting and the citing of authorities to give a cloak of academic respectability to new but unpopular ideas are phenomena not unknown in other disciplines. Nor would it always be difficult to construct academic family trees of discipleship.

Thirdly, although these internal dissensions and theoretical divergences can be regarded as signs of vitality and as evidence that psychoanalysis has not succumbed to the dogmatism of which it is so often accused, they also make it difficult for the uninitiated to know which books on psychoanalysis are definitive, authoritative, and sound and which are controversial, unorthodox, and uninformed – a difficulty which is enhanced by the fact that psychoanalysis has its lunatic and quack fringes and that many unscrupulous writers have been prepared to cash in on a vogue for psychoanalysis and the ubiquity of neurotic suffering. I have, therefore, given bibliographical references throughout this dictionary which will, I hope, help readers to find their way either to the original sources or to clear and reliable expositions. The following notes may also be helpful as a guide to the various psychoanalytical schools:

1. Classical psychoanalysis was summarized by Freud himself in his last work, *An Outline of Psycho-Analysis* (1940).
2. Ego psychology received its initial impetus from Freud's *The Ego and the Id* (1923), and has since been elaborated by Anna Freud in her *The Ego and the Mechanisms of Defence* (1937) and by Heinz Hartmann in his *Ego Psychology and the Problem of Adaptation* (1937; English translation 1958).
3. Kleinian psychoanalysis: Mrs Klein's own writings are not for the uninitiated, but her views have been ably summarized by Hanna

Segal in her *Introduction to the Work of Melanie Klein* (1964), and, more recently, by R. D. Hinshelwood in his *A Dictionary of Kleinian Thought* (1989).

4. Object (relations) theory: W. R. D. Fairbairn's *Psychoanalytical Studies of the Personality* (1952) provides the seminal and most lucid exposition, and H. Guntrip's *Personality Structure and Human Interaction* (1961) the most enthusiastic. For more recent American versions of object theory, see Otto Kernberg's *Object Relations Theory and Clinical Psychoanalysis* (1976) and Greenberg and Mitchell's *Object Relations in Psychoanalytic Theory* (1983). Just to confuse matters, Mrs Klein and D. W. Winnicott are usually, but by no means always, regarded as object theorists. D. W. Winnicott's *Collected Papers* (1958) and Marjorie Brierley's *Trends in Psycho-Analysis* (1951) are also essential reading for anyone who wishes to understand object theory and its connections with classical psychoanalysis and ego psychology.

5. Existential psychoanalysis: Rollo May's *Psychology and the Human Dilemma* (1967) provides a clear account of the issues separating Freudian and existential psychoanalysis, but the writings of R. D. Laing make more lively reading.

6. Jungian psychoanalysis (analytical psychology): As I have already mentioned, Jung's point of view has been clearly summarized by E. A. Bennet in his *What Jung Really Said* (1966). See also Storr's Modern Masters *Jung* (1973) and his *Jung: Selected Writings* (1983). Samuels, Shorter, and Plaut's *A Critical Dictionary of Jungian Analysis* (1986) was partly inspired by the first edition of this present work.

The various controversies and dissensions within the psychoanalytical movement obviously raise the possibility that this dictionary is itself propaganda in favour of some particular theoretical standpoint. It is therefore necessary for me to state my own position briefly and to make explicit the direction of any bias this dictionary may show. In two respects I have already done so. In earlier paragraphs I have made it clear that I ally myself with those analysts who have become sceptical about the validity of applying causal-deterministic principles derived from the physical sciences to the study of living beings who are capable of consciousness and of creative activity; and I have also expressed the opinion that Freud's instinct theory is incompatible with contemporary biological ideas about the nature of instinct. Here I must add that, for reasons which will become clearer during the next section of this Introduction, I believe psychoanalytical theory will eventually have to be re-formulated as a communication theory and that it will have to reflect conceptually the source of its own data. At present, psychoanalysis is formulated *as though* it was based on the objective and detached scrutiny of isolated examples of the species *Homo sapiens* by a totally uninvolved spectator, but in fact, or so it seems to me, its insights arise out of the relationship that develops when two people are gathered together in a psychotherapeutic setting. Of existing psychoanalytical theories, object-relations theory undoubtedly comes nearest to taking account of interpersonal communication, but since most of the data and insights which analysts have accumulated over the last seventy years have been recorded in the language invented by Freud and the first generation of his pupils, anyone who intends to practise psychotherapy of any kind, or who for any other reason is serious about acquiring an understanding of psychoanalysis, remains under a moral obligation to learn that language too.

SOURCES

It remains for me to mention the last stumbling-block lying in the path of anyone who wishes to master the psychoanalytical literature. This is the fact that the source and origin of psychoanalytical ideas lie in a process which it is not easy either to describe or imagine. This difficulty is indeed so great that many analysts, including Freud* himself, have taken the view that psychoanalysis is incomprehensible to anyone who has not themselves been analysed. Although this is an extreme position which, if taken seriously, would compel one to regard psychoanalysis as an esoteric cult with tenets only accessible to the initiated, it does none the less draw attention to an

---

* 'You can believe me when I tell you that we do not enjoy giving an impression of being members of a secret society and of practising a mystical science. Yet we have been obliged to recognize and express as our conviction that no one has a right to join in a discussion of psychoanalysis who has not had particular experiences which can only be obtained by being analysed oneself' – Freud (1933).

important fact about psychoanalysis: its data are derived not from the direct observation of human behaviour in everyday life, but from the analyst's experience of a particular kind of therapeutic relationship invented by Freud. When Freud stopped hypnotizing his patients and instead allowed, indeed encouraged, his patients to talk to him without let or hindrance, he initiated a new kind of human relationship and set in action a number of totally unexpected processes which psychoanalytical theory seeks to explain.

An obvious example of the dependence of psychoanalytical theory on the therapeutic relationship is provided by the concept of transference. This concept seeks to explain a specific clinical observation, viz. that patients whose utterances are allowed to flow freely without being disciplined by reminders of the actual nature of the person they are talking to give unmistakable evidence that they regard him as though he were someone other than the person he is – and that typically this other person is one or other of the patient's parents. To account for this fact, Freud introduced the idea of transference, which enabled him to explain it by saying that his patients transferred on to him emotions, ideas, and expectations which belonged, in the first instance, to their relationship to their parents. Since, however, these emotions and expectations are typically of a kind that one would expect a child and not a grown-up to have, and since, in addition, they indicate a greater degree of preoccupation with their parents than adult patients readily admit to, the concept of transference leads inevitably to three other basic analytic concepts: those of fixation, resistance, and the existence of unconscious mental processes, by means of which transference can be explained as the result of unconscious fixation on significant objects in the patient's childhood.

This example of transference is a particularly telling one since, as we know from his writings, Freud initially regarded it as a disturbing factor which interfered with what he at first thought was the essential analytical process – that of reviving repressed memories and enabling the patient to discharge the pent-up emotions associated with them. It was, indeed, Freud's eventual recognition that 'finally every conflict has to be fought out in the sphere of transference' which transformed psychoanalysis from a quasi-neurological theory about the pathological effects of inhibition into an investigation of the nature and origin of interpersonal relationships.

Rather similarly, the concept of infantile sexuality arose not as the result of direct observations of infants at the breast, or of children at play or being house-trained, but as an attempt to explain themes recurrently encountered in the free associations (spontaneous utterances) of adult patients. The idea that hysterical patients were fixated at the phallic level, that obsessional patients were fixated at the anal level, or melancholic patients at the oral level derives not from studies made in childhood of children who later developed hysterical, obsessional, or melancholic illnesses, but from the fact that adult patients with these illnesses recurrently and obsessively returned to childhood recollections which suggested that they had gone through phases in which they had been preoccupied, both anxiously and pleasurably, with their genitals or their bowel functions; or, in the case of melancholic patients, that they were nostalgic about some unremembered bliss and were curiously preoccupied with their mouths.

This example differs, however, from that of transference in that the concept of infantile sexuality, and its companion, the concept of infantile stages of libidinal development, contains a higher concentration of inference. Whereas transference phenomena can be directly observed, since the analyst has immediate personal experience of his patients treating him as a father- or mother-figure, and may indeed sense paternal and maternal responses being evoked in himself, the concept of infantile sexuality is a construct built up by piecing together fragmentary pieces of evidence, such as obsessive recollections, recurrent dream imagery, and details of symptoms, to form a theoretical pattern. As a result, the theory is in principle capable of criticism, re-evaluation, and revision in two different ways: by discovering whether children do in fact behave in the way which the concept suggests; and by considering whether it is in fact the only or the most satisfactory way of accounting for the analytical data on which it is based.

Criticisms, re-evaluations, and revisions of the concepts of infantile sexuality and infantile stages of development have, of course, frequently been made from both these points of view, but before considering some of them briefly, it is necessary to draw attention to the fact that these developmental ideas are historical concepts which seek to explain phenomena encountered during treatment by reference to presumed events in the patient's past. They attempt to explain the clinical present by the construction of a historical theory which, as it were, unfolds it backwards in time, locating the various aspects of the patient's illness and personality at differing points in his biography, without, as a rule, reference to any documentary or hearsay extra-analytical evidence that may be available. One effect of this procedure is that concepts which have been arrived at by backward extrapolation from adults tend to be formulated in terms of the forward development of a theoretical construct, 'the infant' or 'the child' who looms so large in the analytical literature. The unwary reader who does not realize this may, as a result, be led astray, since it may not occur to him that a chapter entitled, say, 'The Emotional Development of the Child' may be expressing ideas derived from the psychoanalytical treatment of grown-ups and not from direct experience of children; or that an analyst's account of what goes on between infants and their mothers may derive as much from his experience of transference and counter-transference in the psychoanalysis of adults as it does from his direct contact with mothers and babies.

It is true that many analysts have observed children or have treated children psychoanalytically, but it none the less remains important for readers of the psychoanalytical literature to realize that all the basic concepts of classical psychoanalysis derive from the treatment of grown-ups and that, for instance, Mrs Klein's theories about the origins of mental illness in the first year of life derive not from work with infants but from the psychoanalytical treatment of schizoid and depressive adult patients and of children after they have learnt to talk.

This psychoanalytical habit of explaining its data by reference to events which are inferred to have occurred prior to the onset of treatment is, of course, a natural one. Historically speaking, it derives from a straightforward form of medical thinking, that of assuming that illnesses are due either to something that happened to the patient (e.g. trauma and infection) or to some disturbance of growth (e.g. congenital disease and malnutrition). Freud himself regarded the childhood experiences which in his view caused neurosis as traumata which interfered with psychological growth, a view of the origin of neuroses which enabled them to be fitted neatly into the medical scheme of things. Comparatively recently, however, a number of analysts have begun to question whether the neuroses are in fact illnesses in the sense that physical illnesses are, and have pointed out that whereas physical illnesses are the result of things that have happened to the patient's body, or more usually to specific parts of it, the neuroses seem to be disturbances of the whole personality which arise within the context of his relationships with others; the essential difference between the two being that in the case of physical illness the patient is clearly a victim of circumstances which have impinged on his body without his own will being in any way implicated, whereas in the case of the neuroses the patient is suffering the consequences of relationships in which he must have been, to some extent at least, a wilful agent. According to this view, the human ego is not a passive entity, acted upon by environmental and instinctual forces, but an active agent, capable of initiating behaviour, including those ultimately self-defeating forms of behaviour we know as neuroses. If this proves to be true, it will cease to be possible to maintain that everything that goes on between analyst and patient is a scrambled repetition of the patient's childhood, with the analyst acting as a completely detached, though benevolent, observer.

Of the various revisions and elaborations of Freud's developmental concepts, only two need to be mentioned here. The first is the shift in emphasis from instinct and erotic pleasure to ego and object relationships. In Freud's original formulations, development was conceived of as a number of stages during which children were successively preoccupied with their mouth, anus, and genitals, these organs (erotogenic zones) being regarded primarily as sources of pleasurable sensations. Since the 1930s Freudian analysts of all schools have increasingly tended to regard these organs as vehicles by which the child's relationships to its parent are mediated. As a result, the oral phase is now regarded as not only a period during which infants seek oral gratification, as the jargon puts it, but as one during which their relationship to their mothers forms the centre of their being and in which they have yet to be confronted with the fact that they and she are separate beings. Similarly, the anal phase is now regarded not simply as a period during which small children are preoccupied with their anal functions, but also as one during which they are learning mastery of their body and are being confronted with the problem of rendering their behaviour acceptable to the adults around them; while in the phallic and oedipal phases, children are now conceived to be assimilating their first intimations of the existence of a form of relationship between their parents from which they are totally excluded and which is liable to make them envious and jealous and acutely aware of their own physical and emotional immaturity.

It is noteworthy that although both of the predominant schools of contemporary psychoanalysis – ego psychology and object theory – have modified Freud's instinct theory in this direction, the routes they have taken to do so are quite different. Ego psychology has proceeded by emphasizing the growth of the ego and self-awareness and by relating the stages of libidinal development described by Freud to the emergence of a sense of identity, while object theory has proceeded by emphasizing the developing child's need for and constant involvement with objects. It is as though Freud had provided the verbs for a human psychology, and ego psychology and object theory, both sensing that the sentence was incomplete, have concentrated on providing the subject and object respectively. The remarkable confluence of what are, historically and even geographically, very different streams of thought is exemplified by the similarities that can be discovered in the writings of the Vienna-trained American analyst Erik Erikson and D. W. Winnicott in Britain.

The second elaboration of Freud's theories which requires mention consists in the emergence of depression as a central analytical concept. This elaboration is secondary to the one just mentioned, since it is based on recognition that separation from objects (e.g. loss of parents) in infancy and childhood leads not only to anxiety and deprivation but also to grief and mourning, processes which all analysts since Freud (1917) and Abraham (1927) have agreed are the normal analogues of pathological depression. Here again different schools have come to the same conclusion by different routes, the Kleinians having arrived at it by applying concepts derived from the study of depressive states to normal development, while Bowlby and Spitz reached it by follow-up studies of children known to have suffered losses of maternal care during childhood and by direct observation of children in orphanages and hospital. The reader is, however, warned that two incompatible theories about the origin and importance of depression can be encountered in the psychoanalytical literature: the Kleinian school attributing the predisposition to depression to the infant's fear that its innate destructive drives may destroy the object (i.e. the mother) on which it depends, while analysts of other schools attribute it to the child's and infant's actual experience of separation from her.

However, despite these advances, psychoanalysis is still far from realizing 'the dream of a final theory',* one which would, I conceive, heal the Cartesian split between body and mind, would recognize that (the) mind is not a thing that can be pictured in a diagram but a process proceeding through time, and that subjects and objects are not separate entities but inherently 'interpenetrative', inevitably and continuously influencing and modifying one another; that would, in fact, be able to accommodate the insight often better understood by poets and mystics than by scientists, viz. that

> There is no such thing as a single human being, pure and simple, unmixed with other human beings. Each personality is a world in himself, a company of many. That self . . . is a composite structure . . . formed out of countless never-ending influences and exchanges between ourselves and others. These other persons are in fact therefore part of ourselves . . . we are members of one another. [Riviere, 1927; reprinted 1955]

Indeed, so far from having achieved such a 'final theory', psychoanalysis seems, over the past fifty years, to have become as complicated as medieval astronomy was before Copernicus, and later Galileo, proved that the earth and the other planets went round the sun and not the sun and the planets round the earth; and replaced the complex system of cycles and epicycles by one ellipse for each

---

* An allusion to the physicist Steven Weinberg's *Dreams of a Final Theory* (1993). The psychoanalytical equivalent of the final theory sought by contemporary physics would presumably be one that unified instinct theory or ego psychology and object theory. According to Greenberg and Mitchell (1983), such a unification is impossible since they 'rest upon irreconcilable claims concerning the human condition', but Slavin and Kriegman (1992) claim that 'a certain kind of rapprochement of the two traditions is now possible'. The problem is, it seems, analogous to that of reconciling altruistic behaviour with the selfishness of the gene.

planet. Psychoanalysis is, it seems to me, in urgent need of a new and simpler paradigm to replace the present hotchpotch of incompatible theoretical systems: instinct theory, ego psychology, object relations theory, Kleinianism, post-Kleinianism, Winnicottism, self-psychology, and so on and so forth. This babel is, however, the reason why a dictionary such as this one is needed.

C.R.
1968, revised and added to 1994

Abreaction The **discharge** of **emotion** attaching to a previously repressed experience (see **repression**). In the early days of **psycho-analysis**, abreaction was held to be in itself therapeutic, regardless of whether the patient understood the significance of the repressed experience. See Freud (1895). See **insight**.

Abstinence One of the rules of psychoanalytical technique is the so-called *rule of abstinence*, though it is not clear what the patient should be made to abstain from. In Freud (1915a) the phrase, 'The treatment must be carried out in abstinence', refers specifically to the fact that 'analytical technique requires of the physician that he should deny to the patient who is craving for love the satisfaction she demands'. In Freud (1919), however, an almost identical phrase refers to the need to ensure that the patient's suffering is not relieved too quickly. 'If, owing to the symptoms having been taken apart and having lost their value, his suffering becomes mitigated, we must reinstate it elsewhere in the form of appreciable privation; otherwise we run the danger of never achieving any improvements except quite insignificant and transitory ones.' The idea that sexual abstinence in itself causes **anxiety** and **neurosis** occurs only in Freud's earliest papers.

Accessible and inaccessible A patient is said to be accessible if the **psychiatrist** or analyst succeeds in making **rapport** with him, and inaccessible if he fails. The term is pseudo-**objective**, since it implies that the capacity for rapport is a constant, identical in every examining physician. In general, **neurotics** are deemed to be accessible and **psychotics** inaccessible.

Acting out A patient is said to be acting out if he engages in activity which can be interpreted as a substitute for remembering past events. The essence of the concept is the replacement of thought by action and it implies that either (a) the **impulse** being acted out has never acquired verbal representation, or (b) the impulse is too intense to be dischargeable in words, or (c) that the patient lacks the capacity for **inhibition**. Since **psychoanalysis** is a 'talking cure' carried out in a state of reflection, acting out is antitherapeutic. Acting out is characteristic of **psychopathy** and **behaviour disorders** and reduces the accessibility of these conditions to psychoanalysis. See also **active technique**.

Active and passive Freud made extensive use of the idea that there exists a polarity between activity and passivity; **masculinity**, aggression, **sadism** and **voyeurism** being active, and **femininity**, **submissiveness**, **masochism** and **exhibitionism** being passive. As a result there is a tendency in **classical theory** to equate active and masculine, passive and feminine, and to define masculinity in terms of the ability to adopt an active role and femininity in terms of the ability to accept [*sic*] the passive role; and to regard sadism as a masculine propensity and masochism as a feminine propensity. The situation is, however, complicated by a further assumption that instincts can undergo **reversal** into their opposite, in particular that active instincts can become passive, sadism and voyeurism being usually cited as examples of instincts capable of this reversal. See Freud (1915b).

Freud's equation of passive and feminine has been much criticized, particularly by women analysts – Horney (1926), Klein (1948), and Payne (1935) – and is an example of what Jones called Freud's **phallocentric** view of women. Only Hermann (1935) has questioned the active–masculine equation. Attempts to describe heterosexual relationships in terms of male activity and female passivity can lead to absurdity, as when Deutsch (1946) describes 'the active pursuit of passive aims' as a feminine characteristic. There also exists a tendency to assume that mothers are active while their infants are passive, this despite the fact that both sucking and suckling involve activity. In both instances formulations in terms of active and passive roles assume that relationships are collisions rather than interactions and confuse activity with initiation of action and passivity with responsiveness and receptiveness.

Active technique A variation of analytical technique introduced by

Ferenczi in 1924, in which the analyst does not confine himself to **interpretation** but also issues injunctions and prohibitions and provides gratification. If one disapproves of it, it is an example of **acting out**. If one approves of it, it is a modification of **parameters**. See Ferenczi and Rank (1986).

Actual neurosis In his early writings Freud distinguished between **psychoneuroses** and actual neuroses, the former being due to psychological **conflicts** and past events, the latter being the physiological consequences of present disturbances in sexual functioning. He further distinguished two forms of actual neurosis: **neurasthenia**, the result of sexual excess, and **anxiety neurosis**, the result of unrelieved sexual stimulation. See Freud (1894).

Adaptation This almost always refers to adaptation to the **environment** as a whole, i.e. to the capacity to discriminate between **subjective** images (**phantasy**) and external percepts (see **perception**) and to the ability to act effectively on the environment. Since **classical theory** assumes that the human infant satisfies its wishes by hallucinatory **wish-fulfilment** (see also **hallucination**) and has no **ego** or mental structure, adaptation tends to be regarded as a function which is imposed on the developing individual from without as a result of his experience of **frustration**. For the alternative view, that the infant starts life already adapted to the environment it is likely to encounter and that its adaptation increases in complexity as it matures and acquires experience, see Fairbairn (1952), Winnicott (1958), Hartmann (1958). See **environment, average expectable**; **mother, ordinary devoted**; **alloplastic** and **autoplastic adaptation**.

Adlerian 1. A follower of Alfred Adler (1870–1937), early disciple of Freud, who seceded and founded his own movement in 1911. **2.** Adj. referring to ideas formulated by him. See **inferiority complex**; **masculine protest**.

Adultomorphic The adultomorphic fallacy is attributing to infants and young children the thoughts and feelings which an adult would have under analogous conditions. The reference is usually to theories about the psychology of infants which the speaker believes overestimate their level of **development**.

Aetiology and pathology These are frequently confused. *Aetiology* refers to the causes of disease and *pathology* to the abnormal processes inferred to be responsible for the manifest symptoms. For instance, **separation anxiety** and **oral fixation** may form part of a patient's pathology, while a history of **separation** from the **mother** during the oral phase may be part of the aetiology of his illness.

Affect General term for feelings and **emotions**. No generally accepted psychoanalytical theory of affects exists, but a distinction is made between *discharge-affects*, which accompany expression of a drive, and *tension-affects*, which accompany damming-up of a drive. Affects are regarded as being attached to ideas, and not vice versa. The concepts affect and emotion differ in that whereas the former regards them as affixed to ideas, the latter regards them as valid, independent experiences. See Glover (1939), Brierley (1951), Rapaport (1953).

Affectional bond That which **attachment behaviour** strives to create and maintain – and hence that which is disrupted by **loss** and bereavement.

Affective disorder, psychosis Psychiatric diagnostic term for those psychoses which are characterized by disturbance of **mood**. See **manic–depressive psychosis**; **depression**; **mania**.

Afferent Adj. qualifying nerves which conduct **impulses**, messages, towards the centre, in contrast to **efferent** nerves which carry them from the centre to the periphery.

Agape (Gk: brotherly love) Sometimes used in conjunction with **Eros**, to contrast altruistic **love** (*caritas*) with sensual love.

Agent Many of the more puzzling aspects of psychoanalytical theory derive from the fact that one of its basic premises, **psychic determinism**, implicitly denies the possibility that human beings can be agents who make decisions and are responsible for their own actions. As a result we not only have general puzzles about the relationship of causal theories (see **causality**) of human behaviour to moral and legal concepts, but also specific psychoanalytical puzzles such as: (a) What significance can be attached to acts of deciding, choosing, etc., if these acts are already predetermined by

unconscious forces? (b) Who or what initiates a **defence**? Or (c) If the **ego** is built up by **introjection**, who or what introjects the initial introjects? For some of the difficulties involved in applied causal theories derived from physics and chemistry to the behaviour of living organisms capable of **consciousness**, see Szasz (1961), Home (1966), Rycroft (1966), Schafer (1976). See also **creativity**; **meaning**.

Aggression Hypothetical force, **instinct**, or principle imagined to actuate a range of acts and feelings. It is frequently regarded as antithetical to **sex** or **libido**, in which case it is being used to refer to destructive drives. Even when being used as a synonym for destructiveness, controversy exists as to whether it is a primary drive, i.e. whether there is an aggressive, destructive instinct, or whether it is a reaction to **frustration**. Opinion also differs as to whether it is an instinct with its own aims or whether it provides the **energy** to enable the **ego** to overcome obstacles in the way of satisfying other drives. The almost universal tendency of analysts to equate aggression with **hate**, destructiveness, and **sadism** runs counter to both its etymology (*ad-gradior*: I move towards) and to its traditional meaning of dynamism, self-assertiveness, expansiveness, drive. The psychoanalytical usage derives from Freud's later writings, in which he conceived of aggression as a derivative of the **death instinct**. **Ego psychology** uses *aggressification* and *deaggressification* as homologous with *libidinization* and *delibidinization*. For the biology of aggressive behaviour, see Lorenz (1966).

Agitated Agitated **depression** and **melancholia** are **psychiatric** diagnostic terms referring to patients who are both deeply depressed and tense, restless, and anxious.

Agoraphobia Form of **phobia** in which the patient avoids open spaces and becomes anxious (see **anxiety**) when confronted with one.

Aim-inhibition A relationship is said to be aim-inhibited if the **subject** has no conscious **erotic** interest in the **object**. Common examples are friendships, platonic love, and domestic affections between relatives. The concept assumes that, in the absence of inhibition, friendships would be overt **homosexual** relationships, platonic love would be consummated, and **incest** would occur.

Alienation The state of being, or the process of becoming, estranged from either (a) oneself or parts of oneself or (b) others. Freudian **psychoanalysis** tends to concern itself with (a), **existentialism** and Marxism with (b). Since, however, self-alienation limits the capacity to relate to others and alienation from others limits the capacity to discover oneself, (a) and (b) are interdependent.

Alloplastic and autoplastic adaptation Terms introduced by F. Alexander (1930) to distinguish between adaptive responses which alter the **environment** and those which alter the self. **Defence** mechanisms as used in the **psychoneuroses** are the classic examples of autoplastic **adaptation**.

Alpha function Term used by Bion (1897–1979) to describe the conversion of raw sense data into meaningful integrated experiences. Failure of the alpha function leads to the accumulation of 'undigested' 'beta elements'. The alpha function is facilitated by maternal **reverie**. See **perception**. See Bion (1967), Hinshelwood (1989).

Ambivalence Term introduced by Eugen Bleuler (1911) to describe the co-existence of contradictory **impulses** and **emotions** towards the same object. Usually the term refers to the co-existence of **love** and **hate**. Ambivalence has to be distinguished from having mixed feelings about someone. It refers to an underlying emotional attitude in which the contradictory attitudes derive from a common source and are interdependent, whereas mixed feelings may be based on a realistic assessment of the imperfect nature of the object. The curate of the curate's egg story was not ambivalent about the egg though he probably was about the bishop. Although ambivalence is engendered by all neurotic **conflict**, it is mostly easily observed in **obsessional neurosis**, in which an attempt is made to balance the two sides of the ambivalence in **consciousness**; in the other neuroses, one or other side is usually repressed (see **repression**).

Amnesia Loss of the capacity to remember. *Infantile amnesia* is the loss of childhood and **infantile** memories. *Hysterical amnesia* is a

neurotic symptom in which the patient complains of loss of memory, usually for a circumscribed period of time.

Anaclitic (lit. leaning on) Freud (1914) distinguished two types of **object-choice**: narcissistic and anaclitic. *Narcissistic object-choice* (see also under **narcissism**) occurs when a person chooses an object on the basis of some real or imagined similarity with himself, while *anaclitic object-choice* occurs when the choice is based on the pattern of childhood **dependence** on someone unlike himself. According to this formulation, homosexuality is narcissistic, while heterosexuality is anaclitic (see **heterosexual and homosexual**). The implication is that the man rediscovers a mother and the woman rediscovers a father. Alternatively, since Freud considered infantile dependence was a manifestation of the self-preservative instinct (see **self-preservation**), in anaclitic object-choice the sexual choice follows a path laid down by the self-preservative instinct. See also **depression, anaclitic**.

Anal character Type of **character** neurosis inferred to be the result of **fixation** at the **anal stage**. The term is usually used to refer to **reaction-formations** against **anal-erotism**, in particular to **compulsive** obstinacy, orderliness, and parsimony, but can refer to their opposites, viz. compulsive pliancy, untidiness, and generosity. See **obsessional neurosis**.

Anal-erotic, -erotism Refer to sensuous pleasure derived from anal sensations.

Anal-sadistic, -sadism Refer to sadistic phantasies (see **sadism**) inferred to originate in the **anal stage**.

Anal stage, phase Stage of (a) infantile **libidinal development** postulated by **instinct theory**, in which the anus and defaecation are the major source of sensuous pleasure and form the centre of the infant's **self-awareness**; and (b) of infantile **ego development**, in which mastery of the body, particularly of its **sphincters**, and socialization of impulses are the infant's major preoccupations.

Analysand A person who is being analysed. The word owes what little currency it has to the fact that it makes it possible to avoid calling students patients.

Anamnesis Medical term for the history of an illness as given by the patient at consultation, i.e. for his recall of the relevant past.

Anger Primary **emotion**, provoked typically by **frustration**. Surprisingly frequently confused with **hate**, despite the fact that it is a short-lasting emotion readily experienced towards those we **love**, whereas hate is a lasting **sentiment**. See also **humiliation**; **rage**.

Anhedonia Absence of the capacity to experience pleasure.

Anima, animus **Jungian** terms describing the **unconscious** female image in men and the unconscious male image in women.

Anorexia Absence of appetite. *Anorexia nervosa*: **psychogenic** absence of appetite of sufficient severity to threaten health or life.

Anxiety The usual definition of anxiety as irrational fear applies strictly only to *phobic anxiety* (see **phobia**), which is evoked by objects and situations such as open spaces (*agoraphobic anxiety*), closed spaces (*claustrophobic anxiety*), heights, spiders, snakes, thunder, travel, crowds, strangers, etc., to an extent which is out of all proportion to their actual danger. It is better defined as the response to some as yet unrecognized factor, either in the **environment** or in the **self**, and may be evoked either by changes in the environment or by the stirrings of **unconscious**, repressed (see **repression**) forces in the self. **Psychoanalysis** is mainly concerned with the latter. Freud had three theories of anxiety. The first was that it was a manifestation of repressed **libido**, the second was that it represented a repetition of the experience of birth (Freud, 1916), while the third, which can be regarded as the definitive psychoanalytical theory of anxiety, is that there are two forms: *primary anxiety* and *signal anxiety*, both of which are responses of the **ego** to increases of instinctual or emotional **tension** (see also **instinct** and **emotion**); **signal anxiety** being an alerting mechanism which forewarns the ego of an impending threat to its equilibrium, **primary anxiety** being the emotion which accompanies dissolution of the ego. The function of signal anxiety is to ensure that primary anxiety is never experienced by enabling the ego to institute defensive precautions (see **defence**) and it can be regarded as an inwardly directed form of **vigilance**. Primary anxiety represents a failure of defence and occurs in **nightmares**. See Freud (1926), Hoch and Zubin (1950), Rycroft (1968), Rosenberg (1949).

Other forms of anxiety described in the literature are: (a) *Castration anxiety*, provoked by real or imagined threats to the sexual function. (b) *Separation anxiety*, provoked by the threat of separation from **objects** conceived to be essential for survival. (c) *Depressive anxiety*, provoked by fear of one's own hostility towards '**good** objects'. (d) *Paranoid (persecutory) anxiety*, provoked by fear of being attacked by '**bad** objects'. (e) *Objective anxiety*, fear provoked by real, external danger. (f) *Neurotic anxiety*, a term which covers either all forms of the above other than (e), or (a) and (b) in contrast to (c) and (d), which are covered by (g). (g) *Psychotic anxiety*. This last, however, sometimes refers to threats to **identity**. See also separate entries under **castration**; **separation**; **depressive**; **paranoid-schizoid position**; **psychosis**.

Anxiety hysteria Diagnostic term for what is now generally called **phobia**, or phobic illness.

Anxiety neurosis *Either* **1**. one of the two **actual neuroses**, *or* **2**. any **psychoneurosis** in which **anxiety** is the predominant symptom.

Apathy The absence of any **emotion** whatsoever. It is to be distinguished from **despair**, which is the loss of hope, and **boredom**, which is due to blocking of expressive activity, whether for external or **neurotic** reasons. According to Greenson (1949), apathy can be a life-saving defence in extreme situations; by, as it were, putting the mind into neutral, both despair and the exhaustion following unjustified hopefulness can be avoided. See also Fenichel (1954).

Aphanisis Term coined by Jones (1948) to describe the ultimate dread of losing all capacity for **pleasure**.

Aphonia Inability to utter, phonate. When **psychogenic**, a **hysterical conversion** symptom.

Apparatus, psychic(al), mental See **psychic apparatus**.

Archetype Jungian term for the contents of the *collective unconscious*, i.e. for innate ideas or the tendency to organize experience in innately predetermined patterns. It is a shibboleth word, overused by Jungians, actively avoided by Freudians. Freud's **Oedipus complex** is an archetype, since it is, in his Lamarckian view (see **Lamarckianism**), an inherited component of everyone's **unconscious**.

'As if' personality Type of **schizoid** character who behaves *as though* he had normal emotional responses to situations. See Deutsch (1965).

Attachment theory '[A] new and illuminating way of conceptualizing the propensity of human beings to make strong **affectional bonds** to particular others and of explaining the many forms of emotional distress and personality disturbance, including **anxiety**, **anger**, **depression** and emotional detachment, to which unwilling **separation** and **loss** give rise.' Hence *attachment behaviour*. See Bowlby (1980).

Authentic and inauthentic Existential terms (see **existentialism**) used to distinguish between acts which are done in good and bad faith, which are true and false to the **self**. Psychoanalytical theory has no means of making this distinction, nor the similar one between 'sincere' and 'insincere', even though psychoanalytical practice largely depends on the therapist being able to make it. However, inauthentic behaviour is regularly interpreted as defensive (see **defence**), the implication being that the patient's **'real'** feelings and motives are other than he himself realizes, or alternatively, that he was insincere to avoid confronting some aspect of the situation or of himself which would have made him anxious (see **anxiety**). The criteria for deciding whether behaviour which is based on **identifications** is authentic are obscure, though that which is based on identification with a loved **object** is more likely to be authentic than that which is based on identification with a hated or feared object.

Autism, autistic (lit. self-orientated) *Autistic thinking* is thought which is determined solely by the **subject**'s wishes and **phantasies** without reference to the **environment** or to realistic (see **real**) considerations of space and time. *Infantile autism* is a childhood

psychosis in which the patient lacks any capacity to trust or communicate with anyone whatsoever, is either mute or has complex disturbances of speech, and would be diagnosed as mentally defective were it not for his ability to handle inanimate objects. Many, perhaps most, psychiatrists believe it to be an inherited organic disease, but see Bettelheim (1967) and Tustin (1972).

Auto-erotism, -erotic Refer either to pleasurable activity in which the self is used as an **object** (e.g. **masturbation**, thumb-sucking) or to a **libidinal** attitude, orientation, or stage of **development**. In the former case, the words are being used objectively to describe observable behaviour, in the latter they are being used inferentially to describe a hypothesis about the patient's or infant's disregard of external objects. According to classical **instinct theory** infants are auto-erotically orientated, i.e. their attitude towards their **mother** is based solely on self-love and their need for her is based on her capacity to provide them with gratification. When used in this sense, auto-erotic is synonymous with narcissistic (see **narcissism**). **Object theory** is opposed to the idea of an auto-erotic phase in infancy and takes the view that the infant is mother-related from the very beginning, that, to quote Fairbairn (1952), the infant is 'object-seeking not pleasure-seeking'. According to this view, auto-erotic behaviour is substitutive, the **subject** using a part of himself as a symbolic equivalent of someone else.

Autonomous functions of the ego These are functions which have ceased to be directly influenced by the **instincts** of which they are derivatives and which cannot, therefore, be interfered with by **conflicts**. In healthy persons, speech, breathing, walking are autonomous functions of the **ego** and conflict does not produce stammering, asthma, or paralysis of the legs. Activities which have become functionally autonomous are examples of successful **ego development** and **sublimation**, and they use deaggressified and desexualized **energy** (see **deaggressification** and **desexualization**). In **topographical** formulations, autonomous functions occupy the **conflict-free area of the ego**. See Hartmann (1958).

Autonomy and heteronomy Piaget's distinction between the heteronomy of infants and autonomy of adults is made in **psycho-**

analysis by the contrast between **infantile** dependence and adult independence. Neurotic **dependence** is a condition in which an autonomous adult imagines himself to be heteronomous. '*Autonomy v. shame and doubt*' is Erikson's (1963) term for the second of his eight **stages of man**. It corresponds approximately to the **anal stage** of **classical theory**, **sphincter**-control marking the achievement of autonomy.

Autoplastic adaptation See **alloplastic**.

Average expectable environment See **environment, average expectable**.

Bad When qualifying **object**, **breast**, **penis**, **mother**, **father**, this refers to one of the two images or **object-representations** formed by **splitting** of the **internalized** object, breast, etc. Bad in this context is an omnibus word embracing 'frustrating', 'hateful', 'feared', 'malevolent', 'persecuting'. It is sometimes printed 'bad' in quotes.

Basic fault Term used by Balint (1952) to describe an aspect of the pathology of a certain type of patient whose whole development has been faulty and false. According to Balint the basic fault can only be overcome if the patient is allowed to **regress** to a state of oral **dependence** on the analyst (see also **oral**) and experience a **new beginning**. The metaphor is presumably geological not moral.

Basic rule The basic or fundamental rule of **psychoanalysis** governs the patient and not the analyst and is the injunction that he do his best to tell the analyst whatever comes into his mind without reservation. The rule is a counsel of perfection, **resistance** and **defence** manifesting themselves clinically by failures to carry it out. See **free association**.

Basic trust and distrust Terms used by Erikson, Winnicott, and Balint to describe the underlying effects of **good** and **bad** experiences of mothering. Basic trust, which is the first of Erikson's eight **stages of man**, corresponds to the **oral phase** of **classical theory** and to the **primary ontological security** of the existentialists (see **existentialism**). Basic distrust corresponds to some usages of **paranoid anxiety**. See also **mother**.

Behaviour disorder Psychiatric diagnostic term embracing **psychopathy**, the **perversions**, and the addictions, conditions which have in common that their **'symptoms'** consist of behaviour of which society (and sometimes the 'patient' himself when in reflective mood) disapproves. The behaviour disorders raise in acute form problems about the nature of **mental illness**, since the 'symptoms' are, on the face of it at least, voluntary acts for which society as a whole, and the law in particular, holds the patient responsible. (Hence the complete failure in communication which so often occurs when psychiatrists are called as expert witnesses in court.) Theoretically they can be regarded as the opposite of the **neuroses**, since they are characterized by deficiency not excess of **inhibition**. They are, in general, amenable to psychoanalytical explanation, but only infrequently to psychoanalytical treatment.

Behaviour therapy Form of **psychotherapy** based on **learning theory**. It assumes that symptoms are due to faulty learning and conditioning and aims to remove them by deconditioning and reconditioning procedures. Its theoretical basis differs sharply from **psychoanalysis** in rejecting the idea that there is any underlying process or illness of which the symptoms are merely a superficial manifestation. It asserts, on the contrary, that the symptom is the illness. Most of the successes claimed for behaviour therapy have been with **phobias** and **behaviour disorders**, conditions in which it is possible to isolate one specific symptom as the target of therapeutic intervention. Although theoretically an impersonal technique, papers on the role of **transference** in behaviour therapy have appeared, e.g. Crisp (1966). It differs from psychoanalysis in being applicable to unwilling patients. See Eysenck and Rachman (1965).

Belle indifference Psychiatric diagnostic term describing the indifference with which **hysterical** patients often seem to view conversion symptoms (see **conversion hysteria**) which should, on the face of it, be extremely distressing.

Beta elements See **alpha function**.

Birth-trauma The idea that birth is a traumatic experience (see **trauma**) was originally propounded by Otto Rank. It enjoyed a certain vogue for some years and was used, e.g. by Freud (1916), to account for the human predisposition to **anxiety**. It is now only of historical interest. The theory that anxiety is a repetition of the traumatic experience of birth seems to have owed its appeal to the fact that it enabled one universal human experience, viz. anxiety, to be explained by reference to another one, birth; and that it made it possible to regard the **psychoneuroses** as a special form of **traumatic neurosis**.

Bisexual, bisexuality These refer only occasionally to persons who are bisexual in the sense of engaging in both **heterosexual and homosexual** relations, but usually to the presence of **masculine** and **feminine** psychological attributes and attitudes in a single person. Psychoanalytical theory has always assumed that all human beings are constitutionally psychosexually bisexual. Freud took over this idea from his friend Fliess, and it was originally justified by reference to the biological and anatomical data which suggest that males contain vestigial female organs (and vice versa). Contemporary theory, however, tends to explain psychosexual bisexuality by reference to the fact that children identify (to varying degrees) with both parents (see **identification**). The theory of bisexuality assumes that it is possible to attach a sexual connotation to non-sexual functions and to designate as feminine **passive**, **submissive**, **masochistic**, intuitive, and receptive behaviour, and as masculine **active**, assertive, **sadistic**, intellectual, and penetrative behaviour, and that shifts in attitude imply changes in sexual orientation. The problem of bisexuality is bedevilled by social preconceptions about male and female roles. Any satisfactory analysis of bisexuality would have to take into account (a) biological and constitutional factors, (b) identifications with parents and social **stereotypes**, (c) confusions between the active–passive and male–female dichotomies, and (d) the relation of intuitive and analytical modes of thinking to (a) and (b).

Body ego, body image, body schema *Body ego* is Freud's term for that part of the **ego** which derives from the **self**'s self-perceptions (i.e. as opposed to perceptions of external objects). 'The ego is first and foremost a bodily ego', i.e. 'the ego is ultimately derived from bodily sensations, chiefly from those springing from the surface of the body' – Freud (1923). *Body image* is a psychological term for the self's conception of his own body. *Body schema* is a neurological term for the organic representation of the body in the brain.

Borderline personality disorder A borderline case is a patient who is on the border between **neurosis** and **psychosis**, i.e. either one whose **psychopathology** defies categorization or one whose mechanisms are psychotic but whose behaviour does not warrant his being treated as psychotic. The usage arises from the fact that diagnostic systems (see **diagnosis**) assume that neurosis and psychosis are mutually exclusive while clinical observation shows they are not.

Boredom The **emotion** that ensues when an individual fails to find interests and activities which fully engage him. It may arise either as a result of external limitations, e.g. solitary confinement, sensory deprivation, or monotonous work, or as a result of internal **inhibition.** According to Fenichel (1954), neurotic boredom is a state of instinctual **tension** (see also **instinct**) in which the instinctual aim is missing. As a result, the bored person seeks an **object** 'not in order to act upon it with his instinctual impulses, but rather to be helped by it to find an instinctual aim which he lacks'. He knows he wants something, but doesn't know what it is. Hence the irritability and restlessness inseparable from boredom and absent in **apathy**.

Breast This word refers either to the anatomical organ itself or to the idea (**object–representation**) of it existing in the subject's mind. 'The breast' is the object of **oral** wishes, **impulses**, **phantasies**, and **anxieties** and is synonymous with 'the **mother** regarded as a **part object**' or 'the mother regarded as a **need–satisfying object**', i.e. the concept refers not only to the breast as a suckling organ but also to the infant's obliviousness of the mother's person. '*Splitting of the breast*' refers to the psychological process by which the infant divides its image of a complete breast into two, one part becoming 'the **good** breast', conceived to be perfect, lovable, and all-satisfying, the other part being conceived to be hateful and rejecting ('the **bad** breast'). **Splitting** of the breast is a **defence** against recognizing that **love** and **hate** are directed against the same object; it purchases freedom from **ambivalence** at the price of persecutory anxiety (see **persecution**). See **paranoid–schizoid position**; **depressive position**. In the writings of Fairbairn and Klein, both of whom held that all **psychopathology** originates in the relation to the mother, 'the breast' often means 'the primary object' with only a theoretical implication that this was (is) a part of the mother's body.

Bulimia 'A morbid hunger' – *S.O.E.D. Bulimia nervosa*: An eating disorder characterized by binge eating and self-induced vomiting and purging. It can alternate with **anorexia** *nervosa*.

Castrating Word used frequently by analysts in conversation but only rarely in theoretical formulations. It refers to persons who habitually undermine the self-confidence of others. In the first instance, it applies to women who suffer from **penis envy** and therefore disparage or compete with men. In the second instance, it applies to fathers who undermine their sons, but by extension it can even be used to refer to men who habitually make women feel unattractive or incompetent with their children.

Castration, castration anxiety According to **classical theory**, all men and male children are liable to castration **anxiety**, though what the precise nature of this dread is has been subject to both controversy and elaboration. The concept only rarely refers to castration in its anatomical, surgical sense (removal of the testes), but more frequently to either (a) loss of the **penis** – as in *castration threats* used to deter little boys caught masturbating; (b) loss of the capacity for **erotic** pleasure; or (c) demoralization in respect of the **masculine** role.

Although, for obvious reasons, women cannot suffer from castration anxiety in its primary sense, classical theory asserts that they, too, have a *castration complex*, as a result of which they either feel 'castrated', feel a compulsion to prove that they possess an adequate symbolic substitute (see **symbol**) for the penis, or experience anxiety in respect of whatever organ or activity has become a penis-equivalent for them. Freud's own writings on the castration complex of women are imbued with his conviction that vaginal sensations do not occur until puberty and that, therefore, girls interpret their genital anatomy as evidence that they lack a penis. It was left to the women analysts to assert that girls can be aware of their femininity from the earliest days and to point out that boys can be as envious of their mothers' reproductive powers as girls are of the penis. See

feminine; **penis envy**; **phallocentric**. The concept of castration anxiety raises the question of who is the castrator, i.e. whether it tends to be evoked by men or women; and of whether or not it is internalized (see **internalization**), i.e. whether it is evoked by external or internal **objects**. **Object theory** tends to interpret castration anxiety as a variety of **persecutory anxiety**.

Catatonia Form of **schizophrenia** characterized by periods of excitement and stupor.

Catharsis (lit. purging) The reference is usually not to the purging by pity and terror effected by tragedy but to the therapeutic effect of **abreaction**.

Cathexis Neologism invented by Freud's English translators to translate the German *Besetzung* (lit. 'investment') which Freud used to describe the **quantity** of **energy** attaching to any **object-representation** or mental structure. A cathexis is conceived to be analogous to an electric charge which can shift from one structure except in so far as it becomes bound – or to troops which can be deployed from one position to another. Hence the verbs to *cathect*, *decathect*, and *hypercathect*, the last referring to the defensive manoeuvre (see **defence**) of investing in one process in order to facilitate **repression** of another. Hence also *withdrawal of cathexis*, for the process of decathexis. *Object-cathexis* refers to energy invested in external objects as opposed to the self. *Ego* and *id cathexes* are ambiguous; they refer either to cathexes by or of the **ego** and **id**. Hence also *counter-cathexis*, *anti-cathexis*: the energy invested in maintaining repression of a cathected process. Most statements using the word 'cathexis' can be reformulated in terms of 'interest', '**meaning**', or '**reality**'.

Causality The conception that events can be explained as the necessary consequence of prior events, the latter being the causes and the former the effects. **Psychoanalysis** is generally regarded as a causal theory, since it explains present events, symptoms, etc., in terms of the prior experiences of the subject. Its habit of explaining present **conscious** mental events in terms of present **unconscious** forces, motives, etc., is also an example of the conception of causality since it is assumed that the unconscious 'cause' was there first and contains the dynamic of the past. Freud's concept of psychic **determinism** is based on the assumption that unconscious processes can be the cause of conscious ones, but not vice versa. Some aspects of psychoanalytical theory, notably those centring round the **interpretation** of **dreams** and the use of **symbols** are concerned with **meaning** and the grammar of unconscious thinking and not with causation. See Rycroft (1966), Home (1966), Szasz (1961).

Censor, censorship In Freud's first formulations the mental agency responsible for **dream** distortion and **repression** was called the censor. The censor is the theoretical ancestor of the **super-ego**.

Character In analytical writings character usually refers *not* to those of a person's attributes which are most characteristic of him as a unique individual, *but* to those which enable him to be categorized into one of a number of character types. This is owing to the fact that certain *character traits* can be interpreted as either (a) derivatives of specific phases of **libidinal** and **ego development** or (b) analogues of **symptoms**, i.e. as defensive procedures. From (a) derive *oral character, anal character, phallic character, genital character*. From (b) derive *hysterical, phobic, schizoid, obsessional character*. Hence *character neurosis, character disorder, character analysis*. See also separate entries under **oral**; **anal**; **phallic**; **genital**; **hysterical**; **phobic**; **schizoid**; **obsessional**.

Character assassination Term used by Leslie Farber (1966) to describe the misuse of psychoanalytical theory to disparage character and impugn motives. This is done by either (a) interpreting behaviour in terms of **infantile** motives without reference to the modifications of them produced by **sublimation**, education, sophistication, etc., or (b) labelling character traits by reference to whatever psychiatric condition displays them in caricature form.

The first technique typically consists in interpreting the envied behaviour (see **envy**) as a **defence**, without giving the victim the credit for having mastered the primitive **impulse** by constructing the defence. This makes it possible to interpret kindness, considerateness, and gentleness as **reaction-formations** against **sadism**, and efficiency, tidiness and cleanliness as reaction-formations against anality (see **anal**). The second technique makes it possible to designate all the qualities mentioned in the previous sentence as obsessional (see **obsession**), to describe animation, vitality as **manic**, the capacity for objectivity and detachment as **schizoid**, being observant as **paranoid**, spontaneity and emotionality as **hysterical**. Although the motives underlying this abuse of psychoanalysis are envy, hatred, and malice, it is made possible by the fact that whereas **psychoanalysis** claims to be a general psychology, capable of explaining all aspects of human nature, its data are derived from pathology. As a result of this contradiction, concepts and classificatory systems which belong to the consulting-room are all too easily applied without modification outside it. The difficulties in avoiding character assassination are shown clearly by psychoanalytical studies of artists and historical personages, e.g. Freud and Bullitt's study of Wilson (1967). See **pathobiography**.

Child analysis The **psychoanalysis** of children. This differs technically from the analysis of adults in that **play** replaces **free association**. It differs theoretically in that parents and parent-substitutes are still actual, external figures in the patient's life and that **dependence** on them is a social and biological fact not a neurotic symptom. It differs morally in that the relationship between analyst and patient is not one between consenting adults; the decision to have treatment is made not by the patient but by his parents. According to Anna Freud, the real dependence of the child on its parents necessitates modifications in technique; according to Melanie Klein it doesn't. See A. Freud (1959), Klein (1932).

Child sexual abuse Occurs whenever an adult involves a child in sexual activity which the child, by reason of his or her immaturity, can neither fully comprehend nor give informed consent to. The abuse is both physical and psychological; the child's bodily privacy is invaded, and the adult's greater physical and social power precludes the child participating as a free agent. Depending on the amount of force used, the activity engaged in, and the genders of the adult and child involved, child sexual abuse consists of non-accidental injury, **incest,** rape, paederasty, **paedophilia**, or seduction. See Furniss (1991). For the curious role played by child sexual abuse in the history of **psychoanalysis** and the extent to which psychoanalysis may have contributed to society's blindness to the prevalence of child sexual abuse, see **seduction theory**.

Classical analytical technique An analyst is said to practise classical technique if he (a) sees his patients daily, (b) puts them on a couch, (c) eschews all giving of advice, prescribing of drugs, management of their lives, (d) confines his own utterances to **interpretations**, and (e) instructs his patients to obey the fundamental or **basic rule** of **free association**. It is possible to practise classical technique without subscribing to **classical theory**, since theory determines what is said by the analyst and not the setting in which he says it. Some practitioners of classical theory would, however, include (f) interpretation of **defence** in advance of interpretation of unconscious **phantasy** as an essential component of classical technique. **Kleinian** analysts conform to (a)–(e) but not to (f).

Classical technique was designed for the treatment of adult psychoneurotics. Controversy exists as to whether, and if so how, classical technique should be modified when analysing children, adolescents, and psychotics. Planned deviations from classical technique are sometimes called **parameters**. For an exposition of classical technique, see Fenichel (1941).

Classical (analytical) theory Although this concept is frequently encountered in the literature, it is hard, unless one is already familiar with the author's theoretical position, to know precisely to what it refers. The concept implies that there exists a theoretical 'norm' and that other theoretical positions can be placed in relation to it, either as deviations from it or as advances on it. As a result, the concept tends to be used tendentiously, meaning either 'theory which is in line with Freud's basic insights' or 'theory as understood by those old-fashioned Viennese analysts way back in the twenties'. However, classical theory certainly bears some relation to **classical analytical technique** and includes the following concepts: (a) The **structural**, **topographical**, and **economic** formulations of **metapsychology**. (b) The concept of stages of **ego** and infantile **libidinal development**, these stages being related to the primacy of specific **erotogenic zones**. And (c) the idea that the **neuroses** are **regressive** phenomena in which the patient regresses to infantile **fixation points**. Anna Freud in England and Heinz Hartmann in the USA were the heirs or the exponents of classical **Freudian** theory.

Claustrophobia Fear of enclosed spaces. A symptom of **anxiety hysteria** or **phobia**.

Coitus Sexual intercourse. Hence *coitus interruptus*, in which the male withdraws before ejaculation, *coitus prolongatus*, in which male **orgasm** is delayed, and *coitus reservatus*, in which male orgasm is avoided.

Collective unconscious See **archetype**.

Communication As Szasz (1961) has pointed out forcibly, much psychoanalytical theory could, and should, be restated in terms of communication and failures in communication, rather than in terms of functions and disturbances of function of single individuals. This criticism, however, applies more directly to **instinct theory** than to **object theory**, since the latter's emphasis on **object-relations** contains the idea that the individual seeks communication and that the neuroses constitute failures in doing so. See **instinct theory and object theory**; **meaning**; **semantics**; **cause**; **psychic determinism**; **personology**; **conversion**.

Complex A group of interconnected conscious and unconscious ideas and feelings which exert a dynamic effect on behaviour. The **Oedipus** and **castration complexes** are the only ones so called in Freudian **psychoanalysis**. The superiority and **inferiority complexes** are **Adlerian**.

Compromise formation Any mental phenomenon which is the product of **conflict** and which partially expresses both parties to the conflict. Typically, a symptom which effects a compromise between the repressed impulse and the repressing agency (see **repression**).

Compulsive Adj. referring to **conscious** thoughts and actions which the subject feels compelled to think or carry out and which he cannot prevent (or, at least, the omission of which leads to **anxiety**). Compulsive symptoms are characteristic of **obsessional neurosis**. They are either manifestations of 'the return of the repressed', i.e. they correspond to thoughts and wishes which the patient rejects as incompatible with his self-image, or they are a means of keeping such forbidden thoughts out of mind. Compulsive phenomena can be thought of as either due to failure of **repression** or as an indication of **alienation**, since the element of drive in them betokens some force seeking expression while the element of involuntariness indicates that the subject fails to recognize them as part of himself. The opposites of 'compulsive' are 'free', 'voluntary', 'spontaneous', and '**ego-syntonic**'.

Concept The concepts used in psychoanalytical theory can be classified according to the underlying assumptions or **fictions** which are being used to organize the facts into theoretical formulations. For example:

1. '*Principle*' *concepts*, which assume that mental life is actuated by, usually, the **conflict** between opposing forces or principles, e.g. **Eros** and **Thanatos**, **life** and **death instincts**, **sex** and **aggression**, the **reality** and **pleasure principles**. 2. *Structural concepts*: These assume that mental processes are functions of an organism or apparatus consisting of interrelated parts, e.g. the **psychic apparatus** and its components, the **id**, **ego**, and **super-ego**. 3. *Topographical concepts*: These assume that mental processes are localizable on a diagram, e.g. id, ego, and super-ego, **ego boundary**, layers or **strata** of mental content by which **memories**, **impulses**, **phantasies**, etc., are imagined to be at varying distances from the surface. In this instance hypotheses about the accessibility of **unconscious** phenomena to **consciousness** are formulated in terms of their distance from it, it usually being assumed that the longer ago the further down. 4. *Economic concepts*: These assume the existence of some form of mental **energy**, **quanta** of which may be attached to **structures** (bound energy), or may move from one structure to another (free energy), or may be discharged in action (see **discharge**), e.g. **libido**, **aggression**, **destrudo**, **cathexis**, counter-cathexis. 5. *Dynamic concepts*: Those which describe mental activity in terms of process, drive, and development, e.g. **instinct**, **drive**, **impulse**, **sublimation**. 6. *Faculty concepts*: These are hangovers from pre-Freudian psychology, e.g. **memory**, **insight**, both of which can be, but often are not, restated in dynamic terms, i.e. remembering, forgetting, and (perhaps) **introspection**.

All six types of concept do violence to the facts of human experience in as much they formulate them according to **models** which do not arise directly out of its **phenomenology**, i.e. they assume either that the subjective data can be explained as the result of the activity of objectifiable impersonal forces or that non-localizable, temporally organized events can be formulated in terms of a fictitious, space-occupying structure.

Conceptualization The process of deriving concepts from observations, of formulating general statements. A popular term, the virtue of which is that it enables its user to avoid choosing between formulation, generalization, abstraction, and thought.

Condensation The process by which two (or more) images combine (or can be combined) to form a composite image which is invested with **meaning** and **energy** derived from both. It is one of the **primary processes** characteristic of **unconscious** thinking and exemplified in **dreams** and **symptom formation**.

Conflict Opposition between apparently or actually incompatible forces. Internal or psychological conflict may be between instinctual **impulses** (e.g. **libidinal** and **aggressive**, see also **instinct**) or between **structures** (e.g. **ego** and **id**). The idea that all psychological conflict is **neurotic** is not part of psychoanalytical theory; conflicts are only neurotic if one party is unconscious and/or if they are resolved by the use of **defences** other than **sublimation**.

Conflict-free area of the ego **Topographical** formulation by which functions which are not liable to disturbances by neurotic **conflict** are imagined to occupy an area in the ego. See **autonomy**; **ego**; **ego psychology**; **neurotic**.

Confrontation Term occasionally used to describe an analyst's communication in which he draws the patient's attention to some aspect of his behaviour without offering an explanation or **interpretation** of it.

Conscience *Either* a person's system of moral values *or* that part of a person which he experiences as voicing moral values. The word properly refers only to **conscious** values and conscious 'still, small voices' and should not be confused with the **super-ego** which differs from it in being partly **unconscious** and in containing imperatives to which the individual does not consciously subscribe. The two concepts belong, in any case, to different frames of reference.

Conscious According to psychoanalytical theory mental activity can take place in two modes, one conscious, the other **unconscious**, those in the former mode being 'immediate data' which 'cannot be more fully explained by any kind of description', those in the latter mode being inferred. Theory also postulates that the two modes function according to different rules, conscious mental activity obeying the 'grammar' of the *secondary processes* and unconscious mental activity obeying that of the *primary processes* (see **processes, primary and secondary**). *The Conscious*, often abbreviated to 'Cs', is the system, or structure, in which conscious mental activity obeying the secondary processes occurs. Since thoughts belonging to the conscious may at times be unconscious, it is possible for mental activity to be simultaneously *descriptively unconscious* and *dynamically conscious*; such activity is termed *pre-conscious* (see separate entry under **pre-conscious**). The reverse situation occurs in **dreams**, in which we are conscious of manifestations of the unconscious. Contradictions of this kind contributed to Freud's change of terminology in the 1920s, when the conscious became the **ego** and the unconscious became the **id**.

Consciousness 1. The state of being aware, in contrast to being asleep, anaesthetized, in coma. 2. The faculty of **self-awareness** possessed by man in contrast to other animals. When used in sense 2 it is not always clear whether it refers to primary (self-)awareness, i.e. knowing what one is doing, or to reflective self-awareness, i.e. paying attention to one's own mental processes.

Freud's paper on consciousness, which should have been included in his papers on **metapsychology** (1915), is missing; as a result we have only incomplete knowledge of his views on it. We do know, however, that he (a) usually likened it to a sense-organ capable of perceiving **internal** mental events and of discriminating them from external **perceptions**. This function of consciousness he termed **reality-testing**. (b) That he held that consciousness differed from **unconsciousness** in taking cognizance of the categories of space and **time**, in being intolerant of contradictions, and in using bound

energy (i.e. in attributing to images a relatively constant meaning) (see **processes, primary and secondary**). And (c) that he maintained that 'being brought into connexion with verbal images' was an essential prerequisite for the entry of an unconscious thought into consciousness. It is also possible to deduce from his views on treatment and the therapeutic value of making the unconscious conscious that he held that consciousness had an integrative function (see **integration**). See Freud (1915b, 1923). See **word-presentation**.

The tendency of **psychoanalysis** to regard consciousness of secondary importance and to assume that conscious phenomena are the effect of unconscious ones has led to neglect of problems of consciousness. This neglect forms the basis of much existential (see **existentialism**) criticism of **Freudian** psychoanalysis. See **phenomenology**; **ontology**.

Constancy principle Term borrowed by Freud from Fechner to describe the tendency of organisms to maintain a constant level of tension. It corresponds to Cannon's physiological concept of '**homeostasis**'. Although sometimes used by Freud to imply that organisms seek to abolish all internal **tension**, i.e. have a **death instinct**, it is best used to refer to a need to maintain an optimal level of tension. See Freud (1920). See **pleasure principle**.

Constructions in analysis Hypotheses concerning an event in a patient's childhood, reconstructed from data provided by his **free associations** but not recollected by him. Freud's belief in the importance of specific events (**traumata**) in the causation of **neurosis** led him to attach great practical and theoretical importance to accurate and convincing constructions, even when they were of events so early in life that eventual remembering was unlikely. Constructions which *are* later confirmed by recollection or by information acquired from other sources were also highly valued by Freud as confirmation of the historical, scientific accuracy of psychoanalysis (see **science**).

Controversial discussions In psychoanalytical writings this phrase refers to the Scientific Meetings of the British Psycho-Analytical Society between October 1942 and February 1944 at which the differences between **classical** Freudian analysis and **Kleinian** theory were argued. For the texts of the various papers, see King and Steiner (1990). For an account of the discussions and an assessment of their place in the history of **psychoanalysis**, see Grosskurth (1986).

Conversion When used as a technical term, this refers to the process by which a psychological complex of ideas, wishes, feelings, etc., is replaced by a physical symptom. According to Freud (1893), it is the **affect** attaching to the 'ideational complex' which is converted into a physical phenomenon, not the 'ideational complex' itself. Although Freud's discovery that physical '**hysterical**' symptoms are **psychogenic** was the seminal observation from which **psychoanalysis** developed, the 'conversion' hypothesis is unsatisfactory since it leaves unexplained what is sometimes called 'the mysterious leap' from the mental to the physical. The mystery vanishes if hysterical symptoms are regarded as gestures. See Home (1966), Szasz (1961).

Conversion hysteria Form of **psychoneurosis** in which the symptoms are physical complaints. *Conversion symptoms* differ from physical symptoms in that (a) the loss of function corresponds to the patient's idea of how his body works and not to the facts of anatomy and physiology, e.g. a **hysterical** anaesthesia of, say, the hand corresponds to the area embraced by the concept 'hand' (covered by a glove), not to the area served by the nerves to the hand; (b) the symptom can be demonstrated to fulfil a function in the patient's life; and (c) the patient adopts a curious attitude towards the symptom, typically either a histrionic one or one of indifference.

Copro- Relating to faeces, e.g. *Coprophagia*: eating faeces, a symptom occurring in disturbed, deprived children and in **schizophrenia**. *Coprophilia*: pleasure in touching, looking at, or eating faeces.

Counter-cathexis See **cathexis**.

Counter-phobic See under **phobic character**.

Counter-transference 1. The analyst's **transference** on his patient. In this, the correct, sense, counter-transference is a disturbing, distorting element in treatment. 2. By extension, the analyst's emotional attitude towards his patient, including his response to specific items of the patient's behaviour. According to Heimann (1950), Little (1951), Gitelson (1952), and others, the analyst can use this latter kind of counter-transference as clinical evidence, i.e. he can assume that his own emotional response is based on a correct interpretation of the patient's true intentions or meaning. 'He [the analyst] must use his emotional response as a key to the patient's **unconscious**' (Heimann, 1950). Despite its widespread acceptance among **Kleinians**, Klein herself was not enthusiastic about the concept; it was 'elevating subjective feelings into a virtue'. See Grosskurth (1986).

Counter-will See **will** and **negativism**.

Cover Memory See **screen memory**.

Creativity The capacity to arrive at novel but valid solutions to problems. The capacity to create imaginative products (see **imagination**) which are compelling, convincing, significant, etc. From its earliest days, **psychoanalysis** has been tempted to proffer explanations of creative activity, these being invariably based on demonstration of the similarity between creative activity and some **neurotic** process. The simplest version of this procedure is to demonstrate that the content of novels and paintings can be interpreted as an **oedipal** phantasy and then deduce from this that creative activity is a form of neurotic daydreaming (Freud, 1908). The difficulty with this hypothesis is that it fails to explain why all daydreams are not creative and it therefore involves secondary hypotheses as to how the formal and technical aspects of creative work enable private neurotic 'creations' to be converted into publicly acceptable and comprehensible works of art. At the end of his life Freud rejected the idea that psychoanalysis had anything to contribute to creativity. (But see Ehrenzweig (1967) for a contrary view.) More recently, and usually under the influence of **Kleinian** ideas, there have been attempts to prove that creative activity is either **depressive** or **schizoid**, i.e. that it either represents an attempt to make **reparation** for destructive **phantasies** (Klein, 1948; Sharpe, 1950; Levey, 1939), or is in some way analogous to the delusional system-making of **schizophrenics** (see also **delusion**). Here again the reason why some people have the capacity to find creative solutions for their depressive or schizoid problems remains unexplained.

Since classical psychoanalysis designates imaginative activity as primitive, **infantile**, and as a function of the **id**, writers such as Hartmann and Kris have been compelled to describe in terms of **regression** activities which they clearly in fact regard as creative and progressive. This has led to the use of phrases such as 'regression at the service of the **ego**' to describe the '**negative capability**' (Keats) of the creative. Since the results of creative activity are, by definition, novel, unexpected, and therefore unpredictable, creativity is a concept hard to include within a causal–determinist framework (see **causality** and **determinism**); hence presumably the **ambivalence** of psychoanalysis towards it. The concept also raises problems as to whether it is a general aptitude, in which case everyone could become creative if his **inhibitions** were removed, or a special gift, in which case psychoanalysis has to admit exceptions to its categories. For the former view, see Kubie's *Neurotic Distortion of the Creative Process* (1958); for the latter, see Phyllis Greenacre's 'The Childhood of the Artist' (1957), where she argues that gifted persons are different from the beginning of life, that they actively seek objects who will recognize their difference and their gifts, and that, if analysed, they require a different technique than others. See also **meaning**.

Deaggressification The process by which **infantile** aggressive **energy** (see also **aggression**) loses its primitive, aggressive quality when the **impulses** to which it is attached participate in **sublimation**. See **neutralization**; **autonomous functions of the ego**.

Death instinct In his *Beyond the Pleasure Principle* (1920) Freud introduced the concept of a death instinct. 'We . . . have been led to distinguish two kinds of instincts; those which seek to lead what is living to death, and others, the sexual instincts, which are perpetually attempting and achieving a renewal of life.' Despite the fact that, as Jones (1957) points out, 'No biological observation can be found to support the idea of a death instinct, one which contradicts all biological principles', the idea still has a certain currency and forms an essential part of **Kleinian** theory, which conceives of **aggression** as a **projection** of the individual's own innate self-destructive drive. Attempts to work out the death instinct in detail, postulating a death-instinct form of **energy** analogous to **libido**, have never got further than suggesting a name for such energy, e.g. **mortido**, **destrudo**. The concept needs to be carefully differentiated from that of an aggressive or destructive instinct, since the death-instinct concept postulates a wish to dissolve, annihilate *oneself*, while the destructive-instinct concept implies a wish to kill *others*.

Deep and superficial Qualifiers of either '**material**' or **interpretations**. When referring to the former, 'deep' means that the material brought by the patient (i.e. what he talks about) derives either from early in his life or from repressed areas of his personality (see **repression**), while 'superficial' means either 'recent' or 'easily accessible'. When referring to the latter, 'deep' means that the interpretation relates either to early events or to strongly resisted ideas (see **resistance**). The usage derives from the use of geological metaphors to describe differences in accessibility and resistance. The metaphor tends to insinuate the assumption that early events are harder of access and of greater importance than recent ones.

Defence 'A general designation for all the techniques which the ego makes use of in conflicts which may lead to neurosis' – Freud (1926). The function of defence is to protect the **ego**, and defences may be instigated by (a) **anxiety** due to increases in instinctual **tension** (see also **instinct**); (b) anxiety due to a bad **conscience** (**super-ego** threats); or (c) realistic dangers. The concept of defence is usually stated in terms which imply that the human ego is beset by threats to its survival emanating from the **id**, the super-ego, and the outside world, and that it is, therefore, perpetually on the defensive. But the concept is better regarded less negatively and taken to include all techniques used by the ego to master, control, canalize, and use forces 'which may lead to a **neurosis**'. The concept also implies that neurosis is due to a failure of defence; according to this view the **inhibitions** resulting from successful **repression** are not neurotic symptoms. Anna Freud (1937) lists nine defences: **regression**, **repression**, **reaction-formation**, **isolation**, **undoing**, **projection**, **introjection**, **turning against the self**, and **reversal** – plus a tenth, **sublimation**, 'which pertains rather to the study of the normal than to that of neurosis'. **Splitting** and **denial** are also usually listed as defences.

Since **psychoanalysis** holds that anxiety is a spur to **development**, some, perhaps all, of the defences play a part in normal development and it is usually assumed that certain defences belong to specific stages of development, e.g. introjection, projection, denial, and splitting to the **oral** phase; reaction-formation, isolation, and undoing to the **anal** phase. See also **technique**.

Déjà vu The **subjective** sense that a present novel experience has been gone through previously. See Freud (1914).

Delusion Term used in **psychiatry** to refer to a belief voiced by a patient which is both untrue and uninfluenceable by logic or evidence; a fixed idea. A common-sense, clinical concept which turns out to be unexpectedly difficult the moment one asks two questions: (a) How does the psychiatrist know his corresponding belief is true? (b) In what sense does the patient believe his delusion?

(a) can be answered only if it is possible to discover the function of the beliefs in the mental economy of the patient and the psychiatrist. (b) leads to the conclusion that the delusion is a manifestation of a thought–disturbance, viz. loss of the capacity to distinguish between categories of thought – in the simplest instance, between metaphorical and factual statements. If the correct mode can be discovered, delusional ideas can often be shown to make sense.

Delusions of grandeur and persecution occur in **schizophrenia** and **paranoia**. Internally consistent *delusional systems* characterize paranoia. *Delusions of unworthiness*, e.g. the belief in having committed a crime, occur in **melancholia**. See **double bind**.

Dementia paranoides Obsolete term for paranoid **schizophrenia** and **paranoia**.

Dementia praecox Obsolete psychiatric term corresponding approximately to what is now called **schizophrenia**. The term was coined by Kraepelin, the father of modern **psychiatry**, and implied that the illness was incurable, deteriorating, dementing, and began in adolescence.

Dementia, senile and pre-senile Organic diseases of the brain characterized by progressive mental deterioration.

Denial Defence mechanism by which either (a) some painful experience is denied or (b) some impulse or aspect of the **self** is denied. (a) and (b) are not certainly the same process. According to Freud, denial of painful **perceptions** is a general manifestation of the **pleasure principle**, the denial being part of hallucinatory **wish-fulfilment** (see also **hallucination**). As a result, all painful perceptions have to overcome the resistance of the pleasure principle. Denial of aspects of the self is something more complicated, since, according to Klein, it is followed by **splitting** and **projection**, as a result of which the patient denies that he has such and such feelings but goes on to assert that someone else does (see **Kleinian**). *Denial of psychical reality* is a manifestation of **manic defence**; it consists in denying the inner significance of experience, and in particular of **depressive** feelings (see also **reality**). Denial has to be distinguished from **negation**, in which an unpleasant perception is announced by assertion of its negative, e.g. the first sign of a headache is the thought, 'How lucky I am not to have had a headache for so long.'

Dependence, infantile and adult **Infantile** dependence refers either (a) to the fact that children are helpless and dependent on their parents, or (b) to the fact that **neurotics** are fixated on their parents and imagine themselves to be dependent on them (see **fixation**). The use of 'dependence' and 'independence' to make the distinction between the helplessness of the immature and the viability of the mature (which Piaget dealt with by using 'heteronomy' and '**autonomy**') has led to endless confusion and hair-splitting; since adults need objects to satisfy their adult needs, they can be argued to be dependent on them. Fairbairn defined maturation as a progression from infantile dependence to **mature** dependence. In this sense dependence is the antithesis of **narcissism** not of self-reliance. *Oral dependence* is the infant's dependence on its **mother** (see also **oral**).

Depersonalization Psychiatric term for the symptom which leads a patient to complain that he feels unreal. See also **derealization**.

Depression This refers either to an **emotion** or a **diagnosis**. When referring to an emotion, it means in low spirits, gloomy; when referring to a diagnosis, it refers to a **syndrome** of which the emotion 'depression' constitutes one element. **Psychiatry** uses the diagnosis 'depression' to describe what used to be called **melancholia**, the condition in which the patient suffers from low spirits, **retardation** of thought and action, and delusional **self-reproaches** (see also **delusion**). This is one of the affective disorders (see **affective disorder**; **psychosis**), so called because the disturbance is one of **mood**; the other is **mania**. Persons who alternate between depression and mania are said to have a **manic-depressive psychosis**. Psychiatry distinguishes between *endogenous* and *exogenous depression*, the former being presumed to be the result of some (unspecified) constitutional disturbance, the latter being a comprehensible but none the less excessive response to some distressing event (see also entries under **endogenous** and **exogenous**). *Involutional depression* is a depressive illness occurring in the second half of life; its use implies belief in a constitutional origin.

The psychoanalytical literature is unanimous in regarding melancholic depression as a pathological form of **mourning**, the lost object being an 'internal object' not an actual person. This internal object was ambivalently invested (see **ambivalence**), so that the depressed person felt dependent on an object to which he was none the less hostile. In depression he imagines that he has destroyed this object (hence the self-reproaches), but is incapable of surviving without it (hence the depression). This view of melancholic depression assumes that persons subject to it are, even in health, in a state of precarious balance, since their stability is based on a complex, ambivalent relationship towards an internal object. According to Abraham (1927), depression occurs in persons who use **obsessional defences**, and the necessary **infantile** pre-conditions for depression in adult life are (a) ambivalence towards and **fixation** on the **breast**, **introjection** of which creates the 'internal object'; and (b) a severe injury to **self-esteem** occurring later in childhood than weaning, as a result of which the patient fails to achieve self-reliance and reverts to his ambivalent dependence on the breast. See also Freud (1917). Abraham's views on depression formed the basis of Melanie Klein's views (see **Kleinian**) on the **depressive position** and its role in normal **development**.

Neurotic depression refers to the symptom complained of by many neurotics. Sometimes it is a mild form of the condition discussed above; sometimes it refers to a mixture of **anxiety**, **guilt**, and a sense of **inhibition**.

Depression, anaclitic Term coined by Spitz (1946) to describe the state of **depression**, withdrawal, and listlessness into which infants fall when separated from their **mothers**. The 'anaclitic' refers to the fact that the separation, and the resulting depression, occurs at an age at which the infant is still objectively dependent on its mother. See also **anaclitic**.

Depressive When applied to a person or his **character** and/or temperament, the implication is either that he is prone to **depression** or that he has the kind of temperament which leads the speaker to surmise that, if analysed, he would prove to have a **psychopathology** similar to that discussed under depression (see above). *Depressive anxiety* is anxiety concerning the effect of one's own **aggression** on others or on one's **internal objects**.

Depressive illness is a synonym for depression in its diagnostic sense.

Depressive position A **Kleinian** concept. It describes the position reached (in her scheme of things) by the infant (or by the patient in analysis) when he realizes that both his **love** and **hate** are directed towards the same object – the **mother** – becomes aware of his **ambivalence** and concerned to protect her from his hate and to make **reparation** for what damage he imagines his hate has done. Since Klein's system includes the **death instinct** and innate hostility and **envy** of the mother, this crisis is conceived as playing an essential part in every infant's development, regardless of the quality of its mothering, and its outcome is held to determine all later development. Healthy and **neurotic** persons are considered to have passed the depressive position, while persons with depressive problems are fixated at it and persons with **schizoid** and **paranoid** problems have failed to reach it. See **paranoid–schizoid position**. See Segal (1964).

Deprivation The experience of receiving an insufficiency of a necessary commodity. **Psychoanalysis** has concerned itself with two forms of deprivation: *maternal* and *sexual*. Both, but especially in recent years the former, have been adduced as causes of **neurosis**, particularly in Great Britain by Bowlby (1952). The maternal deprivation theory of neurosis exists in various degrees of sophistication, according to how the insufficient commodity is defined. Statistical theories of maternal deprivation have, of necessity, to define the deprivation in terms of the duration of the physical absence of the **mother**. Theories such as Winnicott's (see **Winnicottian**), which are based on both paediatric observation and analytical **constructions**, can define deprivation in terms of love received or not received and can even break up the concept of mothering into sub-categories, e.g. feeding, handling, cuddling, smiling, warmth, as a result of which a mother may fail to be a 'good enough' or ordinary devoted mother (see under **mother**) in one sub-category while succeeding in the others.

Deprivation theories of neurosis imply that deprivation beyond a certain **threshold** produces relatively irreversible effects either by retarding **development** or by initiating **defences**. According to one possible schema, the sequence is deprivation→**frustration**→ **aggression**→**anxiety**→**defence**→**inhibition**→return of the re- pressed→**symptom-formation**; another is deprivation→**fixation** →inhibited development→persistence of the **infantile** need for mothering and **regressive** behaviour. For the effects of gross maternal deprivation, see **separation, mother–child**.

Depth psychology Obsolescent term for **psychoanalysis**, for the psychology of the **unconscious**.

Derealization Psychiatric term for the symptom which leads the patient to complain that the world seems unreal. See also **de- personalization**.

Desexualization The process by which **infantile** libidinal **energy** loses its primitive, **erotic** quality when the **pregenital** impulses to which it is attached participate in **sublimation** and **ego develop- ment**. See **libidinal development, infantile**; **neutralization**; **autonomous functions of the ego**.

Despair The absence of hope. As a pathological phenomenon it occurs in **schizoid** and schizophrenic disorders (see **schizophrenia**), in which it appears to be the result of feelings of unsurmountable **alienation** and **ambivalence**, and in the **neuroses**, in which it is a defensive attitude (see **defence**) designed to reduce **anxiety**. 'There is no hope without fear and no fear without hope' – Spinoza.

Destrudo Rarely used term for the **energy** of the **death instinct** and therefore analogous to the **libido** of the **life instinct**.

Determinism, psychic The assumption made by Freud that mental phenomena have **causes** in whatever sense physical ones do. See Jones (1953–7), vol. I, ch. xvii, for Freud's views on causality, determinism and free will, and their relation to the scientific thought of this time. He seems to have held that demonstration of the existence of **unconscious** mental processes proved the assumption of determinism, since it made it possible to assert that conscious processes were the effects of unconscious ones. He did not, however, regard consciousness as a mere epiphenomenon, but as a regulator capable of a 'more stable control and guidance of the flow of mental processes' – Jones (op. cit.). The assumption of psychic determinism, at least as usually stated, leaves no place in analytical theory for a **self** or **agent** initiating action or **defence** or for the use of explanations other than causal ones.

Most analysts believe that the claims of **psychoanalysis** to be a **science** are based on its use of causal-deterministic assumptions and will have no truck with the idea that it – or at least some parts of its theory – resembles disciplines like linguistics and sociology, which recognize patterns, more than the physical sciences. See Szasz (1961), Home (1966), Rycroft (1966), Gorer (1966). See also **meaning**.

Development **Psychoanalysis** maintains that human behaviour can be viewed developmentally, i.e. that adult behaviour can be interpreted as an elaboration or evolution of **infantile** behaviour, and that complex 'higher' forms of behaviour can be interpreted as elaborations of simple, primitive behaviour patterns and drives. The developmental process as a whole can be seen as resulting from two factors, the evolution of innate developmental processes and the impact of experience on these processes. **Traumata** are experiences which disrupt or pervert development; **fixation points** are circumscribed **inhibitions** of development; satisfactory terms do not exist for experiences which accelerate development (i.e. produce precocity) or for negative experiences (**stimulus**-deprivations) which lead to absences of development. Since **classical analytical theory** is tied to the idea of a division of the **psyche** into an **ego** and an **id**, it is forced to conceive of two parallel forms of development, **ego development** and **libidinal development**, the former consisting in the acquisition of **ego functions** which increase **autonomy**, the latter consisting in the transformation of **pre-genital** sexual and aggressive drives (see **sex** and **aggression**) into adult sexual and sublimated activities (see **sublimation**).

Diagnosis The art of attaching labels to illnesses, of deducing the nature of an illness from the **signs** and **symptoms** presented by the patient. The *differential diagnosis* is the list of labels worthy of serious consideration in any particular instance of making a diagnosis. A *diagnostic formulation* is a more or less complex statement of the **psychopathology** of a psychiatric patient. The concept of diagnosis is a medical one implying that illnesses are specific disease entities, an assumption which is probably invalid when applied to the **psychoneuroses**. See **mental illness**.

Discharge The concept implies a prior build-up or charge of **tension**, **energy**, **impulse**, or **emotion**, the discharge of which lowers tension. The therapeutic effect of **abreaction** was explained by assuming that the damming-up of repressed emotion (see **repression**) led to a state of internal tension which was discharged by the abreactive experience. **Instinct theory** presupposes that instinctual impulses build up a state of tension which is discharged by instinctual activity. *Discharge of affect* is an impersonal, theoretical formulation of what is conceived to occur in the **psychic apparatus** when an emotion is expressed. A *discharge-affect* is an emotion which occurs while an impulse is being discharged, in contrast to a *tension-affect*, which accompanies the damming-up of an impulse. See also **affect**.

Displacement The process by which **energy** (**cathexis**) is transferred from one mental image to another. Displacement is one of the **primary processes** and is responsible for the fact that, for instance, in **dreams** one image can symbolize another (see **symbol**). More generally, the process by which the individual shifts interest from one object or an activity to another in such a way that the latter becomes an equivalent or substitute for the other. Symbolization and **sublimation** depend on serial displacements.

Dissociation 1. The state of affairs in which two or more mental processes co-exist without becoming connected or integrated (see **integration**). **2.** The defensive process (see **defence**) leading to **1**. No hard and fast distinction can be made between dissociation and **splitting**, though there is a tendency to use the former when referring to processes and the latter when referring to **structures**, e.g. dissociation of **consciousness** when talking about dual personalities or hysterical **fugues** (see also **hysteria**), but splitting of the **ego**.

Dora Freud's pseudonym for an eighteen-year-old girl he treated from October to December 1900, and about whom he later published a paper (Freud, 1905). Often regarded as 'the classical analysis of the structure and genesis of **hysteria**' (Erikson, 1962), the paper has recently become a target of feminist criticism (see, for instance,. Lakoff and Coyne, 1993).

Double bind According to Bateson et al. ('Towards a Theory of Schizophrenia', 1956), the childhood of future **schizophrenics** is characterized by repeated experiences of being put into a double bind by, typically, their **mothers**. This experience consists in being made the object of incompatible, contradictory emotional demands in a situation in which there is no avenue of escape and in which no other member of the family rescues the child from the bind by either compensating for or correcting the mother's behaviour or by elucidating it to the child. The schizophrenic's response to a double bind is to lose the capacity to distinguish the logical status of thoughts. In other words, his **defence** against confusion, and his own and his mother's **ambivalence**, is to lose the capacity to understand those nuances which enable one to have **insight** into motives and to appreciate discrepancies between overt and concealed meanings. In lay language, a double bind is an 'impossible' position. Strictly speaking, the double bind is not a psychoanalytical concept, since it refers to an **interpersonal** situation and not to an internal **conflict** or developmental process. Although originally formulated as a theory of schizophrenia, it has been adduced as an explanation of **neurotic** behaviour. The possibility that an analyst may put a patient into a double bind has also been envisaged. See *Family Process* (American journal), Laing (1961), Lidz (1964).

Dream, dreaming Mental activity occurring in **sleep**; a series of pictures or events imagined during sleep. **Psychoanalysis** assumes that dreams have psychological **meaning** which can be arrived at by **interpretation**. According to Freud's original formulations, dreams have (a) a *manifest content*, which is the dream as experienced, reported, or remembered (see also **manifest**), and (b) a *latent content*, which is discovered by interpretation (see also **latent**). He also held that the dreamer performs work (the *dream-work*) in translating the latent into the manifest content, and that, therefore, dream-interpretation is the reverse of dream-work. According to his **wish-fulfilment** theory of dreams, the latent content is a wish, which is fulfilled in the dream in hallucinatory form (see **hallucina-**

tion), the translation into the manifest content being necessitated by two factors: (a) the physiological conditions of sleep which determine that dreaming is, in the main, a visual not a verbal process, and (b) that the wish is unacceptable to the waking **ego**; it has therefore to be disguised in order to pass the **censor**. **Nightmares** and anxiety dreams constitute failures in the dream-work; traumatic dreams (see **trauma**), in which the dream merely repeats the traumatic experience, are exceptions to the theory.

Freud's interest in dreams derived from the fact that they are normal processes, with which everyone is familiar, but which none the less exemplify the processes at work in the formation of neurotic symptoms. These processes – **condensation**, **displacement**, **symbolization**, obliviousness to the categories of space and **time**, and toleration of contradictions – Freud called the *primary processes* in contrast to the *secondary processes* of waking thought. Dream interpretation is, therefore, largely a matter of translating primary-process thinking into secondary-process thinking, of expanding the condensed, non-discursive, mainly visual imagery of the dream into the discursive symbolism of language. See **processes, primary and secondary**.

According to Freud (1900, 1902), the function of dreams is to preserve sleep by representing wishes as fulfilled which would otherwise awaken the dreamer. Recent physiological research suggests, however, that sleep is of two kinds, *dreamless* and *dream sleep* (the paradoxical phase of sleep), that phases of the latter occur recurrently in all extended periods of sleep, and that the function of dream sleep is to process the sensory intake of previous periods of wakefulness. For a rather different view of dreams, see Rycroft (1991).

Dream screen The screen on to which the visual imagery of a dream can be imagined to be projected (see **projection**). According to Lewin's original hypothesis, all dreams are projected on to a screen which is only occasionally visible. This screen Lewin interpreted as a **symbol** of both **sleep** itself and of the **breast**, with which sleep is unconsciously equated, i.e. the screen represented the wish to sleep and the visual imagery represented the wishes disturbing sleep (see **dream**). According to Rycroft and others, the dream screen is not a component of all dreams, but a phenomenon which only occurs in the dreams of persons who are entering a **manic** phase; it symbolizes the manic sense of ecstatic fusion with the breast (**mother**) and denial of hostility towards it. See Lewin (1946), Rycroft (1951), Boyer (1960).

In his later papers Lewin distinguished between screen dreams and *blank dreams*; the latter is a dream characterized by two convictions on the part of the dreamer: (a) that he has had a dream and (b) that the dream had no visual content.

'Dream specimen of psychoanalysis' The phrase (Erikson, 1954) refers to the first **dream** that Freud 'submitted to a detailed interpretation'. He dreamt it on the night of 23–4 July 1895, and his **interpretation** of it occupies fourteen pages of *The Interpretation of Dreams* (1900). Freud wrote as though this dream and his interpretation of it had been a turning-point in his life, and it was for long regarded as the paradigm of dream interpretation. However, in 1966 Schur produced convincing evidence that Freud's published interpretation had been economical with the truth. The dream contains obvious allusion to an occasion on which Fliess, Freud's friend and mentor, operated on one of his (Freud's) patients, and indeed nearly killed her. Freud's interpretation of the dream does not mention this incident. See Schur (1966, 1972), Clark (1980).

Drive No useful purpose is served by trying to distinguish between an **instinct** and a drive. Freud used the word *Trieb*. See Strachey's general preface to the Standard Edition of Freud for his reasons for preferring 'instinct' to 'drive'.

Dual instinct theory See under **instinct**.

Dynamic **Psychoanalysis** is a *dynamic* psychology since its concepts of **process**, **instinct**, and **development** imply movement; in contrast to static psychologies such as faculty psychology, which merely enumerate and define attributes of the mind.

Economic When used as a technical term, economic is the adjective corresponding to the noun **energy**. Economic concepts and formulations refer to the distribution of energy, **libido**, and **cathexes** within the **psychic apparatus**.

Efferent Adj., qualifying nerves which lead impulses away from the centre, in contrast to **afferent**, which lead them towards it.

Ego A **structural** and **topographical** concept referring to the organized parts of the **psychic apparatus**, in contrast to the unorganized **id**. '. . . The ego is that part of the id which has been modified by the direct influence of the external world . . . The ego represents what may be called reason and common sense, in contrast to the id, which contains the passions . . . in its relation to the id it is like a man on horseback, who has to hold in check the superior strength of the horse; with this difference, that the rider tries to do so with his own strength while the ego uses borrowed forces' – Freud (1923). For analysts who do not subscribe to the notion of an undifferentiated id out of which the ego develops, the ego is either (a) the whole psyche: 'The pristine personality of the child consists of a unitary dynamic ego' – Fairbairn (1952); (b) that part of the personality which relates to objects and/or is formed by **introjection** of objects; or (c) that part of the personality which is experienced as being oneself, which one recognizes as 'I'.

Ego and **self** are often confused; they probably belong to different frames of reference, the ego belonging to an **objective** frame of reference which views personality as a structure and self belonging to a phenomenological frame of reference (see **phenomenology**) which views personality as experience.

Ego, anti-libidinal See **saboteur, internal**.

Ego, body See **body ego**.

Ego boundary Topographical concept by which the distinction between **self** and not-self is imagined to be delineated. A patient is said to lack ego boundaries if he identifies (see **identification**) readily with others and does so at the expense of his own sense of **identity**. Analysts who hold that the **infant** lives in a state of primary identification with his **mother**, postulate the gradual development of an ego boundary, i.e. the discovery that objects are not parts of itself.

Ego defect The absence of an **ego function**.

Ego development **Psychoanalysis**'s assumption that the psyche is divisible into an **id** and an **ego** compels it to make a distinction between libidinal and ego development, the former being the progress through various libidinal stages, in which the sources and forms of sexual pleasure change (see **libido**), and the latter being the growth and acquisition of functions which enable the individual increasingly to master his **impulses**, to operate independently of parental figures, and to control his **environment**. Attempts have been made to correlate phases of libidinal and ego development and to describe an **oral** ego, which is entirely pleasure-seeking and dependent on the **mother**, an **anal** ego, which is concerned with control and mastery of impulses, etc. The most ambitious of these is Erikson's **stages of man**, which divides the whole of life from birth to death into eight stages of ego development.

Ego development may also refer to the process by which the ego differentiates out of the id. According to Glover (1939) this occurs by the fusion of a number of originally disparate *ego-nuclei*. On the other hand, according to Fairbairn (1952) the infant starts with a 'unitary, dynamic ego' which reacts to **frustration** by **splitting** into three parts: the *central ego*, the *libidinal ego*, and the *anti-libidinal ego* or **internal saboteur**; the first corresponding roughly to Freud's ego, the second to the id, and the third to the **super-ego** (see **Fairbairn's revised psychopathology**). According to Klein, ego development is a process of **introjection** of objects (see **Kleinian**).

Ego-dystonic Behaviour and wishes are said to be ego-dystonic if they are incompatible with the **subject**'s ideals or conception of himself; i.e. they refer to a value-judgement made by the subject himself.

Ego function Since **psychoanalysis** ascribes all functions to the **ego**, anything which the subject can do is an ego function.

Ego ideal The **self**'s conception of how he wishes to be. Sometimes used synonymously with the **super-ego**, but more often the distinction is made that behaviour which is in conflict with the super-ego evokes **guilt**, while that which conflicts with the ego ideal evokes **shame**.

Ego instinct In Freud's formulations prior to 1920 there were two groups of **instincts**: the self-preservative or ego instincts (see **self-preservation**) and the reproductive or sexual instincts (see **sex**).

Ego-integrity The last of Erikson's eight **stages of man** is ego-integrity v. **despair**. Although Erikson does not use the phrase, 'ego-integrity' seems to mean 'the serenity of old age' and the acceptance of one's own death as natural and as part of the order of things.

Ego libido **Libido** which is invested in the **ego**. It is not always clear whether this refers to the energy available for **ego functions** or to **self-love**.

Ego psychology *Either* 'the psychology of the ego', *or*, more frequently, that variety of psychoanalytical theory which has developed from Freud's *The Ego and the Id* (1923) and Anna Freud's *The Ego and the Mechanisms of Defence* (1937). In this latter sense there is an explicit or implicit contrast with either **instinct theory**, which preceded it, or **object theory**, which has developed contemporaneously with it. Key concepts of psychoanalytical ego psychology are 'autonomous functions of the ego', 'the **conflict-free area of the ego**', 'desexualization', 'deaggressification'. See Hartmann (1958) for a definitive statement.

Ego-syntonic Behaviour and wishes are said to be ego-syntonic if they are compatible with the **subject**'s ideals and conception of himself.

Egotization The process by which a mental process or function becomes part of the **self**, structured or deaggressified and desexualized (see **structural**; **deaggressification**; **desexualization**).

Elation The sense of high spirits and triumph occurring typically after a success. As a pathological term, the emotion accompanying **mania**. Pathological elation is usually interpreted as a reversal of the relationship between **ego** and **super-ego** existing in **depression**. As a result of this reversal, the ego feels as though it had triumphed over (or become fused with) the super-ego; instead of feeling oppressed and alienated it feels liberated and at one with the world. See Lewin (1951) for the **psychopathology** of elation and its relation to enthusiasm and ecstasy.

Electra complex Rarely used term for the **Oedipus complex** of women.

Elusion Term used by Laing (1961) to describe the process by which a person may avoid confrontation with himself and others by impersonating himself, i.e. by playing at the role that he in fact has. He cites Sartre's waiter and Flaubert's Madame Bovary as examples of elusion. 'It counterfeits truth by a double pretence,' i.e. by pretending that **phantasy** is **real**, and then pretending that reality is a phantasy.

Embodied and unembodied Terms used by Laing (1960) to describe two states of being, the embodied state being that possessed by persons with primary ontological security (see **ontology**) who 'feel they began when their bodies began and that they will end when their bodies die', the unembodied being that possessed by persons who lack primary ontological security and have a sense of being detached from their bodies.

Emotion A state of both body and mind consisting of a subjective feeling which is either pleasurable or unpleasant but never neutral, which is accompanied by expressive behaviour or posture and by physiological changes. Psychoanalytical theory tends to assume that emotions are **affects**, i.e. that they are **quanta** of **energy** attached to ideas, that their presence indicates a disturbance in psychic equilibrium, and that they interfere with **adaptation**. 'From the point of view of the psychology of the neuroses, affective action – in contrast to the theoretical ideal of rational action – often appears as a deplorable residue of primitive mental conditions and as a deviation from the normal . . . Yet we do know the crucial role of affectivity in organizing and facilitating many **ego** functions. Freud [1937] implied this when he said that analysis is not expected to free man of all passions' – Hartmann (1958). For some of the complications and paradoxes produced by the 'theoretical ideal of rational action' and the assumption that emotions are primitive and irrational, see Rycroft (1962). **Psychoanalysis** has made little use of McDougall's (1908) distinction between primary emotions, e.g. **fear**, **anger**, tenderness; complex emotions, e.g. admiration, **envy**; and sentiments, e.g. **love**, **hate**, and respect, and tends as a result to interpret simple emotions as manifestations of complex ones, e.g. anger as a manifestation of hate, or to assume that complex emotions can be present at the beginning of life, e.g. to attribute envy to the new-born infant. But for a partial exception, see Brierley (1951).

Empathy (*Einfühlung*) 'The power of projecting one's personality into (and so fully comprehending) the object of contemplation' – *C.O.D.* The capacity to put oneself into the other's shoes. The concept implies that one is both feeling oneself into the object and remaining aware of one's own identity as another person. The word is necessary since sympathy is only used to refer to the sharing of unpleasant experiences and does not imply that the sympathizer necessarily retains his objectivity. Although an occasional analyst has objected to the use of empathy on the ground that it is unscientific and unreliable, the majority opinion is that the capacity to *empathize* is an essential precondition of doing psychoanalytical therapy. It can be, but rarely is, cited as an example of projective **identification**.

Endogamy Custom or law requiring that marriage be with someone within the tribe or **totem** group. See also **exogamy**.

Endogenous Arising from within. See **depression**.

End-pleasure See **fore-pleasure and end-pleasure**.

Energy 'Energy is the only life and is from the body; and reason is the bound and outward circumference of energy' – William Blake. 'We assume, as the other natural sciences have taught us to expect, that in mental life some kind of energy is at work; but we have no data which enable us to come nearer to a knowledge of it by an analogy with other forms of energy. We seem to recognize that nervous or psychical energy exists in two forms, one freely mobile and the other, by contrast, bound' – Freud (1940). Mobile energy is characteristic of the **id** and bound energy characteristic of the **ego**.

Freud's concept of psychical energy is *not* designed to explain phenomena such as mental fatigue, differences in vitality, etc., but to elucidate problems of shifts in attention, interest and attachment from one object or activity to another. These are explained by postulating that **quanta** of energy are invested in the mental **representations** of **objects** and that these quanta vary in their mobility. *Bound energy* is relatively immobile and is characteristic of structured parts of the **psychic apparatus**, i.e. of the ego and the **secondary processes**, while investment with free or *mobile energy* characterizes unstructured parts of the psychic apparatus, i.e. the id and the **primary processes**. In other words, in primary-process thinking, e.g. **dreaming**, ideas and images are relatively interchangeable, so that one idea or image readily symbolizes another (see **symbol**), while in the secondary-process thinking of conscious rational thought, images, ideas, and words have relatively constant value and meaning. It is hard to avoid the conclusion that Freud's theory of bound and mobile energy has little to do with the concept of energy as used by the 'other natural sciences', but that it is really a theory of **meaning** in disguise. Freud's reasons for trying to explain thinking in terms of movements of energy derive from his *Project for a Scientific Psychology* (1895), where he attempted to explain psychic processes in terms of quanta of energy moving from one **neurone** (brain cell) to another.

The adjective corresponding to 'energy' is '**economic**'. Quanta of energy invested in particular mental representations are '**cath-exes**'; as a result, representations to which energy is attached are described as being 'cathected', and those from which energy has been withdrawn are described as being 'decathected'.

A problem which has exercised **psychoanalysis** is the question as to whether different **instincts** or **structures** use different forms of energy. When Freud held that there were two groups of instincts, the sexual (see **sex**) and the **ego instincts**, he held that the energy of the sexual instincts was **libido**, but never came to a clear opinion as to whether the ego-instincts also used libido or some other kind of energy. Similarly, when he believed that the two groups of instincts were the **life** and **death instincts**, he held that libido was the energy of the life instincts but never coined a term for the energy of the death instinct. According to the **ego psychologists**, the id is invested with sexual and aggressive energy, whereas the ego uses energy borrowed from the id which has been desexualized and deaggressified (see **desexualization** and **deaggressification**).

Engulfment Term used by Laing (1960) to describe a form of **anxiety** suffered by persons who lack primary ontological security (see under **ontology**), in which relationships with others are experienced as overwhelming threats to their **identity**.

Enuresis Incontinence of urine. Bed-wetting is, strictly, *nocturnal enuresis*.

Environment That which is outside the organism, person, under consideration. A distinction needs to be made, especially when considering the psychology of animals and infants, between the *Umwelt*, the total environment as perceptible by the observer, and the *Merkwelt* (perceptual environment) of the subject being observed. The latter consists solely of those aspects of the total environment which are perceptible and relevant to the subject. Failure to appreciate this distinction leads to anthropomorphic and **adultomorphic** fallacies. In the psychoanalytical literature 'external **reality**' and 'outer **world**' are often used as synonyms of environment. **Psychoanalysis** tends to concern itself solely with human aspects of the environment. But see Searles (1960).

Environment, average expectable Term used by Hartmann (1958) to describe the kind of environment for which the infant has built-in expectations and to which maturational processes are geared. In some respects it corresponds to Winnicott's less abstract *ordinary devoted* **mother**. The concept makes a break with Freud's view that the infant starts life totally maladapted and assumes, on the contrary, that he is born with a number of built-in patterns of response and behaviour and that development 'can count on average expectable stimulations (environmental releasers)'.

Environment, facilitating Winnicott's (1971) term (see

Winnicottian) for the setting provided by the *ordinary devoted mother* which enables the infant to mature along its own lines; in contrast to one which forces the infant to adapt to a preconceived pattern of behaviour.

Envy 'Grudging contemplation of more fortunate persons' – *C.O.D.* According to McDougall (1931), 'it is a binary compound of negative self-feeling and of anger'. According to Freud *penis envy* occupies a central position in the psychology of women (see under **penis envy**), while according to Melanie Klein innate **envy** of the **breast** of the **mother** and its **creativity** is a primary cause of all mental illness (see **Kleinian**). Both propositions create more problems than they solve. The former raises the question of how feelings of bodily incompleteness can arise in an intact body, i.e. it raises problems about the **body-image** of girls, while the latter raises questions as to how an **emotion**, and a complex one at that, can be innate and present from birth. Freud's views on penis envy are an example of his **phallocentric** view of women and are linked with his conviction that vaginal sensations (see **vagina**) never occur in females until puberty. See **castration**.

Epinosic Occurs only in the phrase 'epinosic gain', which is synonymous with 'secondary gain'. See **gain, primary and secondary**.

Epistemophilia Pleasure in gaining knowledge. There is a tendency to regard the thirst for knowledge as either a derivative of **scopophilia**, i.e. as an extension of sexual curiosity, or as a **sublimation** of **oral** drives.

Eros Greek God of Sexual Love used by Freud to personify the **life**-force and the sexual instincts. In his later writings, Eros was contrasted with **Thanatos**, the God of Death, the personification of the **death instinct**. Freud's use of Eros is poetic metaphor rather than science. The appropriateness of the metaphor derives from (a) the fact that Eros was the secret lover of **Psyche** and (b) the fact that 'his role was to co-ordinate the elements which constitute the universe. It is he who "brings harmony to chaos" and permits life to develop. This primitive deity, a semi-abstract personification of cosmic force . . .' – *Larousse Encyclopedia of Mythology*.

Erotic Sexual, libidinal, pleasurable (see **sex** and **libido**). According to **psychoanalysis** all bodily functions accessible to consciousness may be sources of erotic pleasure, while those which involve the *erotogenic zones* habitually are (see also **erotogenic zone**). Hence **oral**, **anal**, **urethral**, **phallic**, **genital**, etc., erotism. Bodily functions which are not normally sources of erotic pleasure may by displacement become *eroticized*; if this happens, the eroticized organ may become the site of a **neurotic** or **psychosomatic** symptom, since it is, as it were, serving two masters. Psychoanalysis's use of 'erotic' as a bridge concept between 'sexual' and 'pleasurable' can lead to confusion; only according to context can one tell whether 'erotic' refers to pleasure which is experienced as having a sexual quality or to pleasure which is inferred to have some connection with sex.

Erotogenic zone Any area of the body from which **erotic** sensations may arise. Typically, the sexual organs and the mucous membrane surrounding bodily openings.

Essentialism The opposite of **existentialism**. Freudian **psychoanalysis** is an essentialist theory since it explains phenomena in terms of essences, i.e. in terms of forces underlying the phenomena.

Ethology Nowadays *not*, as some dictionaries have it, the science of character-formation, *but* the study of animal behaviour under natural conditions. The relevance of ethology to **psychoanalysis** derives from (a) the possibility that it will provide it with a theory of **instincts** based on observation of non-human species and (b) the possibility that some of its techniques will prove applicable to the study of infants and children, thereby enabling psychoanalytical hypotheses about infantile **development** to be tested by direct observation. Psychoanalytical writers such as Spitz (1959), who base their work on direct observation of infants rather than on therapeutic work, are arguably human ethologists rather than psychoanalysts. See Lorenz's *On Aggression* (1966) for some points of convergence between psychoanalysis and ethology. See also Bowlby (1969, 1973, 1980).

Exhibitionism 1. Sexual **perversion** consisting in the exposure, by the male, of his **genitals** to a female. **2.** Similar behaviour by male children. **3.** By extension, all behaviour which is motivated by pleasure in being looked at, in self-display, in showing off, etc. Although Freud lists exhibitionism as a component-instinct and as a normal component of **infantile sexuality**, exhibitionism in senses **1** and **3** is regularly interpreted as **neurotic** and defensive (see **defence**); its function being to prove that one has got something by compelling some object to react to it. The generalized exhibitionism of women, which society tends within limits to accept as normal, is often interpreted as a derivative of **penis envy**; as being based on the need to prove that one has something despite not having a penis. Latter-day analysts are, however, more likely to regard it as a **manic defence** against **depression**, **frigidity**, or fear of loss of **identity** ('I must be **real** because I'm being looked at'). True exhibitionism of the genitals is almost unknown in women.

Existentialism Philosophical theory which gives priority to **phenomenology** and **ontology** over **causation**, which rejects explanations in terms of essences imagined to actuate behaviour from within in favour of study of the phenomena themselves. Whereas psychoanalysts claim to observe and explain mental phenomena, existentialists aim to understand experience. For general discussions of the relationship between existential and **Freudian** psychoanalysis, see Hartmann (1964), May (1967), and the writings of R. D. Laing. See also **essentialism**.

Exogamy Custom or law requiring that marriage be with someone outside the tribe or **totem** group. See also **endogamy**.

Exogenous Arising from outside. See **depression**.

Externalization The process by which a mental image is imagined to be outside the **self**, by which an 'internal **object**' (see also **internal**) is *projected* on to some figure in the external world. In this sense, synonymous with **projection** and the opposite of **introjection** not **internalization**. Fairbairn, however, uses externalization and internalization in a somewhat individual sense to describe the location of objects outside and inside the self during his transitional stage of development. See **Fairbairn's revised psychopathology**; **technique**; **quasi-independence**.

Extraversion and introversion *Either* **1.** as used by Jung, personality types differing in the importance attached to external perceptions and internal ideas. *Or* **2.** as used by Eysenck, a dimension of personality, according to which all individuals can be placed at some point along an extraversion–introversion axis. According to Eysenck (1965), extraversion corresponds to the choleric and sanguine, and introversion to the melancholic and phlegmatic temperaments of Galen. He also endorses the popular equation of 'extravert' with 'outgoing' and 'introvert' with 'introspective'. Neither term is used much by either analysts or psychiatrists, though there is a tendency to equate 'introverted' with 'withdrawn' or **'schizoid'**. According to Eysenck's findings *psychopaths* and *hysterics* tend to score highly for extraversion and *phobic* and *obsessional patients* tend to score highly for introversion.

Faeces Excrement, shit. Since the **anal** is the second of the **pre-genital** phases of **libidinal development**, and the acquisition of **sphincter** (bowel) control is the achievement of the corresponding phase of **ego development**, the words 'faeces' and 'defaecation' feature prominently in all psychoanalytical case histories. Anyone inclined to be sceptical as to whether faeces and defaecation really play such an important part in our mental life as the literature implies, should reflect on the extent to which obscene language calls on faecal terms to express abuse, contempt, and disparagement.

Fairbairn's revised psychopathology Fairbairn (1941) in his *Revised Psychopathology of the Psychoses and Psychoneuroses* describes mental **development** in terms of **object–relationships** and asserts that the various **psychoses** and **neuroses** differ not, as **classical psychoanalytical theory** maintains, in **regressions** to different stages of **libidinal development**, but in the use of different **techniques** during his second stage of development, the Stage of Transition or **quasi-independence**. During his first stage, the Stage of **infantile dependence**, the infant is objectively totally dependent on the **mother** (**breast**), towards whom he has initially a non-ambivalent relationship (see **ambivalence**). The unavoidable experiences of **frustration** and rejection at her hands lead, however, to the **schizoid position**, during which the infant's **ego** splits into three, two parts of which, the *libidinal ego* and *anti-libidinal ego* (**internal saboteur**), become attached to two antithetical conceptions of the breast, the accepted (exciting) object and the rejected (rejecting) object respectively. The third part of the infant's ego becomes the *central ego*, which corresponds to the ego of classical analysis. The libidinal ego corresponds to the **id** and the anti-libidinal ego, less precisely, to the **super-ego**. **Schizophrenia** and **depression** are in Fairbairn's view aetiologically (see **aetiology**) related to disturbances of development during the Stage of Infantile Dependence, but the other neuroses reflect the operation of different techniques during the next stage, the Stage of Transition or Quasi-independence, during which the child achieves partial independence of the mother by manipulations of the accepted and rejected objects created during the schizoid position. In the **obsessional technique**, he conceives both to be inside himself, thereby achieving a measure of independence at the cost of having to control a 'bad' **internal object** (the rejected object); in the hysterical defence (see **hysteria**), he conceives the accepted object to be outside himself, and the rejected object to be inside himself; in the phobic (see **phobia**), he conceives both rejected and accepted object to be outside himself; and in the **paranoid**, the accepted to be inside, and the rejected outside. Fairbairn's third and last stage is the Stage of Mature Dependence. See also **futility, sense of**.

Family The family in **psychoanalysis** is always what anthropologists call the *nuclear family*, consisting of **mother**, **father**, and children, who regard themselves, and are regarded by society, as a basic unit; and not the *extended family* of clan or tribe. As a result, phenomena such as the **Oedipus complex** and sibling-rivalry (see under **sib**) are always defined in terms that would make no sense if applied to cultures in which uncles and grandparents are no less significant than fathers or cousins and sibs are not clearly differentiated. As a result, too, phenomena such as adolescent **identity** crises, which apparently only occur in nuclear families, are defined as though they were inherent in human nature. *Family therapy* is **psychotherapy** which regards the family, not the individual 'presenting' patient, as the therapeutic object. *Family Process* is the American journal in which research based on the assumption that the neuroses are intra-familial disturbances is published. The *family romance* is the childhood **phantasy** that one's apparent parents are not one's real ones, and that one is really of noble or royal birth.

Fantasy and phantasy According to the *O.E.D.*, 'In modern use *fantasy* and *phantasy*, in spite of their identity in sound and in ultimate etymology, tend to be apprehended as separate words, the predominant sense of the former being "caprice, whim, fanciful invention", while that of the latter is "imagination, visionary notion".' Since the psychoanalytical concept is more akin to **imagination** than to whimsy, English psychoanalytical writers use *phantasy* not *fantasy*, but few, if any, American writers have followed them in doing so.

Father Although Freud's own writings attach central importance to the father and the **Oedipus complex**, almost all contemporary analytical literature centres round the **mother** and **pre-oedipal** phases of development. Whether this is a reflection of social change or a real advance in knowledge remains uncertain. 'The father' means either the patient's father or his internal image of his father, the latter being 'the **internal** father', which may by **splitting** exist in two forms: 'the **good** father' and 'the **bad** father'. The 'primal father' is the leader of the 'primal horde', whose murder by his sons evoked the primal inherited sense of **guilt**; see **totem** and **taboo**. Hence: *father-figure, father-complex.*

Fear Primary **emotion** evoked by impending danger and accompanied by the wish to flee. Despite the fact that fear is one of the elemental human experiences and that flight is undoubtedly one of the basic biological responses, **psychoanalysis** has little to say about fear. There are two reasons for this. First, its primary concern has been with pathology; as a result fear has been overshadowed by **anxiety**, though this is sometimes defined as irrational fear; alternatively fear is sometimes defined as 'objective anxiety'. Secondly, Freud's insistence on dual instinct theories (see under **instinct**) left no place for a third primary instinct; as a result psychoanalysis has much to say about how **love** and **hate** can **conflict** with one another, **inhibit** one another, and even at times reinforce one another (**sadism**), but little to say about how fear can interact with love and hate. In view of Freud's passion for antitheses and opposites, it is worth noting that a case could be made for regarding fear as the opposite of both love and hate.

Feminine, femininity Referring to patterns of behaviour, attitudes, etc., presumed to be psychological secondary sexual characteristics of the female. **Classical theory** tends to assume that femininity has an essential connection with **passivity** and **masochism** and that feminine psychology centres round the difficulties involved in taking up a helpless position. Whereas, as the jargon has it, men 'adopt the masculine role', women 'accept the feminine role' reluctantly and only after 'renouncing the **penis**'. As Jones pointed out, this view of femininity is an example of Freud's '**phallocentric**' bias and it has been criticized by many but not all the women analysts. See Payne (1953) for a concept of femininity based on the idea of receptivity. See **masculine** for some of the obstacles to discovering what mental characteristics are innately masculine or feminine. See also **active and passive**; **bisexual**; **castration**; **gender**; **male and female**.

Fetish 1. Inanimate object worshipped by savages for its magical powers or as being inhabited by a spirit. Hence 2. an **object** which a *fetishist* endows with sexual significance and in the absence of which he is incapable of sexual excitement. A sexual fetish is either an inanimate object or a non-sexual part of a person, the inanimate ones usually being clothes, footwear, or articles of adornment, the animate ones being typically feet or hair. Fetishists can be said to regard their fetish as being 'inhabited by a spirit', since the fetish is clearly associated with a person without being one, and as having 'magical powers', since its presence gives them the potency they otherwise lack. Fetishism is a classical example of primary-process thinking influencing behaviour since (a) the fetish has multiple meanings derived by **condensation**, **displacement**, and **symbolization** from other objects, and (b) the fetishist behaves as though it actually were these other objects and is no more disturbed by incongruity or absurdity than a dreamer is while dreaming (see **dream**). See **processes, primary and secondary**; **splitting**. See also Freud (1938).

Fiction Some but not all psychoanalytical **concepts** are fictions, i.e. they formulate mental phenomena *as if* they were phenomena of some other kind. The central fiction of **classical theory** is the **psychic apparatus**, which enables mental processes to be conceived as functions of a hypothetical thing or **structure**. The tendency to use fictions seems to derive from the assumption that formulations which sound **objective** are more scientific (see **science**) than those which admit openly that mental phenomena are subjective. See **model**; **reification**.

Fixation The process by which a person becomes or remains ambivalently attached (see **ambivalence**) to an **object**, this object being one which was appropriate to an earlier stage of **development**. Fixation is therefore evidence of failure to progress satisfactorily through the stages of **libidinal development**. The concept assumes that the fixated person has a tendency (a) to engage in **infantile**, outmoded patterns of behaviour or to regress (see **regression**) to such patterns under stress; (b) to choose compulsively (see **compulsive**) objects on the basis of their resemblance to the one on which he is fixated; and (c) suffers impoverishment of available **energy** as a result of his investment in the past object. Excessive **frustration** and **satisfaction**, excessive **love** and **hate** have all been adduced as causes of fixation. Hence *oral fixation*, *mother fixation*, *anal fixation*, *father fixation* (all of which q.v.).

Fixation point That phase, period, or point of infantile **development** at which a person has become fixated (see **fixation** above), through which he has not completely passed, and to which he remains liable to regress (see **regression**).

Flight The instinct or innate behaviour pattern of flight does not feature in psychoanalytical theory. See **anxiety**; **fear**; **instinct**.

Flight into health Phrase used to describe the rapid symptomatic recovery sometimes displayed by patients who wish to avoid psychoanalytical investigation. Probably a **manic defence**.

Flight into illness Phrase used to describe the escape from conflict achieved by developing symptoms.

Focal therapy Modification of psychoanalytical therapy in which one specific problem presented by the patient is chosen as the focus of **interpretation**. See Malan (1963).

Forensic Used in courts of law. Hence *forensic medicine*, *forensic psychiatry*.

Fore-pleasure and end-pleasure These terms enable the **pleasure** associated with **erotic** activity to be divided into (a) that associated with mounting **tension**, *fore-pleasure*, and (b) that associated with reduction of tension, *end-pleasure*, the former being a

tension–affect, the latter a **discharge–affect**. According to Freud (1905), the fore-pleasure of heterosexual intercourse, i.e. the kissing and cuddling, represents the survival into adult life of those forms of **infantile sexuality** which are aesthetically acceptable. He also argued that fore-pleasure from the infantile **erotogenic zones** (see also **infantile**) fulfilled the 'new function' of creating sufficient tension to enable genital **satisfaction** to be achieved. 'This pleasure then leads to an increase in tension which in its turn is responsible for producing the necessary motor energy for the conclusion of the sexual act.' Fore-pleasure refers strictly only to those activities which enhance the desire for end-pleasure and not to those which distract from it. Fore-pleasure is a striking example of a phenomenon which is extremely difficult to reconcile with Freud's **pleasure principle**, since (a) the tension produced by it is pleasurable not painful and (b) it shows that desire can be dependent on external stimulation and not solely on internal pressure.

Forgetting Usually discussed under the headings of **amnesia** and **parapraxes**. There is a tendency to assume that *all* forgetting is due to **repression**, though the idea that in perfect health we would remember every experience throughout our lives, however trivial, seems improbable on *a priori* grounds. If, as biological theory maintains, the function of remembering is to make available past experiences while making present decisions, forgetting is only pathological if it occurs in respect of facts which are relevant to the present.

Free association Brill's mistranslation of Freud's *freier Einfall*, which has, however, become the accepted term in English. *Einfall* means 'irruption', 'sudden idea', not 'association', and the concept refers to ideas which occur to one spontaneously, without straining. When used as a technical term, free association describes the mode of thinking encouraged in the patient by the analyst's injunction that he should obey the '**basic rule**', i.e. that he should report his thoughts without reservation and that he should make no attempt to concentrate while doing so. Free association technique relies on three assumptions: (a) that all lines of thought tend to lead to what is significant; (b) that the patient's therapeutic needs and knowledge that he is in treatment will lead his associations towards what is significant except in so far as **resistance** operates; and (c) that resistance is minimized by relaxation and maximized by concentration. It was Freud's adoption of free association technique which enabled him to abandon **hypnosis**. Resistance manifests itself during sessions by failures in the patient's capacity to associate freely. Some accounts of analytical technique make it depend entirely on free association and the resultant emergence of the relevant pathogenic '**material**', but this is an over-simplification since (a) the analyst makes **interpretations**, and the following utterances of the patient are associations *to* his intervention and not free; and (b) the analyst's interventions compel the patient to scan his free associations in **identification** with the analyst, i.e. the patient does two things at once, or in rapid oscillation: free association and reflection. An alternative formulation is that the patient oscillates between being the **subject** and **object** of his experience, at one moment letting thoughts come, the next moment inspecting them. See also **splitting**.

Freudian Follower of Freud and, therefore, according to context, not of Jung, Adler, Klein, Winnicott, Fairbairn, etc.

Neo-Freudian Term used to describe a number of American writers who attempted to restate Freudian theory in sociological terms and to eliminate its connections with biology. Karen Horney, Erich Fromm, and Harry Stack Sullivan are the best-known neo-Freudians. Horney and Fromm were concerned with the relations of personality and individual development to social structure. Sullivan was concerned with the role of **interpersonal** relations in determining behaviour and personality and could be classified as an object theorist (see **object theory**). See Brown (1961).

Contemporary Freudians A group of London-based analysts, descendants of the Viennese who settled in England in the late 1930s under the leadership of Anna Freud. They are proponents of **ego psychology** and influenced by **self-psychology**. See also **Independent Group**.

Frigidity Although some writers use the word 'frigidity' to describe all sexual inhibitions in women, including the inability to have vaginal **orgasms** (see also **vagina**), it is best restricted to the inability to be in any way sexually aroused. Since many women enjoy sexual intercourse without coming to a climax, the wider definition leads to the absurdity of designating as frigid women who are sexually responsive. See 'Medica' (1955), Gorer (1966). Frigidity can only be regarded as a **neurotic** symptom (a) if it is persistent or (b) if it occurs even under the most favourable circumstances; otherwise it is a sign of either inexperience or insincerity (on the part of either the woman or her partner).

Frustration The state of being or having been balked, baffled, or disappointed. Frustration and **deprivation** are often confused, but, strictly speaking, frustration refers to the effect of non-satisfaction of a drive or failure to achieve a goal, while deprivation refers to the lack of the commodity or opportunity necessary for satisfaction. Frustration and deprivation theories of neurosis tend none the less to be identical on the assumption that deprivation leads to frustration, frustration leads to **aggression**, aggression leads to **anxiety**, anxiety leads to **defences** . . .

Although **psychoanalysis** is popularly supposed to maintain that frustration is harmful, this is not the whole story since it also maintains that **ego development** is initiated by frustration. In fact, frustration theories of **neurosis** assume that both frustration and deprivation *beyond a certain threshold of intensity* are pathogenic (see **threshold**).

Fugue Psychiatric term for the process by which a person wanders off, not knowing who or where he is. Fugues are generally categorized as **hysterical** and cited as examples of **dissociation** of consciousness. A rare condition, most of the cases cited in psychiatric textbooks have occurred in persons such as boys in boarding schools and conscript soldiers who feel trapped in situations in which they are no longer free agents.

Fundamental rule See **basic rule**.

Furor therapeuticus Disparaging term for therapeutic enthusiasm. According to Freud, *furor therapeuticus* is against the long-term interests of patients being analysed. But see Malan (1963) for its value in short-term therapy.

Fusion and defusion According to Freud's later speculative writings, **instincts** are not only in **conflict** but are also capable of fusing and defusing. 'We never have to deal with pure **life instincts** and **death instincts** at all, but only with combinations of them in different degrees. Corresponding with the fusion of instincts there may under certain conditions occur a defusion of them' – Freud (1920). Analysts who accept this point of view assume that in health the life and death instincts are fused with the life instincts preponderating, that in sadistic (see **sadism**) and masochistic (see **masochism**) perversions they are fused with the death instinct preponderating, and that in **obsessional neurosis** defusion occurs, the patient's life instinct becoming the object of his death instinct.

Futility, sense of Phrase used especially by Fairbairn (see **Fairbairn's revised psychopathology**) to describe the predominant **affect** in **schizoid** disorders.

Gain, primary and secondary (paranosic and epinosic) The primary (paranosic) gain of a **symptom** is the freedom from **anxiety** and **conflict** achieved by its formation. The secondary (epinosic) gain consists of the practical advantages which can be achieved by using the symptom to influence or manipulate others. For instance, the primary gain of **agoraphobia** is the freedom from anxiety and conflict about **ambivalence** towards parental figures achieved by not being able to leave home; the secondary gain is the possibility of using the symptom to avoid unpleasant commitments or to compel others to act as one's companion. Relatives of patients tend to be acutely aware of the secondary gains of **neurosis** but to be oblivious to its primary gains.

Gender Grammatical term for the division of nouns into masculine and feminine (and, in some languages, neuter). Modern English is unusual in having '"natural" as opposed to "grammatical" gender, i.e. nouns are masculine, feminine or neuter according as the objects they denote are male, female, or of neither sex' – *S.O.E.D.* **Psychiatry** and **psychoanalysis** have borrowed this grammatical term to make the distinction between a person's gender identity, i.e. his conception of himself as **masculine** or **feminine**, and his biologically given male or female **sex** (see **male and female**). See Stoller (1985). In feminist and sexological literature gender is increasingly used as a synonym for sex, e.g. in phrases like 'gender studies', 'gender differences', and even 'same gender sexual contact among men'!

Generativity v. stagnation Erikson's term for the seventh of his eight **stages of man**. It corresponds to middle age. 'Generativity is primarily the interest in establishing and guiding the next generation or whatever in a given case may become the absorbing object of a parental kind of responsibility. When this enrichment fails, a regression from generativity to an obsessive need for pseudo-intimacy, punctuated by moments of mutual repulsion, takes place, often with a pervading sense (and objective evidence) of individual stagnation and interpersonal impoverishment' – Erikson (1963).

Genetic In the psychoanalytical literature this almost always means 'ontogenetic', related to the development of the individual, and not 'phylogenetic', relating to the development of the species. Hence the word's associations with 'genetics' and 'genes' should be ignored and it should be regarded as synonymous with 'developmental' (see **development**).

Genital character Hypothetical or ideal character displayed by a person who has been fully analysed, who has fully resolved his **Oedipus complex**, who has 'worked through' (see **working through**) his *pre-genital* ambivalence and achieved the post-ambivalent **genital level** of **psychosexual** development (see also **ambivalence**). A genital character would, if such a person existed, be totally free of **infantile dependence** and would be distinguishable from a **phallic character** by the fact that he attached equal importance to his own and his **object**'s satisfaction – to attach more to his object's than his own would reveal him as a masochist (see **masochism**). Although there is something absurd about the concept, which illustrates vividly the difficulties inherent in describing healthy phenomena in terms of a language rooted in pathology, it is a logical necessity for anyone who thinks that maturity should be definable in terms of **instinct theory**. Evans (1949) has pointed out the close similarity between the analytical ideal of the genital character and the English ideal of a gentleman. See also **genitality**.

Genitality 'While psychoanalysis has on occasion gone too far in its emphasis on genitality as a universal cure for society and has thus provided a new addiction and a new commodity for many who wished to so [*sic*] interpret its teachings, it has not always indicated all the goals that genitality actually should and must imply. In order to be of lasting social significance, the utopia of genitality should include:

'1. mutuality of orgasm
'2. with a loved partner
'3. of the other sex

'4. with whom one is able and willing to share a mutual trust
'5. and with whom one is able and willing to regulate the cycles of
  'a. work
  'b. procreation
  'c. recreation
'6. so as to secure to the offspring, too, all the stages of a satisfactory
  development' – Erikson (1963).

Genital level According to **classical theory**, the last phase of **libidinal development**; after progressing through or up the **pre-genital** stages of development and passing through the latency period, the individual reaches or achieves the genital level – presumably a plateau from which no further ascent is possible. Erikson (1963), however, discusses **genitality** in connection with the sixth of his eight **stages of man**, **intimacy** *v.* **isolation** (Young Adulthood), and reserves **maturity** for his eighth, which is only reached in old age. See **genital character**; **ego integrity**.

Globus hystericus The subjective sense of a lump in the throat occurring in absence of any palpable lump.

Good When used technically 'good' refers to a particular class of **internal objects**, viz. those which are conceived to be benevolent towards the subject, in contrast to '**bad**' objects, which are imagined to be malevolently disposed towards him. The two types of object, good and bad, arise as a result of **splitting** of the primary or original introjected object (see **introjection**), i.e. the subject divides his conception of the **breast**, **mother**, **father**, **penis**, etc., into two, the good and bad breast, etc., thereby defending himself against the **ambivalence** which would ensue if he recognized that he experienced **satisfaction** and **frustration** from and **love** and **hate** towards the same object. Although this usage derives its wide currency from the writings of Klein and Fairbairn, its origins are to be found in the work of Freud, Abraham, and Rado on **melancholia**. See also **idealization**; **depressive position**; **paranoid–schizoid position**; **Kleinian**; **Fairbairn's revised psychopathology**.

Gratitude 'A binary compound of tender emotion and negative self-feeling' – McDougall (1931). 'A warm feeling of goodwill

towards a benefactor' – *S.O.E.D.* According to Klein (1957) gratitude is counterpoised to **envy**, and in her view both **emotions** are
present from birth. Most non-**Kleinian** analysts doubt whether
infants are capable of such sophisticated emotions. Both McDougall's
and the *S.O.E.D.* definitions imply that the recipient has some
awareness of the benefactor's greater power, i.e. that he/she was in a
position *not* to grant the favour.

Grid Invention of Bion's. He plotted all possible kinds of **communication** on two co-ordinates, one displaying relations at different
levels of abstraction, the other displaying the way these could be
used. See Bion (1963).

Grief Sorrow; the **emotion** accompanying **mourning**.

Group A number of persons united for some purpose or possessing
common interests, aspirations, functions, or fears which enable them
to be differentiated as a social entity both by themselves and by
others.

Group psychology: That branch of psychology concerned with the
behaviour of groups and with the psychology of membership of
groups. Probably not distinguishable from social psychology or
Massenpsychologie. Psychoanalytical formulations stress **identification** between members, identification of members with a leader,
and the relationship with the common enemy, all three factors
playing an important role in diminishing the disruptive effects of
rivalry between members.

Group psychotherapy: Any form of **psychotherapy** in which
more than two patients are present. In most forms of group
psychotherapy the group is initially an artefact created by the
therapist selecting the members, but it is assumed that the common
relationship to the therapist will lead to the formation of a genuine
group situation. Group psychotherapy of 'natural' groups, e.g. of
whole **families**, seems to be a rarity.

Group analysis: Group psychotherapy in which the therapist re-
stricts his activities to **interpretation** of the dynamics of the group.
See Foulkes and Anthony (1957).

Guilt **Psychoanalysis** is concerned not with the fact of guilt but
with the sense of guilt, i.e. with the **emotion** which follows

infringement of a moral injunction. More specifically, it is concerned with the **neurotic** sense of guilt, i.e. with those experiences of feeling guilty which are not explicable in terms of infringements of the patient's conscious values. According to **classical theory** the neurotic sense of guilt arises as a result of conflict between the **super-ego** and **infantile** sexual and aggressive wishes (see **sex** and **aggression**), this conflict being an internalized **representation** and perpetuation of conflicts between the child and his parents (see also **internalization**); the situation is, however, complicated by the fact that the super-ego is conceived to derive its energy from the child's own **aggression**; as a result the sense of guilt is influenced directly by the extent to which the individual expresses his aggressive feelings by taking them out on himself in moral condemnation.

Guilt differs from **anxiety** in that (a) anxiety is experienced in relation to a feared future occurrence, while guilt is experienced in relation to an act already committed, and (b) the capacity to experience guilt is contingent on the capacity to internalize objects whereas the capacity to experience anxiety is not; animals and infants may feel anxious, but only human beings with some aware-ness of time and of others can feel guilty. Neurotic guilt and anxiety may, however, be indistinguishable owing to the fact that the neurotic sense of guilt is associated with dread of punishment and retribution.

Analysts who believe in an innate destructive instinct also believe inevitably in an inherent sense of guilt derived from awareness of the wish to destroy what is also loved, to defy what is also submitted to.

All **defences** used to reduce anxiety can also be used to reduce the sense of guilt, but one defence, **reparation**, the making good of damage imagined to have already been done, is used specifically to reduce the sense of guilt. See **shame**.

Hallucination 'Apparent **perception** of an external object not actually present' – *O.E.D.* A subjective image which the patient experiences as an external phenomenon. Owing to the failure in '**reality-testing**' involved in hallucinating it tends to be regarded as **psychotic**, though this is not always so. Hallucinations can occur as a result of fever, brain disease, drugs, and sensory deprivation as well as for psychotic reasons. Hallucinations of all senses can occur, those of touch being known as '**haptic**'. **Dreams** are the hallucinations of the normal.

'Hans, Little' Pseudonym of the three- to five-year-old boy, whose analysis by his father from 1906 to 1908 was described by Freud (1909a) in his *Analysis of a Phobia in a Five-year-old Boy*.

Haptic Relating to touch.

Hate 1. A principle or inner force conceived to actuate behaviour. 2. An **affect** characterized by an enduring wish to injure or destroy the hated **object**. Hate is often confused by analysts with **anger**, despite the fact that the latter is a passing not an enduring emotion which can be felt in relation to someone one loves. According to McDougall (1908), hate is a **sentiment** and anger a simple, primary **emotion**. According to Freud (1915), hate is the response to threats to the **ego**, but in his later speculative writings he viewed it as a manifestation of the **death instinct**. Analysts influenced by these later ideas tend to regard **love** and hate as opposites and to see the psyche as a battleground between these two opposed principles. See also **humiliation**; **rage**.

Health Health and normality (see **norm**) are often confused, but, strictly speaking, health refers to states of wholeness and **integration** while normality refers to states corresponding to whatever norm the writer is taking as his standard of comparison. When, however, the writer takes as his norm the ideal of mental health, the two terms become synonymous. In phrases such as 'the mental health movement', health means freedom from ascertainable **mental illness**. Health is both a medical and a religious term, *vide* the Book of Common Prayer's 'We have left undone those things which we ought to have done; and we have done those things which we ought not to have done; and there is no health in us.'

Hebephrenia Form of **schizophrenia** characterized by withdrawal, bizarre mannerisms, and neglect of the person.

Hermeneutics 'The art or science of interpretation, espec. of Scripture' – *S.O.E.D.* '[A] discipline concerned with the interpretation of human products and experiences . . . Modern hermeneutics provides methodological guidelines for asking and answering questions' – Steele (1982).

Heteronomy See **autonomy and heteronomy**.

Heterosexual and homosexual These two words seem to have entered English in 1892 with the translation of Richard von Krafft-Ebing's *Psychopathia Sexualis*. When used as adjectives, they refer to desires and actions directed towards a member of the opposite or same **sex**. When used as nouns, they insinuate an assumption that is not true, viz. that every human being can be categorized as belonging intrinsically to one or other of two classes. See **bisexual**, **homosexual**, **perversion**.

Holism Word invented by General (later Field-Marshal Lord) Smuts (*Holism and Evolution*, 1926) to describe 'the tendency in nature to produce wholes from the ordered regroupings of units' – *S.O.E.D.* Also used for the idea that the whole is implicit in its parts. See Brierley (1951) for the suggestion that **psychoanalysis** is an holistic theory. Although recently a vogue word, as in *holistic medicine*, which claims to treat the whole person not just his bodily organs or his mind, the idea is ancient and related to that of holiness.

Homeostasis The tendency of organisms to maintain themselves in a constant state. According to Cannon (1932), who coined the term: 'Organisms, composed of material which is characterized by the utmost inconstancy and unsteadiness, have somehow learned the methods of maintaining constancy and keeping steady in the presence of conditions which might reasonably be expected to prove profoundly disturbing.' Freud's **pleasure–pain principle**, and his use of Fechner's **constancy principle**, are usually regarded as psychological concepts analogous to the physiological concept of homeostasis, i.e. they imply an in-built tendency to keep psychological **tension** at a constant optimal level, similar to that which makes the body keep its blood–chemistry, temperature, etc., constant.

Homosexual 1. Adj. referring to sexual behaviour in which the **subject**'s object is a person of the same sex. According to Freud (1914), homosexual love differs from heterosexual love in being narcissistic (see **narcissism**), since the **object** is loved on account of its similarity to what the subject is, once was, or hopes some time to become, as opposed to heterosexual love, which is **anaclitic**, being dependent on the object providing what the subject cannot himself be. **2.** By extension, adj. referring to all attitudes, feelings, etc., directed towards persons of the same sex. Hence *homosexuality*, which may be male, female (lesbianism), **active** (in which the subject behaves as a man and treats his object as though he were female), **passive** (in which the subject behaves as a woman and treats his object as a man), **manifest**, **latent**, **aim-inhibited**, and **sublimated**. The latter three terms are used to refer to phenomena which the laity would not regard as homosexual. *Latent homosexuality* is the odd one out since it refers not to repressed homosexual feelings (see **repression**) which become manifest during psychoanalytical treatment, but to defensive submissive attitudes (see **defence** and **submission**) adopted towards more powerful males. The justification for the concept derives from the theoretical assumption that the defence is regressive (see **regression**), that it consists in reactivation of passive, **feminine** wishes towards the **father** during the negative oedipal phase (see **negative Oedipus complex**). Latent homosexuality can, however, be regarded as a defence against **paranoid anxiety** and as analogous to the intimidated, appeasing, submissive attitude adopted by animals when attacked by a member of their own species. See Lorenz (1966).

The 'homo' in homosexual derives from the Greek *homos*, meaning 'same', and not from the Latin *homo*, a 'man'; hence 'homo-sexual' can be applied to women as well as men. See **heterosexual and homosexual**.

Humiliation In psychoanalytical language, humiliating experiences are 'injuries to the **ego**' and *narcissistic wounds*. Responses to humiliation are **hate** and narcissistic **rage**. The assumption of both **classical** and **Kleinian** theory that hate is an **instinct** has led to neglect of the importance of humiliation as a cause of hatred. But see Kohut (1972).

Hypnagogic Adj. referring to the drowsy state occurring while falling asleep (see **sleep**) and to experiences such as **hallucinations** occurring during this state.

Hypnoid Sleep-like. According to Breuer, Freud's collaborator in *Studies on Hysteria* (1895), hypnoid states occur frequently in women who engage in activities such as housework which do not engage their full attention and predispose to **hysteria**.

Hypnopompic Adj. referring to the drowsy state occurring while awakening from **sleep** and to experiences such as **hallucinations** occurring during this state.

Hypnosis Artificially induced **sleep**. The **trance**-like state induced by **hypnotism**.

Hypnotism The process of putting a person into a state of **trance**, in which he is awake but suffers an impoverishment of his critical faculty and is amenable to *hypnotic suggestion*. According to Ferenczi (1909), the hypnotic state is a **transference** phenomenon, in which the hypnotist temporarily acquires the authority of a parent, some techniques being paternal (the authoritative, imposing voice *à la* Svengali), others maternal (stroking the forehead, the soothing voice). Hypnotism played an important part in the history of **psychoanalysis**, since it was Freud's dissatisfaction with it which led him to discover the technique of **free association**.

Hypochondriacal Adj. referring either to a person who imagines he is suffering from a physical illness or to the **delusions** or **phantasies** of such a person. Hence *hypochondriasis*, a **psychosis** of which the main symptom is the patient's belief that he has an incurable physical illness.

Hypomania Psychiatric term for the condition of persons who display in mild form the **elation** and **psychomotor acceleration** of **mania**. Differentiation of hypomania from exuberant and inde-fatigable vitality depends on demonstrating that the patient uses **manic defences** against **depression**.

Hysteria 1. Medical diagnostic term for illnesses characterized by (a) the presence of physical **symptoms**, (b) the absence of physical **signs**, or any evidence of physical pathology, and (c) behaviour suggesting that the symptoms fulfil some psychological function. The notion of hysteria derives from the ancient Greeks, who applied the term solely to diseases of women, which were explained as being due to malfunctioning of the **uterus** (*hysteron*). According to one theory, the uterus is a mobile organ capable of moving about the body and pressing on other organs; according to another, sexual abstinence leads to 'starvation of the womb' or to retention of unused animal spirits which passed out of the uterus leading to disturbance in other organs. One of the effects of psychoanalysis has been to demolish uterine theories of the causation of hysteria while retaining the idea that it is in some way connected with **sexuality**. For the history of the medical concept, see Veith (1965). **2. Classical theory** distinguishes between two forms of hysteria: *conversion hysteria* (q.v.), which corresponds to the traditional medical concept, and *anxiety hysteria* (q.v.), which is now more commonly known as **phobia**. Hysteria occupies an important place in the history of **psychoanalysis**, which began with the publication of Freud and Breuer's *Studies on Hysteria* (1895), in which hysterical symptoms were explained as the result of repressed memories (see **repression**) and the **conversion** of ideas into physical symptoms.

Although both these concepts survive in psychoanalytical theory, no contemporary analyst would maintain that they provide an adequate explanation of hysteria. A curious fact, to which Wisdom (1961) has drawn attention, is that Freud never wrote a definitive formulation of his views on hysteria and that it is extremely difficult to discover what the classical theory of hysteria is. There is, however, a tendency to assume that it asserts that the hysterical

fixation point is during the oedipal phase (see **Oedipus complex**) and that its characteristic **defence** mechanisms are **repression** and **dissociation**. Melanie Klein was also silent on the subject of hysteria and the only object-theorist to concern himself with it has been Fairbairn (1952), who labelled one of his defensive **techniques** 'the hysterical' and held that the origins of hysteria lay in the **schizoid** position (see **paranoid-schizoid position**). According to Veith (1965), hysteria is an almost extinct disease which only occurs among 'the uneducated of the lower social strata' who have not been influenced by the dissemination of psychoanalytical ideas. (Psychoanalysts who work in private practice are none the less quite familiar with hysterical phenomena.)

Hysterical 1. When applied to a symptom, see **hysteria** above. **2.** When applied to a personality, the reference is either to a predisposition to produce **conversion symptoms** or to a histrionic quality in the patient's behaviour. In both cases the implication is that the observed phenomena should not be taken at their face value and that they are intended either to draw or distract attention. **3.** When applied to **defences**, the reference is either to the tendency to produce conversion symptoms, or to the use of **dissociation** (**splitting**), or to simultaneous use of **idealization** and **repression**. According to Fairbairn (1952) the *hysterical technique* consists in **externalization** of the **good** object and **internalization** of the **bad** object, as a result of which the hysterical person regards some external **object** as ideally good and his own impulses as bad.

I When used simply as the nominative of the first person singular, 'I' creates no difficulties, but when used substantively to refer to a **structure**, viz. 'the I', its relations to 'the **self**' and 'the **ego**' are not always clear. In German, indeed, 'the I' and 'the ego' are identical: *das Ich*. However, given the fact that the English language permits a choice between 'the I' and 'the ego', it seems logical to use 'the I' for the self when it is the **subject** of experience, i.e. for that part of the self which can assert 'I am', and the 'ego' for the self or person when it is the **object** of scrutiny.

I–thou relation Term used by Martin Buber to describe mutual experiences of reciprocity, of shared relations in which the self discovers itself in relation to the other. The 'I–Thou' relation is contrasted by existentialist writers (see **existentialism**) with **classical theory**'s conception of **object-relations** between genital **characters** (see also **genital**) whose **egos** are distinct entities. 'Buber's emphasis upon the relation between selves, rather than upon the individual self in its relations to the world, constitutes an obvious difference from Freudian psychology.' See 'Martin Buber and Psychoanalysis', in Farber (1966).

Id The Latin word for 'it', used by Freud's translators to translate his *das Es*, the term he borrowed from Groddeck (1923) and used to designate unorganized parts of the **psychic apparatus**. (Groddeck's translators prefer 'the **it**'.) Historically the id is the descendant of the **unconscious** in the same way as the **ego** is the descendant of the **conscious**. According to **classical theory** the id is developmentally anterior to the ego, i.e. the **psychic apparatus** begins as an undifferentiated id, part of which develops into a structured ego. The id 'contains everything that is present at birth, that is fixed in the constitution – above all, therefore, the instincts, which originate from the somatic organization and which find a first psychical expression here [in the id] in forms unknown to us' – Freud (1940). 'It is the dark, inaccessible part of our personality; what little we know of it we have learnt from our study of the dream-work and of the construction of neurotic symptoms, and most of that is of a negative character and can be described only as a contrast to the ego. We approach the id with analogies: we call it a chaos, a cauldron full of seething excitations ... it is filled with energy reaching it from the instincts, but it has no organization, produces no collective will, but only a striving to bring about the satisfaction of instinctual needs subject to the observance of the pleasure-principle' – Freud (1933). The concept is one of many examples of Freud's passion for explaining mental phenomena in terms of the opposition of antithetical forces. The id is primitive, the ego civilized; the id is unorganized, the ego organized; the id observes the **pleasure principle**, the ego the **reality principle**; the id is emotional, the ego rational; the id conforms to the **primary processes** which ignore differences and are oblivious of contradictions and of space and time, the ego conforms to the **secondary processes** which are analytical and respect the principles of contradiction and the categories of space and time. For a summary of the arguments *against* conceiving of mental life in terms of such antitheses and in favour of the view that the psyche has structure from the very beginning, see Rycroft (1962).

Idealization Defensive process (see **defence**) by which an ambivalently regarded (see **ambivalence**) (**internal**) **object** is split into two (see **splitting**), one resulting object being conceived of as ideally **good**, the other as wholly **bad**. The concept includes two notions: the construction of an ideal, perfect object and the **reification** of an idea. Idealization in its wider and non-technical sense of regarding some person as perfect and wonderful involves **projection** as well as idealization. Idealization differs from admiration in that (a) the idealizing person needs a perfect person to exist and ignores (denies, see **denial**) the existence of those attributes of the idealized person which do not fit the picture, and (b) it leads to **dependence** on and subservience to the idealized person and not to emulation and imitation. Idealization is a defence against the consequences of recognizing ambivalence and purchases freedom from **guilt** and **depression** at the cost of loss of **self-esteem**. Failure of the defence leads to disillusion and depression. See Rycroft (1955).

Identification The process by which a person either (a) extends his **identity** *into* someone else, (b) borrows his identity *from* someone else, or (c) fuses or confuses his identity *with* someone else. In analytical writings it never means establishing the identity of oneself or someone else.

Four types of identification are distinguished: primary, secondary, projective, and introjective. *Primary identification* is the state of affairs presumed to exist in infancy when the individual has yet to distinguish his identity from that of his **objects**, when the distinction between 'I' and 'you' is meaningless. *Secondary identification* is the process of identifying with an object the separate identity of which has been discovered. Unlike primary identification, secondary identification is a defence since it reduces hostility between the self and the object and enables experiences of **separation** from it to be denied. None the less, secondary identification with parental figures is held to be part of the normal developmental process (see **development**). *Projective identification* is the process by which a person imagines himself to be inside some object external to himself. This again is a defence since it creates the **illusion** of control over the object and enables the subject to deny his powerlessness over it and to gain vicarious satisfaction from its activities. *Introjective identification* is either the process of identifying with an **introject** or the process by which a person imagines another to be inside and part of him. In some usages this is indistinguishable from secondary identification and introjection.

Identification is often confused with **introjection, internalization**, and **incorporation**. See Koff (1961), and Fuchs (1937) for attempts to define the term accurately. See also **ego**; **ego development**; **ego boundary**.

Identity The sense of one's continuous being as an entity distinguishable from all others. According to Erikson (1953), many aspects of **ego development** can be formulated in terms of the growth of the sense of identity, an *identity-crisis* of greater or lesser severity being characteristic of late adolescence and early adulthood. The sense of identity is lost in **fugues** and perverted in schizophrenic **delusions** of identity (see also **schizophrenia**) in which, typically, an underlying sense of nonentity is compensated for by delusions of grandeur. Many of the problems about identity centre round the part played by **identifications** in enhancing or diminishing identity. Failure to identify with parents, particularly the parent of one's own sex, during childhood is held to diminish the sense of identity, but failure to disidentify with them in adolescence has a similar effect. The sense of identity is probably synonymous with **self-awareness** and can be regarded as the subjective equivalent of the **ego**, which psychoanalytical theory tends to use only objectively. It is not clear whether the *search for identity* which preoccupies many American writers is a search for a role or for enhanced self-awareness. See Erikson (1953), Wheelis (1958), Lynd (1958). See also **self**; **I**; **identity *v*. role diffusion**.

Identity *v*. role diffusion The fifth of Erikson's eight **stages of man**. It corresponds to adolescence and early manhood, during which, according to Erikson, the individual has to redefine his identity, particularly in relation to the parents he is growing away from and the society he is growing into. 'Role diffusion' refers to the adolescent tendency to 'over-identify, to the point of apparent complete loss of identity, with the heroes of cliques and crowds' – Erikson (1953).

Illusion 'A subjective perversion of the objective content' of a perception. It differs from a **hallucination** in that it is due to misinterpretation of an actual experience, and from a **delusion** in that the question of belief does not arise. Illusions are not pathological phenomena and are of more interest to psychologists, particularly to students of perception, than they are to psychiatrists and psychoanalysts. The word is, however, used by Winnicott (see **Winnicottian**) in a somewhat special sense to describe the infant's experience on those happy occasions when the **mother** succeeds in realizing his expectations, i.e. when the infant's wish-fulfilling hallucinations (see **wish-fulfilment**) are met by actual mothering. According to Winnicott, healthy development is dependent on such experiences of illusion. See Winnicott (1958). Patients who use the defence of **idealization** can also be said to be in a state of illusion. See Rycroft (1955).

Imagination The process, or faculty, of conceiving **representations** of objects, events, etc., not actually present. The process produces results which are either (a) *imaginary*, in the sense of being fictitious, unreal, etc., or (b) *imaginative*, in the sense of providing solutions to problems which have never previously been so solved or, in the arts, creating artefacts which none the less reflect or enhance experience. The psychoanalytical literature tends to subsume imagination under the heading of **phantasy** and has the same difficulty as do the arts in deciding whether and when phantasy (imagination) is escapist or creative, defensive or adaptive (see **creativity**, **defence**, and **adaptation**). It is generally accepted, however, that creative imaginative activity involves the participation of unconscious non-verbal phantasy.

Imago Word used by Freud to describe (unconscious) **object-representations**. Not to be confused with an insect after its final metamorphosis.

Implosion Term used by Laing (1960) to describe the fear of being annihilated by reality which is experienced by persons who lack primary ontological security (see **ontology**). Such persons feel like vacuums, long to be filled, but fear that whatever could fill them would destroy their **identity**.

Impotence When describing a symptom, sexual incapacity of the male is always intended. Sexual impotence may be due to either physical or psychological factors. **Psychoanalysis** is only concerned with the latter. **Psychogenic** impotence can only be regarded as a **neurotic** symptom if it is persistent, if it defeats the patient's conscious intentions and occurs even under the most favourable conditions. Otherwise it is the result of either inexperience or insincerity.

Impulse The psychoanalytical usage of this word derives from **neurology**, where it refers to the wave of electrical charge passing along a nerve fibre. In **classical theory** instinctual impulses are similarly conceived to pass from some point in the **id** along channels leading into the **ego**, where they are either (a) discharged in action (see **discharge**), (b) inhibited (see **inhibition**), (c) diverted by the operation of **defence** mechanisms, or (d) sublimated (see **sublimation**) into non-instinctual channels. When used correctly the concept is an **economic** one, used to describe the movements of psychic **energy** within the **psychic apparatus**, but in fact it is often used as a synonym for wish, desire, or drive, all of which refer to subjective experiences.

Inaccessible See **accessible and inaccessible**.

Incest Sexual relations between blood relatives; the prohibited degree of relationship being determined by canon or secular law. For Freud's views on the origins of the incest **taboo**, see his *Totem and Taboo* (1913). The **Oedipus complex** implies that all individuals have *incestuous phantasies*. In conversation, analysts and persons who have been in close contact with psychoanalytical circles habitually use 'incestuous' for 'in-bred', to refer, for instance, to the social atmosphere created by the fact that everyone and his wife has been in analysis with everyone else.

Incorporation Although sometimes used synonymously with **internalization** or **introjection**, incorporation properly refers only to a **phantasy**, viz. to the phantasy that the subject has ingested an **external object**. Incorporation-phantasies are typically **oral**, i.e. that the subject has swallowed the object, but they may also occur in relation to other openings of the body, including such organs as the eye and ear which can be imagined as openings. The confusion with introjection arises from the fact that the structural process of introjection may be accompanied by the phantasy of incorporation. When used as a technical term, incorporation never refers to the process of assimilating something into a previously existing structure or to the combining of units to form a larger body or structure. Incorporation-phantasies were first described as occurring in melancholic (**depressive**) patients (see **melancholia**), whose introjections (**identifications**) are made during the oral stage of **libidinal development** and are accompanied by cannibalistic phantasies. See Freud (1917), Abraham (1927).

Independent Group The Independent Group consists of those members of the British Psycho-Analytical Society who are neither *contemporary* **Freudians** nor **Kleinians**. Until his death in 1971 Winnicott (see **Winnicottian**) was its most prominent member, but he consistently denied that he was its leader. See Kohon (1986) for papers written by members of the group; Rayner (1990) for its history and achievements.

Individuation The process of becoming an individual, or of becoming aware that one is one. As used by Jung, the term seems to include not only the idea of becoming aware that one is separate and different from others, but also the idea that one is oneself a whole, indivisible person. According to Jung, individuation is one of the tasks of middle age. See Bennet (1966).

Industry v. inferiority The fourth of Erikson's eight **stages of man**. It corresponds to the **latency period** of **classical theory**. The 'industry' refers to the preoccupation with acquiring physical skills characteristic of the phase (ages 8–13) and the 'inferiority' to the danger of being discouraged by a sense of inferiority in comparison with grown-ups. See Erikson (1953).

Infantile When applied to behaviour, **emotions**, **phantasies**, etc., infantile means **pre-genital** and not childish or immature. *Infantile sexuality* embraces sexual phenomena assumed to be normal, ubiquitous, and inevitable during the infantile phases of **libidinal development** and which persist into adult life only in so far as (a) the **Oedipus complex** has not been resolved, (b) **sublimations** have not occurred, and (c) the activities have not been integrated into the **fore-pleasure** of adult sexuality. The psychoanalytical usage of 'infantile' to mean pre-genital, **pre-oedipal**, unsublimated is accompanied by an analogous use of 'infant' to mean any child under, say, 4 or 5. In medical and statistical literature, 'infant' means 'a child under 1 year of age'.

Inferiority complex Originally an **Adlerian** term describing the cluster of ideas and feelings which arise in reaction to the sense of *organ inferiority*. Now a popular term for the sense of inadequacy.

Inhibition A process or function is said to be in a state of inhibition if it is being rendered quiescent by the operation of some other process or function. In **neurology**, a reflex response is said to inhibit another if its operation precludes the possibility of the other occurring. Fear can also be said to inhibit appetite, sexual desire, etc. The essence of the notion is that of holding in check. In **psychoanalysis** the term is usually used to refer to instances in which the state of inhibition can be regarded as a symptom, the inhibiting agency usually being the **ego** or **super-ego** and the inhibited process being an **instinctual impulse** or a sublimated derivative thereof (see **sublimation**). In some contexts, however, inhibition is contrasted with **symptom**, the former referring to a loss of function, the latter to disturbance of function. See Freud's *Inhibitions, Symptoms and Anxiety* (1926). Inhibition and **repression** differ in that the former implies that something is switched off, the latter that something is being held back.

Initiative v. guilt The third of Erikson's eight **stages of man**. It corresponds to the oedipal phase (see **Oedipus complex**) of **classical theory**, the 'initiative' manifesting itself *inter alia* in 'anticipatory rivalry with those who have been there first', leading 'to a climax in a final contest for a favoured position with the mother; the inevitable failure leads to resignation, **guilt**, and **anxiety**' – Erikson (1953).

Insanity See **sanity and insanity**.

Insight 1. In **psychiatry**: the capacity to appreciate that one's disturbances of thought and feeling are subjective and invalid. Loss of insight characterizes **psychosis**, retention characterizes **neurosis**. 2. In **psychoanalysis**: the capacity to understand one's own **motives**, to be aware of one's own **psychodynamics**, to appreciate the **meaning** of symbolic behaviour (see **symbol**). Analysts distinguish between *intellectual insight*, the capacity to formulate correctly one's own **psychopathology** and dynamics, and *emotional insight*, the capacity to feel and apprehend fully the significance of '**unconscious**' and symbolic manifestations. Intellectual insight is usually classified as an **obsessional defence** since it enables the subject to understand and control aspects of himself from which he remains alienated (see **alienation**). Emotional insight, on the other hand, is evidence of freedom from alienation and of 'being in touch with the unconscious'. It is possible to have insight in sense 1 and to lack it in sense **2**, i.e. to be sane and yet clueless. Although insight refers in the first instance to **self-awareness** and self-knowledge, it is also used to refer to the capacity to understand others. Insight is a faculty necessary for the practice of psychoanalysis.

The aim of psychoanalytical treatment is sometimes defined in terms of the acquisition of insight, though Freud himself never used this formulation, preferring the idea that its aim is to make **conscious** the **unconscious**. Both definitions imply that consciousness has an integrating function (see **integration**). According to Fonagy (1991), insight is a 'reflexive self-function' dependent on the capacity for 'metacognitive monitoring'.

Instinct An innate biologically determined drive to action. According to **classical theory**, an instinct has (a) a biological source, (b) a supply of **energy** derived therefrom, (c) an aim, viz. carrying out the behaviour specific to the instinct, leading to *instinctual satisfaction* (see also **satisfaction**) and **discharge** of the energy invested in it, and (d) an **object**, in relation to which the aim can be achieved. Failure to find an object and to achieve the *instinctual aim* leads to *instinctual frustration* (see also **frustration**) and increase in instinctual **tension**, the heightened tension being experienced as **pain**. In accordance with the **pleasure principle**, this pain leads either to increased activity in pursuit of relief or to the introduction of **defence** mechanisms to reduce the tension. The **ego** reacts to the threat of instinctual tension over and above its **threshold** of tolerance by **anxiety** (**signal–anxiety**), which is the ego's **stimulus** to institute defensive measures. According to Freud (1915), an instinct may undergo four vicissitudes, viz. (a) **reversal** into its opposite, typically the replacement of an active role by a passive one; (b) **turning against the self**, i.e. use of the self as the instinctual object; (c) **repression**, a term which in 1915 included all the defence mechanisms, later described; and (d) **sublimation**, as a result of which the instinctual energy is eventually discharged in activities bearing only a symbolic connection (see **symbol**) with the primary instinctual aim. This conception of instinct is clearly only applicable with any degree of plausibility to the sexual and aggressive drives (see **sex** and **aggression**), and attempts to apply it to other innate behaviour patterns, such as sleep or nutrition, would lead to immediate and obvious absurdities. In fact it was constructed with the sexual disorders of hysterics in mind (see **hysteria** and **hysterical**), though the relation of instinctual tension to signal-anxiety derives from study of the defences against aggression occurring in **obsessional neurosis**.

Freud was consistently a proponent of a *dual instinct theory*, holding that instincts could be categorized into two groups, which tended to be antagonistic towards one another, and that the conflicts between the two groups were responsible for neurosis. He was not, however, consistent in his view as to what the two (groups of) instincts were. Until the early 1920s they were the *ego-instincts* (see **ego-instinct**) and the *sexual instinct*, corresponding to the self-preservative and reproductive instincts of biology (see **self-preservation**), but in his later speculative writings they were the **life** and **death instincts**. The scheme outlined above was never intended to apply to ego-instincts, and it is not clear whether it was meant to apply to the death instinct – though there certainly exists a tendency among analysts to assume that there is an instinct and a form of energy both called 'aggression' to which it does. Many analysts have pointed out that, although the notion of **conflict** implies the existence of at least two drives, there is no particular reason for preferring a dual to a triple or even a multiple instinct theory. Contemporary animal psychology (**ethology**) postulates at least seven instincts or innate behaviour patterns: nutrition, **sex**, fighting, parental, **sleep**, **territoriality**, and grooming. The last two are unrepresented in psychoanalytical theory. According to Anna Freud (1937), there is an 'innate hostility between the ego and the instincts which is primary and primitive'.

Instinct, component According to **classical theory**, the adult sexual **instinct** 'gradually develops out of successive contributions from a number of component instincts which represent particular **erotogenic zones**' – Freud (1940).

Instinct theory and object theory These terms are used to distinguish between formulations which concern themselves with **instincts** and their vicissitudes and those concerned with the individual's relations with his **objects**. Formally the distinction is a false one, since instincts are directed towards objects and objects can only be of significance if the individual has some drive to relate to them. In practice, however, it is a real one, viz. between theories which assume that the individual acquires the capacity to relate to objects at some stage of **development** and those which assume that he is born related to an object (the **mother**); between those which assume that **adaptation** is a reluctantly learned process and those which assume that the infant is born adapted; between those which assume that the value of objects lies in their capacity to give instinctual pleasure and those which assume that the value of pleasure lies in its capacity to enrich relationships. *Instinct theory* provides psychoanalysis with a link with biology; *object theory* gives it one with the social sciences. Classical **psychoanalysis** is an instinct theory; the **Kleinian** and Fairbairnian (see **Fairbairn's revised psychopathology**) systems are object theories. Hartmann's **ego-psychology** has some aspects of both. See Klein (1948), Fairbairn (1952), Hartmann (1958).

Integration The process by which parts are combined into a whole. According to **classical theory** the human psyche starts as an unintegrated, unorganized **id** and becomes integrated as a result of **ego development**. According to **object theory** the infant begins life in a state of primary integration. 'The pristine personality of the child consists of a unitary, dynamic ego' – Fairbairn (1952). All **defences**, other than **sublimation**, operate at the expense of integration, purchasing freedom from **anxiety** at the price of **splitting** off or **repression** of parts of the potential integrated **self**. Psychoanalytical treatment aims to restore lost parts to the self and to increase integration. See Fairbairn (1952), Rycroft (1962), Storr (1960).

Internal This is frequently used as a synonym for 'psychical', 'mental', on the assumption that mental processes are located in an inner space. Hence *internal reality*, *internal conflict*, *internal object* (see also **reality**, **conflict**, **object**), all of which are conceived and defined in contrast to their 'external' equivalents.

Internalization Although sometimes used synonymously with **introjection**, it is best used only to describe that process by which **objects** in the external world acquire permanent mental **representa-**

tion, i.e. by which **percepts** are converted into images forming part of our mental furniture and structure. See also **externalization**.

Internal saboteur Term used by Fairbairn (1952) to describe one of the three parts into which the original 'unitary, dynamic **ego**' becomes split. The internal saboteur is anti-libidinal, is attached to the **internal** 'rejecting **object**', and is the precursor of Freud's **super-ego**.

Interpersonal 1. *Interpersonal theories* and concepts are concerned with how persons interact on one another, in contrast to the *intrapersonal theories* of **classical theory**, which are concerned with how single individuals develop and behave. **2.** *Interpersonal relationships* are relationships between persons; the 'inter' is redundant unless a contrast is being made with relationships between parts of a person. A man's relation to (with) his boss is interpersonal, to his **super-ego** is intrapersonal.

Interpretation The process of elucidating and expounding the **meaning** of something abstruse, obscure, etc. Psychoanalytical interpretations are statements made by the analyst to the patient in which he attributes to a **dream**, a **symptom**, or a chain of **free associations** some meaning over and above (under and below) that given to it by the patient. The paradigm of interpretation is *dream-interpretation*, the activity of discovering the **latent** content of meaning of a dream by analysis of its **manifest** content. The assumptions underlying this activity are (a) that the dream has meaning; (b) that this can be elucidated by a person familiar with symbolism (see **symbol**) and the **primary processes** (the rules governing **unconscious** mental activity), with the circumstances of the dreamer and with his associations to the dream; and (c) that the dreamer can confirm the accuracy of the interpretation by his response to it – in the most simple instance by recollecting some event corresponding to one surmised by the interpreter. It is assumption (c) which prevents dream-interpretation from becoming an arbitrary and dogmatic procedure.

Transference-interpretations relate the patient's behaviour and associations to his relationship to the analyst. *Content interpretations* refer to unconscious **impulses** and **phantasies** without reference to the defensive processes which have been keeping them unconscious. *Direct interpretations* are based solely on the analyst's knowledge of symbolism without reference to the patient's associations. *Correct interpretations* are those which both (a) explain adequately the '**material**' being interpreted and (b) are formulated in such a way and communicated at such a time that they have actuality for (make sense to) the patient. *Premature interpretations* are 'true' interpretations communicated to the patient before they can make sense to him. *Mutative interpretations* alter the patient. (See Strachey (1934) for an explanation as to why interpretations have a therapeutic effect and for the preconditions necessary for an interpretation being effective.) The function of interpretation is to increase **self-awareness** and therefore facilitate **integration** by making the patient **conscious** of processes within himself of which he was previously unconscious.

Analysts habitually talk as though *all* their utterances were interpretations, but this is not, strictly speaking, the case. Some are **confrontations**, i.e. remarks which draw the patient's attention to something without explaining it, while others reflect what the patient is saying and show that the analyst is still 'with' him.

See Freud (1900, 1902), for the original account of psychoanalytical dream interpretation. See Sharpe (1937, 1950), for vivid pictures of an analyst at work. See Rycroft (1958), for a discussion of the emotional significance of interpretations.

Intimacy v. isolation The sixth of Erikson's eight **stages of man**. It is during this stage that the healthy individual reaches the **genital level** of classical psychoanalysis (see **classical theory**) and becomes capable of intimate love and creative work. It apparently lasts from the early twenties to early middle age. The hazard of this phase is 'the fear of **ego** loss in situations which call for self-abandon' and a resulting sense of isolation. See **genitality** for an extended quotation from Erikson's description of this phase. See Erikson (1953).

Intrapsychic Adj. referring to processes occurring within the **mind**. *Intrapsychic conflict* refers to **conflict** occurring between two parts of the same mind, in contrast to conflict between persons.

Introjection The process by which the functions of an external **object** (see also **externalization**) are taken over by its mental **representation**, by which the relationship with an object 'out there' is replaced by one with an imagined object 'inside'. The resulting mental structure is variously called an *introject*, an *introjected object*, or an *internal object*. Introjection is preceded by **internalization**, may or may not be accompanied by the **phantasy** of **incorporation**, and may be followed by secondary **identification**. The **super-ego** is formed by introjection of parental figures and it may be analysed into a number of component introjects (the **good** (**bad**) **internal father** (**mother**)). Introjection is both a **defence** and a normal developmental process; a defence because it diminishes **separation anxiety**, a developmental process because it renders the subject increasingly **autonomous**.

Introspection Looking inwards, examining one's thoughts and feelings. It is sometimes distinguished from **self-observation** by using the former to describe worried or narcissistic self-preoccupation (see **narcissism**), the latter objective self-scrutiny. According to this distinction, one of the aims of psychoanalytical treatment is to decrease introspection and to increase the capacity for self-observation.

Introversion, introvert See **extraversion and introversion**.

Intuition 'The immediate apprehension of an object by the **mind** without the intervention of any reasoning process' – *S.O.E.D.* This definition assumes that intuition and reason are distinct, separatable faculties. In a psychoanalytical context, it would be necessary to qualify 'reasoning' with the adjective **conscious** to arrive at an acceptable definition. Intuition is comparable to **empathy** in that findings based on it can be dismissed as unscientific and unreliable.

Invert, inversion *Sexual inversion* is an obsolescent term for male **homosexuality**; hence *invert* for male homosexual.

Isakower phenomenon **Hypnagogic** experience first described by Isakower (1938) in which the subject imagines soft, doughy masses to be moving towards his face. Isakower interpreted this phenomenon as a revival of the infant's experience of being at the **breast**. See Lewin (1946) for an account of its relevance to his **dream screen** concept and the psychology of **sleep**.

Isolation Defence mechanism by which the subject isolates an occurrence, preventing it from becoming part of the continuum of his significant experience. 'When something unpleasant has happened to the subject or when he has done something which has a significance for his neurosis, he interpolates an interval during which nothing further must happen – during which he must perceive nothing and do nothing . . . the experience is not forgotten, but, instead, it is deprived of its **affect**, and its associative connections are suppressed or interrupted so that it remains as though isolated and is not reproduced in the ordinary processes of thought' – Freud (1926). Isolation is used typically by obsessional neurotics (see **obsessional neurosis**) in whom it plays the same role as does **repression** in **hysteria**. It has connections with **splitting** and **dissociation**.

'It, the' The English translators of Groddeck (1866–1934), from whom Freud borrowed the concept of the **id** (*das Es*), use 'the It' to refer to Groddeck's original concept, which Freud modified considerably. Although 'the Id' and 'the It' have in common the idea of an impersonal force within, with which the **ego** has to come to terms, they differ in that 'the id' is a *psychological* concept, that part of the **psychic apparatus** within which the instinctual and innate are mentally represented and out of which the ego arises, while 'the *Es*' is a *psychosomatic* concept: 'the body and mind are a joint thing which harbours an It, a power by which we are lived, while we think we live . . . The It, which is mysteriously connected with sexuality, Eros, or whatever you choose to call it, shapes the nose as well as the hand of the human, just as it shapes his thoughts and emotions . . . And just as the symptomatic activity of the It in hysteria and neurosis calls for psychoanalytical treatment, so does heart trouble and cancer.' See Grossman (1965), Groddeck (1923).

Jealousy Differs from **envy** in that it involves three parties: the **subject**, an **object** whom the subject loves, and a third party who arouses **anxiety** in the subject about his security of tenure of the second party's affections; whereas envy involves only two parties: the subject and an object whose good fortune or possessions the subject envies. *Jealousy* is related to possessiveness of the other, *envy* to comparison of the self with the other. It is typically evoked by the oedipal triangle and forms part of the **Oedipus complex**. *Pathological jealousy*, i.e. persistent, unfounded, delusional jealousy (see also **delusion**), appears to have some intrinsic connection with **homosexuality** and **paranoia**. According to Freud (1911), the jealousy and the paranoia are defences against the homosexuality, but the contemporary tendency is to regard the paranoia as the primary member of the triad.

Jungian 1. N. a follower of C. G. Jung (1875–1961), Swiss psychiatrist who was a disciple of Freud's from 1907 to 1913 but later founded his own school and system of **psychopathology**. Jungian therapists are correctly called *analytical psychologists* and not psychoanalysts, though this is far from being general usage. **2.** Adj. referring to ideas propounded by Jung. See Bennet (1966) for a comprehensible summary of Jung's ideas, and Samuels et al. (1986).

Kleinian 1. N. a follower of Melanie Klein (1882–1960), pioneer of **child analysis** and of research into **depressive** and **schizoid** states. 2. Adj. referring to ideas and theories formulated by Melanie Klein. Although the *Kleinian school* of **psychoanalysis** remains within the Freudian fold, its theories differ in several fundamental respects from **classical theory**. The main differences are: (a) The **death instinct** is taken seriously as a clinical concept; innate **ambivalence** is assumed, the destructive component of the ambivalence being interpreted as a defensive **projection** (see also **defence**) outwards of the innate self-destructive instinct. (b) **Ego development** is regarded as a process of continual **introjection** and **projection** of **objects** and not as progress of the self through a number of stages in which a variety of defences are used. (c) The origins of **neurosis** are held to lie in the first year of life and not in the first few years and to consist in failures to pass through the *depressive position*, and not to **fixation** at a variety of stages (**fixation points**) through childhood. As a result, the depressive position plays the same part in Kleinian theory as the **Oedipus complex** does in classical theory. (d) Kleinian theory is an **object theory** not an **instinct theory** in as much as it attaches central importance to resolution of ambivalence towards the **mother**, the **breast**, and regards ego development as being based primarily on introjection of the mother and/or breast. It differs, however, from the object theories of Fairbairn (see **Fairbairn's revised psychopathology**) and Winnicott in attaching little importance to the infant's actual experience of mothering, this being overshadowed in the Kleinian view by the infant's difficulties in overcoming its innate ambivalence towards the breast. Being endowed with both innate **envy** of it and the need to use it as the recipient of its own projected death instinct, the infant has first to work through its fear and suspicion of the breast (the **paranoid-schizoid position**) and then work through its discovery that the breast it hates and the breast it loves are the same breast (the **depressive position**). (e) It assumes that the infant has a much more vivid, violent **phantasy** life than does classical theory and that the main task of analysis is to interpret **unconscious** phantasies rather than to interpret **defences** against unconscious impulses. Phantasies are, however, regarded as the psychic representatives of libidinal and destructive instincts and to be the processes against which defences are erected. In summary, Kleinian analysis resembles classical analysis in subscribing to a dual **instinct** theory and indeed in being more **Freudian** than the Freudians in its use of the death instinct but differs from it in rejecting the concepts of stages of development and fixation points in favour of a theory of positions and in attributing greater importance to the first year of life than to childhood as a whole. See Segal (1964) and Hinshelwood (1989) for expositions of Kleinian theory, and Glover (1945) for sharp criticism of it from a classical point of view.

Kohut, Heinz (1913–81) Viennese-born American analyst. Originator of **self-psychology** in opposition to **ego psychology**. 'It is a hybrid offshoot of **object relations theory**, notable chiefly for its metapsychological focus on issues of **narcissism**' – Rudnytsky (1991). Kohut is widely believed to have been more influenced by Fairbairn and Winnicott than he admitted (see **Fairbairn's revised psychopathology** and **Winnicottian**). See also **metapsychology**; **narcissistic personality disorder**; **rage**.

Lacanian psychoanalysis The ideas and theories propounded by Jacques Lacan (1901–81). Lacan became a member of the Société Psychoanalytique de Paris (SPP) in 1934 and was briefly its president in 1953. That same year he resigned from the SPP and his membership of the International Psycho-Analytical Association lapsed. From then onwards he was *persona non grata* to the psychoanalytical movement, despite becoming a cult figure in French intellectual circles. One objection held against him was his habit of cutting therapeutic sessions short when it suited him – a procedure rather obviously capable of abuse. His ideas are 'heretical' and anomalous since there is no way in which they can be accommodated within any of the main streams of psychoanalytical thought – **classical theory**, **ego psychology**, **object relations theory**, or **self-psychology**.

Lacan rejected all biological, evolutionary, and developmental concepts and denied the significance of the **environment** and of pre-verbal experience. His best-known ideas are **1**. The **mirror** stage. According to Lacan, the crucial experience of childhood, and indeed of life, is the first time a child sees his/her reflection in a mirror; he is captivated by his 'specular image', becoming for ever alienated from his body, which from then on has less reality for him than his mirrored image. **2.** That the **unconscious** 'is structured in the most radical way like a language'. Since Lacan ignores the body and pre-verbal experience, this is not the same as the idea, first mooted by Sharpe (1937), that Freud's **primary processes** are analogous to figures of speech (see **metaphor**). **3.** The idea that the phallus (not the **penis**) is *the* privileged signifier of desire. For elucidation, see Bowie (1991, ch. 5). Lacanian concepts do not lend themselves to dictionary definition since, as Bowie (1991) points out, Lacan placed 'a continuous positive valuation upon ambiguity', thought that 'students of the **unconscious** mind, when they become writers, are somehow morally obliged to be difficult', and was 'defiantly self-congratulatory' about his own reputation for being difficult. For discussion of the relationship of Lacan's ideas to those of Winnicott (see **Winnicottian**), **Kohut**, and Klein (see **Kleinian**), see Rudnytsky (1991).

Lamarckianism Evolutionary theory, first stated by Lamarck (1744–1829), which asserts that characteristics acquired by the individual can be inherited by his descendants. This theory of the 'inheritance of acquired characteristics' is generally held to be incompatible with the Darwinian theory that evolution occurs by natural selection, i.e. by the survival and transmission of chance variations. Much to the embarrassment of most of his followers Freud was a Lamarckian. 'In spite of innumerable similar strictures Freud remained from the beginning to the end of his life what one must call an obstinate adherent of this discredited Lamarckism,' wrote Jones (1957). This adherence explains his anthropological theory that the sense of guilt of contemporary man derives from **parricide** committed in prehistoric times; and his historical theory that the consciousness of **guilt** which pervades Jewish history is an inherited, **unconscious** memory of the guilt felt by Moses' murderers. Jones (1957), vol. III, ch. 10, is at a loss to explain this aberration of Freud's. See Freud (1913, 1939). See **ontogeny and phylogeny**; **totem**; **taboo**; **primal**. See also Yerushalmi (1991).

Latency period Developmental phase postulated by **psychoanalysis** in which psychosexual maturation marks time. It occurs after the **oedipal** phase and ends at puberty and is a period of emotional quiescence between the dramas and turmoils of childhood and adolescence. It is unclear whether the latency period is an innate, universal phenomenon related to the prolonging of biological immaturity which characterizes human development or whether it is confined to repressive cultures (see **repression**) in which **infantile** and immature sexual behaviour is subject to restriction. The latency period corresponds to the fourth of Erikson's eight **stages of man, industry v. inferiority**, a formulation which emphasizes the preoccupation of this stage with acquiring skills.

Latent See **manifest and latent**.

Lay analyst A **psychoanalyst** who is not medically qualified. It was Freud's opinion that **psychoanalysis** should become a profession independent of medicine, 'a profession of lay curers of souls who need not be doctors and should not be priests'. This quotation is exceptional in that 'lay' here means 'non-clerical' and not 'non-medical'.

Learning theory 1. Any theory which attempts to explain learning. 2. (And more usually) that body of psychological theory which seeks to explain behaviour in terms of learned responses to environmental stimuli – in contrast to **dynamic** theories such as **psychoanalysis** which explain it in terms of innate or instinctual developmental processes. In sense 2 learning theory is the heir of Pavlov's work on conditioned reflexes and of Watson's behaviourism, which it resembles in rejecting introspective data and in regarding **psychology** as a 'purely **objective** experimental branch of natural **science**'. Learning theory provides the theoretical basis for **behaviour therapy**, which proceeds from the assumption that **neurotic** behaviour is the end-result of faulty, maladaptive learning and can, therefore, be modified by deconditioning and relearning techniques. Learning theorists claim that its reliance on experiment and sophisticated statistical techniques gives it a scientific respectability which psychoanalysis, with its clinical origins, sadly lacks. See Eysenck (1965).

Libidinal and libidinous The former is the correct form for the adjective corresponding to the technical term **libido**.

Libidinal infantile development Classical theory postulates a series of phases of libidinal development through which the individual passes from infancy until he reaches the **latency period**, these phases being synchronous with a parallel series of phases of **ego development**. In most formulations the phases are the **oral**, **anal**, **phallic**, and **oedipal**, the first three being conjointly '**pre-oedipal**'. The oral, anal, and phallic phases are so named because during them the mouth, anus, and penis are respectively the main source of libidinal pleasure; according to some formulations they are narcissistic (see under **narcissism**), on the ground that only in the oedipal phase does the capacity for **object-love** emerge. In some formulations the oral phase is subdivided into *oral-sucking* and *oral-*

biting substages, and the anal phase divided into *anal-expressive* and *anal-retentive*. **Object theory** continues to use the terms 'oral' and 'anal' to describe phases or aspects of the **mother**–child relationship, despite its abandonment of the classical notion that the infant is narcissistic and pleasure-seeking – and despite its rejection of the distinction between an **id** in which libidinal development occurs and an **ego** in which ego development takes place. See also **instinct theory and object theory**; **libido**.

Libido Hypothetical form of mental **energy**, with which processes, **structures** and **object–representations** are invested. Libido is conceived as having a source, the body or the **id**, as existing in various forms related to specific **erotogenic zones** (i.e. **oral**, **anal**, **genital** libido), as being distributed between various structures or processes, which are *libidinized* (or, alternatively, carry a *libidinal cathexis* (see **cathexis**)). In Freud's first formulations, libido was the energy attached specifically to the sexual instincts (see **sex**), but later the **ego** was assumed to possess libido, this *ego-libido* being derived from libido attached to object-representations (object-libido). This rather curious formulation derives from two others: viz. (a) that the ego differentiates out of the id; hence ego energy must be a differentiated form of id energy; (b) that the development of the ego is the result of **frustration** by parental objects, and is accompanied by **identification** with and **introjection** of them; hence the libido originally attached to them becomes attached to the ego, **self-love** and **self-awareness** increasing as the attachment to the parents decreases. This formulation implies that the ego is its own object; hence the distinction made by Federn (1952) between *subject-libido*, the energy available to the self *qua* subject, and *object-libido*, the energy available for investment in objects. Object-libido invested in the ego is *narcissistic libido*. Believers in the **life instinct** and **death instinct** are logically compelled to contrast libido, the energy of the life instincts, with another form of energy specific to the death instinct. Although attempts have been made to introduce '**mortido**' and '**destrudo**' to fill this gap, neither has caught on.

Libido theory See **libido**; **instinct theory**.

Life instinct In his later speculative writings Freud abandoned his earlier idea that the two groups of **instincts** were the sexual (see **sex**) and the **ego instincts**, corresponding to the reproductive and self-preservative instincts of biology (see **self-preservation**), in favour of the **life instinct** and **death instinct**, the life instinct including both the sexual and the self-preservative instincts, the death instinct being the drive to return to the inanimate state.

Linking, attacks on In the definition of Bion (1959, in Bion, 1967): 'destructive attacks which the patient makes on anything which is felt to have the function of linking one object with another'. 'The prototype for all the links of which I wish to speak is the primitive **breast** or **penis**.'

Loss See **Object-loss**; **mourning**; **attachment theory**.

Love Psychoanalysts have as much difficulty defining such a protean concept as do others. It appears in the literature as (a) **Eros**, a personified force or principle; (b) an **instinct** or group of instincts liable to come into **conflict** with either self-preservative (see **self-preservation**) or destructive instincts; (c) an **affect** more often contrasted with **hate** than with **fear**; and (d) a capacity or function liable to **inhibition**, **perversion**, and **sublimation**. **Instinct theory** assumes that all forms of loving are, in the last resort, derivatives of instinct and that their function is to provide instinctual **satisfaction**; **object theory** assumes that they are all manifestations of the need to relate to objects. The distinction between love which recognizes the needs and reality of the other and that which fails to is usually made by contrasting **object-love** and **infantile** or dependent love (see **dependence**). A *love-object* is an object whom the subject loves in contrast to either (a) an object whom he hates or to whom he is indifferent, or (b) a need-satisfying object. *Oedipal love* is love for a parent or for a parent-substitute. *Genital love* is not a synonym for sexual desire but the form of love of which a person who has reached the **genital level** is capable.

Magic Primitive, superstitious practices based on the assumption that natural processes can be affected by actions which influence or propitiate supernatural agencies, or, as in the case of *sympathetic magic*, by actions which resemble those which the magician wishes to induce. See **omnipotence**; **obsessional neurosis**; **ritual**.

Male and female Adj. referring to persons of the **sex** capable of begetting or bearing offspring respectively; or to the sexual organs necessary for begetting or bearing offspring. Or, alternatively, to those of the sex capable of producing spermatozoa and ova respectively; or to those sexual organs necessary for fertilization and parturition to occur. Not to be confused with **masculine** and **feminine**. See also **gender**.

Malignant In medicine, cancerous growths are *malignant*, in contrast to non-cancerous ones, which are *benign*. Severe **hysteria** is sometimes termed *malignant hysteria*, possibly partly because of the unconcious malice so often present.

Mania **Psychosis** characterized by **elation**, **psychomotor acceleration**, i.e. gross acceleration of both physical and mental activity leading to excitement, severe insomnia and eventual exhaustion, and flight of ideas, i.e. rapid thought in which the connections between one idea and the next are based on superficial associations and which is undisciplined by self-criticism. Acute and chronic forms are described and the illness is regarded as being a phase of **manic-depressive psychosis**. The few psychoanalytical studies made of mania suggest that its **psychopathology** is the reverse of that of **depression** and that the elation is due to a sense of triumph at having overcome the **super-ego** (**internal objects**), whose imagined hostility is responsible for the depression of the **depressive** phase of the psychosis. See Abraham (1927), Lewin (1951).

Manic defence Form of defensive behaviour (see also **defence**) exhibited by persons who defend themselves against **anxiety**, **guilt**, and **depression** by (a) **denial** of the guilt, anxiety, and depression; (b) the operation of a **phantasy** of **omnipotent** control, by means of which they imagine themselves to be in control of all situations which might provoke anxiety or feelings of helplessness; (c) **identification** with objects from whom a sense of power can be borrowed; and (d) **projection** of 'bad' aspects of the self on to others. Manic defences purchase freedom from guilt and anxiety at the expense of depth of character and appreciation of the motives and feelings of others.

Use of the manic defence is not confined to persons liable to develop **mania** or a **manic–depressive psychosis**. The concept belongs to **object theory**. According to Fairbairn it is an emergency defence brought into operation when the non-specific **techniques** (**paranoid**, **obsessional**, **hysterical**, and **phobic**) have failed to protect the **ego** against the onset of a depressive state (see **Fairbairn's revised psychopathology**).

Manic-depressive psychosis **Psychosis** in which periods of **mania** and **depression** alternate. According to Kraepelin, the major mental illnesses could be divided into two groups, **dementia praecox** and manic-depressive psychosis, the latter being a cyclical illness in which the patient suffers a series of attacks of **elation** and depression with intervening normal intervals. The concept is descriptive and prognostic (see **prognosis**) and has no psychopathological implications (see **psychopathology**). Contemporary psychiatry tends to prefer **affective psychosis** or affective disorder, terms which exclude the implication of an in-built cycle of moods.

Manifest and latent The *manifest content* of a **dream** is the dream as reported by the dreamer; the *latent content* is its meaning as revealed by **interpretation**. Freud seems to have believed that dreams have, as it were, an original text, the publication of which encounters **censorship** so that the dream has to be redrafted in a form that the censor cannot understand. The original draft is the latent content, the redrafting is the dream–work, and the final, published draft is the manifest content. The distinction between manifest and latent can also be applied to a **symptom** and its unconscious **meaning**. The distinction between manifest and latent homosexuality is, however, anomalous; *manifest homosexuality* refers to overt **homosexual** behaviour, *latent homosexuality* refers to submissive attitudes adopted by **neurotic** men towards men imagined to be more powerful than themselves (see **submission**). Since manifest homosexual behaviour is regarded as defensive (see **defence**), its latent equivalent is not homosexuality but **fear** of either men or women. Since latent homosexuality describes a form of behaviour it cannot be latent. What has happened is that a hypothesis about the cause of submissiveness, viz. that it is a manifestation of latent (i.e. **unconscious**) homosexuality, has been introduced into its description.

Masculine, masculinity Referring to patterns of behaviour, attitudes, etc., presumed to be psychological secondary sexual characteristics of the male. **Classical theory** tends to assume that masculinity has an inherent connection with activity, aggressiveness (see **aggression**), **sadism**, and competitiveness; and further that all these propensities are related to **sex**; e.g. aggressiveness and competitiveness are related to the **Oedipus complex** rather than to a non-sexual instinct such as **territoriality**. The question as to what forms of behaviour and what mental characteristics are innately masculine is bedevilled by (a) the assumption that all characteristics must be either masculine or feminine; (b) the absence of human societies in which any individual comes to **maturity** without being influenced by social **stereotypes**; and (c) the absence of any neutral neuters to view the issue without bias. See **active and passive**; **bisexual**; **feminine**; **male and female**.

Masculine protest **Adlerian** term for reactive behaviour in women who feel they are members of an inferior sex. See **envy**; **penis envy**.

Masochism **1.** Sexual **perversion** in which the subject claims to get **erotic** pleasure from having pain inflicted upon himself. **2.** Character-trait presented by persons who bring ill-treatment, humiliation, and suffering upon themselves. **3.** *Moral masochism*: term used by Freud to describe the tendency to submit to one's own sadistic **super-ego** (see **sadism**). The concept hinges on the idea that the super-ego derives its moral force from instinctual aggressive **energy** (see also **instinct** and **aggression**) which is discharged by 'taking it out on' the **ego**. Masochism is either a real or an apparent exception to the **pleasure principle**. It tends to be explained in terms of either (a) **reversal** of sadism; (b) **identification** with the sadistic partner; (c) alleviation of **guilt** by experiencing punishment and pain simultaneously with pleasure; (d) eroticization of a submissive role (see **erotic** and **submission**) originally adopted to appease authority figures; and (e) the **death instinct**.

Classical theory assumes an intrinsic connection between masochism, passivity (see **passive**), and **femininity**. In doing so it confuses abandoning oneself to the **will** of another with experiencing pain.

Masturbation Although the word literally means genital excitement, it is only used to refer to self-induced genital excitement. Hence:

Masturbation phantasy The imaginative activity accompanying masturbation.

Infantile masturbation Masturbation occurring in childhood.

Masturbation equivalent or substitute Activity inferred to be an equivalent or substitute for masturbation.

Material Analysts often refer to material brought by patients. This means their utterances. The usage derives from the fact that what the patient says is used by the analyst as evidence on which to base **interpretations**. As a result a patient can be thought of as producing material for the analyst to interpret, **oral** material being evidence making possible interpretations at the oral level, etc. Although this elision of the notions of utterance and evidence is convenient and natural, it also encourages the tendency of analysts to think of their work as inspection of some*thing* rather than as **communication** with some*one*.

Mature and immature Although these tend to be words of praise or abuse, they have in biology precise meanings. A mature individual (organism) is one in whom **development** is complete; an immature individual is one in whom it is incomplete: a child is immature and a grown-up is mature. When applied to psychological processes and behaviour, their use seems always to imply comparison with **norms**, the origins of which are unclear; to label someone immature implies that one knows what sort of behaviour is appropriate to his age and that he is in fact behaving in a way appropriate to someone younger.

Meaning Although **psychoanalysis** is usually presented as a **causal** theory which explains psychological phenomena as the consequences of prior events, a number of analysts, notably Szasz (1961), Home (1966), Rycroft (1966), have argued that it (or some aspects of it) is really a theory of meaning, and that Freud's crucial observation that **hysterical** symptoms were psychogenic was really the discovery that they have meaning, i.e. that they could be interpreted as gestures and **communications**. Advocates of this view argue that theories of causality are only applicable to the world of inanimate objects and that Freud's attempt to apply deterministic principles derived from the physical sciences to human behaviour fails to take account of the fact that man is a living **agent** capable of making decisions and choices and of being creative (see **creativity**). They also hold (a) that Freud was misguided in supposing that his discovery of **unconscious** mental processes and of the '**primary processes**' governing them proved that mental life demonstrated the principle of psychic **determinism**; and (b) that in so supposing he involved psychoanalysis in a contradiction, viz. that of maintaining both that **conscious** processes are determined by unconscious ones and that making unconscious processes conscious increased the individual's freedom of choice and action. In some aspects of his work Freud clearly realized that he was concerned with meanings and not causes. He entitled his most famous book *The Interpretation of Dreams*, not the 'Cause of Dreams', and his chapter on symptoms in his *Introductory Lectures* is 'The Sense of Symptoms'. See Schafer (1976).

Melancholia Obsolescent term for what is now called **depression** (particularly **endogenous** depression), **depressive** illness, or the depressive phase of **manic–depressive psychosis**. When *melancholic* qualifies depression, the implication is that the patient is not simply in low spirits but is also retarded, suicidal, and self-reproachful (self-accusatory) (see **retardation**; **suicide**; **self-reproaches**).

Memory Memory fulfils the biological function of enabling organisms to respond to present circumstances in the light of past experience and thereby to replace simple, automatic, 'instinctual' reactions by complex, selective, learned responses. Freud's theory of memory is in reality a theory of **forgetting**. It assumes that all experiences, or at least all significant experiences, are recorded, but that some cease to be available to **consciousness** as a result of **repression**, this mechanism being activated by the need to diminish **anxiety**. Although this theory explains those instances of forgetting that can be demonstrated to be related to neurotic **conflict**, other factors presumably contribute to the fact that **amnesia** for infancy and very early childhood is universal and is not decreased by even the 'deepest' analysis.

Menarche The onset of menstruation in puberty.

Mental illness This term embraces the **psychoses**, the **psychoneuroses**, and the **behaviour disorders**, three clinical entities which differ in kind. Some at least of the psychoses are illnesses similar in kind to physical illnesses; they have demonstrable physical **causes** which explain the **symptoms** without reference to either the patient's personality or to any motives which he might have for wishing to be ill. The neuroses resemble physical illnesses in that they have symptoms of which the patient complains, but they are inexplicable without reference to the patient's personality and motives, i.e. they are creations of the patient himself and not simply the effects of causes operating on him. The behaviour disorders are conditions in which there are no symptoms in the sense of phenomena of which the 'patient' himself complains; it is society not the patient who objects to the disordered behaviour. The idea that the neuroses – and, *a fortiori*, the behaviour disorders – are illnesses is a useful social fiction since it enables neurotic phenomena to be dealt with therapeutically, but it is based on a confusion of thought, viz. the equation of **unconscious** motives with causes. See Szasz (1961), Home (1966), Rycroft (1966).

Metaphor The figure of speech by which one thing or process is described in terms of some other thing or process. The ability to use metaphor depends on the capacity to see a similarity between things that are otherwise dissimilar. 'A good metaphor implies an intuitive perception of the similarity in dissimilars' – Aristotle. The **primary processes**, **condensation**, **displacement**, and **symbolization** can all be regarded as examples of (or analogous to) metaphorical expression. See Sharpe (1937), Rycroft (1991).

Metapsychology Term invented by Freud to describe what other sciences call 'general theory', i.e. statements at the highest level of abstraction. Metapsychological formulations describe mental phenomena in terms of the fictive **psychic apparatus** (see **fiction**) and ideally contain references to the **topographical**, **dynamic**, and **economic** aspects of the phenomenon in question; the topographical referring to its location within the psychic apparatus, i.e. whether in the **id**, **ego**, or **super-ego**, the dynamic to the **instincts** involved, and the economic to the distribution of **energy** within the apparatus. Metapsychology is part of **classical theory** and is not used by object theorists (see **object (relations) theory**).

Migraine Correctly, severe one-sided headache with *photophobia* (painful sensitivity to light) and *castellations* (visual images resembling the battlements of a castle).

Mind In Strachey's translation of Freud, 'mind' translates *Seele* and 'psyche' translates *Psyche*. The two terms are, however, synonymous, as are also 'psychical' and 'mental'. As Brierley has pointed out, **psychoanalysis** regards mind as a process and not a thing, despite Freud's habit of relating mental phenomena to a **psychical apparatus**. 'The general theory of psycho-analysis, in its most abstract definition, is a psychology of mental processes and their organization. For such a psychology, mind has ceased to be a static structure or a substantial thing and has become a dynamic entity, a nexus of activities and a sequence of adaptive responses' – Brierley (1951). Psychoanalysis also regards mind (mental processes) as being in some way intrinsically connected with body (bodily processes). Despite conforming to the linguistic conventions which compel one to talk of a body and a mind which are different and yet interact, it contains a number of concepts which tie its psychology to physiology and biology. Among these are **instinct**, **id**, **unconscious**, **affect**, sexuality (see **sex**), **erotogenic zones**, and **symbolism**. In his *Freud and Man's Soul* (1983), Bruno Bettelheim criticized Strachey for translating *Seele* as 'mind', asserting that he would have been truer to the spirit of Freud if he had translated it 'soul'.

Mirror According to Lacan (see **Lacanian psychoanalysis**), the human infant is captivated by its first sight of its own reflection in a mirror. According to Winnicott (see **Winnicottian**) the infant finds itself reflected in its **mother**'s face.

Mneme Memory. Hence *mnemic image*, the psychological equivalent of a memory-trace.

Model When analysts talk of constructing models, they are referring to the formulation of a system of concepts which can be expressed diagrammatically. The classic example of a psychoanalytical model is Freud's **psychic apparatus**, in which the relations between the **id**, **ego**, **super-ego**, and the **environment** are represented topographically (see **topographical**). The danger of models is that they may be taken too seriously; the fact that mental activity and conflict *can* be conceived of in terms of a visible diagram, parts of which are labelled id, ego, and super-ego, leads all too readily to the conviction that there really are things called the id, ego, and super-ego. See **reification**.

Mood Psychiatry only recognizes two moods – **elation** and **depression**. Disturbances of mood characterize the **affective disorders**. See **mania; manic-depressive psychosis**.

Mortido Term coined by Federn (1952) to describe a form of **energy** belonging to the **death instinct** and analogous to **libido**. Although such a concept is logically necessary for analysts who believe in the **life** and death instincts, no one, not even Federn himself, has had the nerve to work out the implications of conceiving of a **psychic apparatus** in which two opposed instincts are simultaneously at work, and two different forms of energy circulate.

Mother Since psychoanalytical theory is formulated in terms of what anthropologists call the *nuclear family*, consisting of **father**, mother, and children, it assumes that the person who mothers a child and the person who gave it birth are identical. Hence formulations about mothering are stated in terms of 'the relationship to the mother', the real-life complications arising from the contributions of grandmothers, aunts, nurses, elder sisters, and *au pair* girls being dealt with, if at all, by calling them 'mother-figures'. Even fathers may on occasion be mother-figures.

According to most formulations, the mother is the central person in the child's life throughout the **pre-oedipal** phases of **development**, though Melanie Klein (see under **Kleinian**) dates the onset of the **Oedipus complex** in the first year of life, i.e. during what **classical theory** holds to be the **oral phase**. Again according to most, but not all, formulations, the mother is a **need-satisfying** or **part object** during the first few months of life, i.e. she is 'loved' solely for her capacity to provide **satisfaction** and only later does she become a **whole object**, whose own personality and needs are in any way recognized by the infant. The phrases '*the good mother*' (see also **good**), '*the bad mother*' (see also **bad**), '*the ideal mother*', and '*the persecuting mother*' all refer to conceptions of the mother existing in the infant's mind formed by **splitting** of the mother image. The *phallic mother* (see **phallic woman**) is also, strictly speaking, a conception in the infant's mind, though the term is sometimes also applied to women whose personality encourages such a conception. '*The rejecting mother*' and '*over-protective*' and *schizophrenogenic mothers* are actual mothers, so described by psychiatrists and analysts who attribute to them pathogenic effects on their offspring (see entries under **over-** and **schizophrenogenic**). The *ordinary devoted mother* is Winnicott's (1958) term (see **Winnicottian**) for the mother who provides her child with mothering adequate for his development and who is capable of *primary maternal preoccupation*. For the effects of maternal deprivation and of separation from the mother, see **deprivation**; **separation, mother–child**.

Motive That which drives a person towards an end or goal. The concept does not distinguish between 'internal' factors, such as **instincts**, and 'external' ones, such as incentives. See **will**.

Mourning 'The psychological processes that are set in train by the loss of a loved object and that commonly lead to relinquishing of the object' – Bowlby (1961). It follows bereavement, is accompanied by **grief**, and may or may not be followed by attachment to a new object; it is typically accompanied by (a degree of) **identification** with the lost object (see **object–loss**). Although terminologies differ, mourning seems to be divisible into three stages: (a) That of protest or **denial**, in which the subject attempts to reject the idea that the loss has occurred, feels incredulous, and experiences anger, reproaching himself, the dead person, or his medical attendants for having allowed the loss to occur. Darwin called this stage 'frantic grief'. (b) That of resignation, acceptance, or despair, in which the reality of the loss is admitted and **sorrow** supervenes. (c) That of detachment in which the subject relinquishes the object, weans himself from it, and adapts himself to life without it. If mourning occurs 'normally', the subject 'gets over' the loss and becomes capable of reattaching himself to a new object.

All schools of **psychoanalysis** regard mourning as the normal analogue of **depression**, the loss in depression being not that of an actual person but of an ambivalently invested '**internal object**' (see also **ambivalence**). See Freud (1917), Abraham (1927). According to Bowlby (1951, 1961), infants and children react to separation from their mothers by mourning processes which predispose to psychiatric illness in later life.

Muscle erotism Pleasure in bodily activity.

Narcissism **1.** Sexual **perversion** in which the **subject**'s preferred **object** is his own body (first used in this sense by Havelock Ellis and Näcke). **2.** By extension, any form of self-love.

Classical theory distinguishes between *primary narcissism*, the love of self which precedes loving others, and *secondary narcissism*, love of self which results from introjecting and identifying with an object (see also **introjection** and **identification**). The latter is either a defensive activity or attitude (see **defence**), since it enables the subject to deny (see **denial**) that he has lost the introjected object, or part of the developmental process (see **development**). A major difficulty of the concept is that, on the one hand, the word 'narcissism' has inescapable disparaging overtones, while, on the other hand, it is used as a technical term to categorize all forms of investment of **energy** (**libido**) in the **self**. Hence the not infrequent references to 'healthy narcissism' to distinguish proper self-respect from 'over-valuation of the **ego**'.

Narcissistic object-choice is based on the object's similarity to the subject. A *narcissistic wound* is an injury to self-esteem. A *narcissistic neurosis* is one in which the patient is incapable of forming a **transference**. *Narcissistic supplies* are indications of affection, flattery, praise, etc., which enhance self-esteem. Narcissism also on occasion means egocentrism or **solipsism**, i.e. it can refer to the tendency to use oneself as the point of reference round which experience is organized. In this sense the discovery that one is not the only pebble on the beach and that the world was not constructed solely for one's own benefit involves a loss of narcissism.

See **auto-erotic**.

Narcissistic personality disorder Diagnostic category much popularized by **Kohut** (1972, 1978). It embraces persons who have suffered intense injuries to self-esteem in early life, who have compensated for this by developing a grandiose conception of themselves, and who respond to attacks on their inflated self-image with **rage**. According to **classical theory**, such persons do not form **transferences** and are, therefore, unanalysable, but, according to Kohut, they form **self–object** transferences, i.e. they identify their analyst with some part of themselves, and can therefore be analysed. See Kohut and Wolf (1978).

Need-satisfying object **Object** which is 'loved' solely for its capacity to satisfy instinctual needs without cognizance being taken of *its* needs or personality.

Negation Process by which a **perception** or thought is admitted to **consciousness** in negative form, e.g. the onset of a headache is registered by the thought, 'How lucky I am to have been free from headaches for so long'; the fact that a figure in a **dream** stands for the **mother** is admitted by the statement, 'It wasn't my mother anyhow.' (The point here is that none the less the idea that it might be the mother must have occurred for it to be denied.) Not to be confused with **denial**; **negativism**.

Negative Often used as synonym for 'hostile', but see below.

Negative capability The phrase always alludes to Keats's 'negative capability, that is, when a man is capable of being in uncertainties, mysteries, doubts, without any irritable reaching after fact and reason' – a passage from one of his letters not uncommonly quoted by British analysts when describing the attitude of receptive expectation an analyst should take up towards patients.

Negative Oedipus complex Form of **Oedipus complex** in which the subject wishes to possess the parent of its own sex and regards that of the opposite sex as its rival.

Negative therapeutic reaction Technical term for a fortunately rare hazard of psychoanalytical treatment, viz. exacerbation of the patient's symptoms in response to precisely those **interpretations** which are expected to alleviate them. Although the phenomenon has been used as evidence in favour of the existence of primary **masochism**, it is more usually explained in terms of **guilt** provoked by the prospect of **health** achieved at the expense of someone else.

Negativism Counter-suggestibility; cussedness; rejection of over-tures of help. Attitude displayed by patients who have a compulsion to oppose their **will** to that of others, even to the extent of 'cutting off their nose to spite their face', and who react to the prospect of therapeutic change as though it would be a defeat. It is not synony-mous with **negative therapeutic reaction**.

Neo-Freudian See **Freudian**.

Neurasthenia 1. Obsolescent medical and psychiatric term for a state of excessive fatiguability and lack of vigour once supposed to be due to exhaustion or malnutrition of the nerves. **2.** In Freud's writings, one of the **actual neuroses**.

Neurology That branch of medicine concerned with disorders of the nervous system. Freud was a neurologist before he became a psychoanalyst and many psychoanalytical concepts derive from neurology, notably **impulse**, **inhibition**, **discharge**, and **cathexis** – the last being a transposition of the idea that neural activity consists in the movement of **quanta** of **energy** from one **neurone** (nerve-cell) to another into the field of psychology, so that 'ideas', 'mental **representations**', 'images' are treated as the unit structures (neurones) of a **psychic apparatus** analogous to the nervous system. See Freud's *Project for a Scientific Psychology* (1895) for his attempt to base a psychology directly on the movement of energy from neurone to neurone. The *Project* was never published in Freud's lifetime and is now only of interest in showing to what extent **psychoanalysis** developed out of neurology.

Neurone A nerve-cell, the basic structural unit of the central nervous system, consisting of a cell-body and processes along which **impulses** pass.

Neuropsychiatry That branch of medicine concerned with the treatment of nervous and psychological disorders. A *neuropsychiatrist* is at home both in **neurology** and **psychiatry** and is primarily interested in the interrelations of the two disciplines.

Neurosis This term, which dates from the second half of the eighteenth century, originally meant a disease of the nerves. Then later, in the nineteenth century, it was used to describe 'functional disorders', i.e. diseases believed to be due to functional disturbances of the nervous system which were unaccompanied by structural changes. Since Freud's discovery that one of the neuroses, **hysteria**, was a disorder of the personality and not of the nerves, it has been used to describe precisely those mental disorders which are *not* diseases of the nervous system. **Classical theory** distinguishes the following types of neurosis:

Actual neurosis Due to present causes and explicable in terms of the patient's sexual habits (see also entry under **actual neurosis**).

An *anxiety neurosis* is either any neurosis in which **anxiety** is the major symptom or one of the actual neuroses (see also entry under **anxiety neurosis**).

Character neurosis In which the '**symptoms**' are **character** traits.

Infantile neurosis Neurosis in childhood (see also **infantile**). Classical theory assumes that all neuroses in adult life have been preceded by one in childhood.

Narcissistic neurosis Neurosis in which the patient is incapable of forming a **transference** (see also entry under **narcissism**).

Organ neurosis A rarely used term for a **psychosomatic** illness (see also entry under **organ neurosis**).

Psychoneurosis Due to past causes and explicable only in terms of the patient's personality and life history. There are three types of **psychoneurosis**: **conversion hysteria**, **anxiety hysteria** (**phobia**), and **obsessional neurosis**.

A *transference neurosis* is either a neurosis in which the patient is capable of **transference**, or the obsessive interest in the analyst which develops during the course of psychoanalytical treatment.

Traumatic neurosis Due to shock (see also entry under **traumatic neurosis**).

Neurotic 1. Adj. from **neurosis**. According to context, it is used to assert that the phenomenon so qualified is not healthy (**normal**), not **organic** (physical), not **psychotic**, and is capable of psychological explanation. 2. Popularly: 'nervy', 'anxious', 'tense', 'highly-strung', with the implication that the state referred to has a psychological explanation.

Neutralization The process by which **infantile** sexual and aggressive **impulses** (see **sex** and **aggression**) and **energies** are desexualized and deaggressified (see **desexualization** and **deaggressification**) and lose their infantile quality. Sublimated activities (see **sublimation**) and **autonomous functions of the ego** use *neutralized energy*. The concept belongs to **ego psychology**. See Hartmann (1958).

New beginning Term used by M. Balint to describe the start of the process of recovery occurring in patients whose cure necessitates a **regression** to extreme **dependence** on the analyst. It corresponds to what Winnicott (1958) calls emergence of the true self (see **true and false**). See **basic fault**.

Nightmare 1. A **dream** of being sat upon and in danger of being suffocated by a female monster. 2. The female monster herself; an incubus. 3. Loosely: any terrifying dream. Nightmares are an example of gross failure of **defence** against internal forces, and as a result of this failure, the dreamer experiences terror rather than **anxiety**. Nightmares are commoner in childhood than in adult life. The suffocating monster is a good example of a **bad** internal **object** (see also **object, bad**; **object, internal**), since it is a mental **representation**, a phantom (a **phantasy** image), which the dreamer's **ego** responds to as though it were a person. See Jones (1931), Rycroft (1991).

Norm, normal, and abnormal A norm is that member of a class by comparison with which other members are described. In medicine, **psychoanalysis**, **psychology**, and sociology there is a tendency to use as the norm some ideal member of the class and to designate as abnormal any member who deviates appreciably from this norm. In medicine, the norm is 'health' and signs and symptoms are abnormal (hence the medical abbreviation 'N.A.D.' – nothing abnormal detected). Behaviour is designated abnormal by psychologists, sociologists, and psychoanalysts if it deviates from the behaviour considered normal by either the society in which the subject lives, or by the theory to which the scientist subscribes. For instance, **homosexual** behaviour may be described as abnormal either because society considers **heterosexuality** the norm or because theory regards it as a **perversion** of **development**. In the former case, 'abnormal' means 'socially deviant', in the latter 'unhealthy'. Workers who accept society's values are tempted to confuse these two conceptions of normality and to regard as 'unhealthy' all behaviour which is deviant and to equate 'health' with conformity and adjustment. The links between psychoanalysis and biology compel psychoanalysts to define normality in terms of **health** (i.e. in terms of **integration** and freedom from **conflict**), and not in terms of successful adjustment to any particular society. See *neo-Freudian* under **Freudian**.

Nucleus 'Central part or thing around which others are collected'; 'beginning meant to receive additions' – both *C.O.D.* According to Glover (1939), the **ego** begins as a number of discrete nuclei which fuse during **development**, i.e. subjectively: experience of the **self** is at first fragmentary and discontinuous, islands of self-awareness only gradually becoming fused to form a continuous sense of **identity**; and objectively: integrated behaviour patterns are at first partial and only gradually fuse to form an integrated person. This idea belongs to **classical theory** and **ego psychology** and is, apparently at least, in striking contrast to **object theory**'s assumption of an original unitary ego liable to fragmentation. See also **Fairbairn's revised psychopathology**.

The rarely encountered *nuclear complex* refers to the constellation of ideas and feelings relating to the parents and originating in childhood, which form the kernel of the subject's **psychopathology**. See **Oedipus complex**.

Object N. That towards which action or desire is directed; that which the **subject** requires in order to achieve instinctual **satisfaction**; that to which the subject relates himself. In psychoanalytical writings, objects are nearly always persons, parts of persons, or **symbols** of one or the other. This terminology confuses readers who are more familiar with 'object' in the sense of a 'thing', i.e. that which is not a person. Hence:

Object, bad An object whom the subject hates or fears, who is experienced as malevolent. A **bad** object may be either an internal or an external object (see below).

Object-cathexis Investment of **energy** in an external object, in contrast to its investment in the self (narcissistic **cathexis**, see also **narcissism**).

Object-choice Narcissistic *object-choice* is based on **identification** with an object similar to the subject. *Anaclitic object-choice* is based on the object's difference from the subject (see also **anaclitic**).

Object-constancy The ability to maintain a lasting relationship with a specific, single object; or, inversely, the tendency to reject substitutes for a familiar object, e.g. an infant who displays object-constancy rejects mothering from anyone other than his **mother** and misses her specifically when she is absent.

Object, external An object recognized by the subject as being external to himself; in contrast to an internal object (see below).

Object, good An object whom the subject loves, who is experienced as benevolent. A good object may be either **internal** or **external**.

Object, internal **Object-representation** which has acquired the significance of an external object (see above). Internal objects are phantoms, i.e. they are images occurring in **phantasies** which are reacted to as '**real**'. They are derived from external objects by

introjection and are conceived to be located in internal (psychical) reality.

Object-libido **Libido** which is invested in objects, as opposed to *narcissistic libido* which is invested in the self.

Object-loss The loss of, usually, a good external object. The event which precedes introjection and/or **mourning**. See also **attachment behaviour**.

Object-love Love of an object which is recognized as a person other than oneself, in contrast to **self-love** and **identification**. And *love-object*: an object who is loved, who is the object of object-love.

Object, need-satisfying An object whom the subject 'loves' solely on account of its capacity to satisfy needs and whom the subject fails to recognize as a person. The term is only used when discussing the nature of an infant's attachment to its *mother*.

Object, part An object which is part of a person, e.g. a **penis** or a **breast**. The distinction between whole and part object is sometimes used to make what would at first sight appear to be a very different distinction, that between recognizing an object as a person whose feelings and needs are as important as one's own and treating an object as existing solely to satisfy one's own needs. See whole object (below) and need–satisfying object (above).

Object-relations(hip) The relation of the subject to his object, *not* the relation between the subject and the object which is an *interpersonal* relationship. This is because psychoanalysis is a psychology of the individual and therefore discusses objects and relationships only from the point of view of a single subject. An object-relationship may be either an external or an internal object (see above).

Object (relations) theory Psychoanalytical theory in which the subject's need to relate to objects occupies the central position; in contrast to **instinct theory**, which centres round the subject's need to reduce instinctual **tension**. Until the 1970s an entirely British school of thought, but in the past twenty years various American and Americanized versions have appeared, e.g. Kernberg (1976), Greenberg and Mitchell (1983). For the purest and seminal version, see **Fairbairn's revised psychopathology**. For versions complicated by their originators' need to assert that they were loyal

followers of Freud and not dissidents, see **Kleinian** and
Winnicottian.

Object-representation The mental **representation** of an object.
Strictly speaking, all **economic** concepts, e.g. object–**cathexis**,
object–**libido**, refer to the mental representations of objects and
not to objects themselves; otherwise one would have to envisage
the possibility of mental *energy* being attached to **structures** outside
the **psychic apparatus** and even perhaps the possibility of energy
passing from one apparatus to another. See **internalization**.

Object, transitional Object which the subject treats as being half-
way between himself and another person, typically a doll or piece
of cloth which a child treasures and uses as a comforter but which
does not have to be treated with the consideration appropriate to a
person. The concept is Winnicott's (1958), who regards such objects
as helping children to make the transition from **infantile** narcissism
to object–love and from **dependence** to self-reliance. See
Winnicottian.

Object, whole An object whom the subject recognizes as being a
person with similar rights, feelings, needs, etc., as himself.

Objective and subjective 'Are terms of philosophy and physiology distinguishing concepts and sensations that have an external
cause from those which arise only in the mind' – Fowler, *A
Dictionary of Modern English Usage* (1965). Hence physical **pain** is an
objective phenomenon, **dreams** and **hallucinations** are subjective.
Psychoanalysis is largely concerned with the interconnection between objective and subjective phenomena and is sometimes described as a mixed **psychology** on the grounds that it takes
cognizance of both types of phenomenon and uses concepts derived
both from observation of behaviour and from **introspection** (either
by the observer, i.e. the analyst, or by the subject, i.e. the patient).
In this it differs sharply from behaviourism, which attempts to
construct a psychology without reference to **consciousness**, and
less sharply from **phenomenology** which is concerned solely with
how the subject experiences himself and his relation to the external
world. The fact that psychoanalysis uses subjective data is used as
the starting-point of criticisms of it on the grounds that it is
unscientific. This criticism only holds if one defines **science** in a

way that only applies to the natural sciences and excludes the moral sciences such as linguistics, **semantics**, sociology, and anthropology. See Eysenck (1965), Szasz (1961), Rycroft (1966). See also **behaviour therapy**; **causality**; **meaning**; **subject**; **object**.

Obsession When used as a technical term: an idea or group of ideas which persistently obtrudes itself on the patient's **consciousness** despite his **will** and despite the fact that he himself recognizes its abnormality. Obsessions (syn. obsessive or **compulsive** ideas) are the major symptom of **obsessional neurosis**.

Obsessional character A person whose personality contains traits which can be interpreted as equivalent to an **obsessional neurosis**; who uses **obsessional defences** but does not have obsessional symptoms. Conscientiousness, tidiness, meanness, pedantry, rationality combined with cluelessness about human emotions, respect for the letter rather than the spirit of the law and for red tape rather than creative achievement are all liable to be called obsessional character traits. The common feature of these is that control is valued more highly than expressiveness. The justification for calling them obsessional derives from the theoretical inference that **anxiety** about losing control lies at the back of them. See **anal character**.

Obsessional defences This term embraces **reaction-formation**, **isolation**, and **undoing**, defences which have in common their tendency to keep the **ego** uncontaminated by instinctual forces (see **instinct**). See **defence**.

Obsessional neurosis Form of **psychoneurosis** of which the predominant symptoms are *obsessive thoughts* and *compulsive behaviour* (*obsessional rituals*, see also **ritual**). Obsessional thoughts differ from 'normal' thoughts in that they are experienced by the patient himself as unspontaneous, distracting, repetitive, ruminative, and as coming from elsewhere than himself; their subject-matter is typically absurd, bizarre, irrelevant, and obscene. **Compulsive** behaviour is repetitive, stereotyped, ritualistic, and superstitious.

According to **classical theory**, the **psychopathology** of obsessional neurosis centres round **regression** to the **anal-sadistic** stage and **ambivalence** towards parental figures and their **introjects**. More recent formulations centre round the high degree of

internalization and the need to control all **impulses**, the symptoms constituting failures to achieve control, i.e. they are examples of 'return of the repressed' (see under **repression**). It can also be regarded as a disorder occurring in persons whose personality development has been based on **alienation** from **instinct** and **emotion**, the obsessional **ego** being anti-libidinal, anti-impulsive, anti-emotional, etc., and the symptoms being either breakthroughs from the alienated aspects of the self (obsessional thoughts) or **defences** against such breakthroughs (obsessional rituals).

Obsessional neurosis has occupied an important place in the history of psychoanalysis since Freud's *The Ego and the Id* (1923), in which he first described the personality as a tripartite structure consisting of an **id**, **ego**, and **super-ego**, and his *Inhibitions, Symptoms and Anxiety* (1926), in which he first described **signal anxiety**, were both written with obsessional neurosis in mind. 'Obsessional neurosis is unquestionably the most interesting and repaying subject of analytic research,' he wrote in the latter.

Obsessional technique One of the four **techniques** described by Fairbairn in his *A Revised Psychopathology of the Psychoses and Psychoneuroses* (see **Fairbairn's revised psychopathology**). These techniques are used by the subject to effect the transition from **infantile** to mature **dependence**. According to Fairbairn, the infant constructs two images of the **mother** (**breast**) on whom he is originally dependent, one being that of her as a **good**, satisfying **object**, the other that of her as a **bad**, frustrating object, and the four techniques differ in *where* the subject locates these two objects. In the obsessional technique, he locates both inside himself – in Fairbairn's terminology he *internalizes* both the accepted and the rejected object (see **internalization)** – identifying with the good object (see **identification**) but regarding the other as an alien 'content' within him which he must control. As a result, the subject achieves '**quasi-independence**' from the mother based on identification with her, but only reaches the stage of 'mature dependence' if identification with her is replaced by a relationship to her – or rather some adult, 'genital' equivalent. Since this technique, like the other three, can be regarded as a **defence** against **separation anxiety** it tends to be called *the obsessional defence*, though it is clear from Fairbairn's own text that he regarded it as a normal developmental process. See Fairbairn (1952).

See **genitality**; **instinct theory and object theory**.

Obsessional thinking This term refers *not* to obsessional thoughts (see above) but to a form of thinking displayed typically by **obsessional characters** and accepted by them as a valid form of mental activity. Its function is to reconcile ambivalent attitudes (see **ambivalence**), and it tends therefore to consist of highly abstract formulations designed to reconcile contradictions or of statements, typically linked by 'buts', which tend to cancel one another out. Alternatively, all assertions may be so qualified by references to exceptions, conditions, or hints as to the possibility of another and better formulation that the subject in fact avoids committing himself to them.

Oceanic feeling Phrase used by Romain Rolland in a letter to Freud to describe the mystical, cosmic emotion which (according to Rolland) is the true source of religious sentiments (see **religion**). Freud could not discover this feeling in himself. See Freud (1930), where he offers an interpretation of it, viz. that it is a **regression** 'to an early phase of **ego**-feeling', and revives the experience of the infant at the **breast** before he has learnt to distinguish his ego from the external world.

Oedipus complex Group of largely **unconscious** ideas and feelings centring round the wish to possess the parent of the opposite sex and eliminate that of the same sex. The complex emerges, according to **classical theory**, during the *oedipal phase* of **libidinal** and **ego development**, i.e. between the ages of three and five, though oedipal manifestations may be present earlier – even, according to Melanie Klein (see **Kleinian**), during the first year of life. The complex is named after the mythical Oedipus, who killed his father and married his mother without knowing that they were his parents. According to Freud, the Oedipus complex is a universal phenomenon, built in phylogenetically (see **phylogenetic**), and is responsible for much unconscious **guilt**. *Resolution of the Oedipus complex* is achieved typically by **identification** with the parent of the same sex and (partial) temporary renunciation of the parent of the opposite sex, who is 'rediscovered' in his (her) adult sexual object. Persons who are fixated at the *oedipal level* are *mother-fixated* or *father-fixated*, and reveal this by choosing sexual partners with obvious resemblances to their parent(s). Oedipal rivalry with the **father** is a cause of **castration anxiety**.

Freud first mentioned the Oedipus complex in a letter to his friend Fliess in 1897, and the idea arose out of the self-analysis which he conducted after the death of his father. Its first published appearance was in *The Interpretation of Dreams* (1900). It remained a cornerstone of psychoanalytical theory up to, say, 1930, but since then **psychoanalysis** has become increasingly mother-orientated and concerned with the *pre-oedipal relationship to the mother*, and the modern tendency is to regard the Oedipus complex as a psychic structure itself requiring interpretation in terms of earlier conflicts rather than as a primary source of **neurosis** itself. However, even the most enthusiastic supporters of psychopathological systems (see **psychopathology**) centring round the **mother** have to take account of the fact that children have two parents, that in our society at least they grow up in close proximity to both and are confronted with intimations of their sexual life together and their own exclusion from it.

Omnipotence *Omnipotent phantasies* are **phantasies** that the subject is omnipotent. *Omnipotence of thought* refers to the belief that thoughts can of themselves alter the external world. According to some accounts, all infants believe in the omnipotence of thought and learn by their experience of **frustration** to accept the **reality principle**. According to others, it is a symptom of **alienation** and the **dissociation** of phantasy from any contact with the external world. According to Freud (1912), belief in the omnipotence of thought underlies animism, **magic**, religious practices (see **religion**), and **obsessional neurosis**, the **rituals** of the latter two being attempts to *control* the omnipotence of, in the one case, God, in the other, the **subject** himself (i.e. of the alienated part of himself, see **alienation**). Omnipotence of thought is also invoked as an explanation of the fact that wishes can arouse as much **guilt** as actions.

Oneiromancy Divination by means of **dreams**; not to be confused with dream **interpretation**, which makes no claim to be predictive and uses the dream solely as evidence of the dreamer's state of mind. *Oneirology* is a rarely used word for the scientific study of dreams.

Ontogeny and phylogeny The former refers to the development of the individual, the latter to the development of the race or species. In biology the formulation 'ontogeny recapitulates phylogeny' is used to describe the fact that the general pattern of embryological development in the individual is only explicable in terms of the evolution of the species. The idea that this formula might also be applicable to human psychological development was responsible for Freud's incursions into anthropology and for his drawing parallels between infantile **phantasies** (see also **infantile**) and modes of thinking with those of primitive man. As Jones (1930) put it: '. . . when psycho-analytic methods are applied to data obtained from savage races and from mythology and archaeology, it becomes difficult to resist the conclusion that there is an extensive resemblance between the phantasies and mental peculiarities of our young children and what one must infer to have been characteristic of the race as a whole in primitive times; the ideas of cannibalism, of incest, and of father-murder are prominent among the many I am referring to. Freud himself views these conclusions, perhaps rather uncritically, in the Lamarckian manner.' The reference to **Lamarckianism** is to Freud's belief that acquired characteristics could be inherited and that, therefore, modern man's **neurotic** sense of **guilt** could be attributed to ancestral crimes committed in prehistoric times. See **incest**; **omnipotence**; **parricide**; **primal**; **totem**.

Ontology The science or study of being. According to Rollo May (1967), the American existential analyst (see **existentialism**), man has four ontological characteristics: (a) 'he seeks to preserve some center'; (b) 'the human being's centeredness depends on his courage to affirm it', i.e. it is not automatically maintained as in plants and animals; (c) 'he has the need and possibility of going out from his centeredness to participate in other beings'; and (d) **self-consciousness**, that development of the awareness possessed by animals which enables man to be aware that he is the being who has a centre, who affirms and who participates in other beings – and which enables him to use abstractions and **symbols** to transcend the immediate situation. Existentialist philosophers and analysts criticize Freudian **psychoanalysis** on the ground that it neglects ontology and that its preoccupation with the past and with the **unconscious** has led to neglect of problems of **consciousness** and self-consciousness. These criticisms are characteristically levelled at **instinct theory** and **ego psychology** and not at **object theory**. See May (1967), Sartre (1956), Laing (1967). See also **identity**.

Hence: *Primary ontological security*, term used by Laing (1960) to describe the existential position of a person with a 'centrally firm sense of his own and other people's reality and identity'. According to Laing it is this that the psychotic basically lacks (see **psychosis**).

Optimism and pessimism According to Frieda Goldman Eisler (1953), quoted by Carstairs in his 1963 Reith Lectures, optimism is significantly associated with prolonged **breast**-feeding and pessimism with early weaning. Clinically, optimism, in the sense of under-estimating obstacles, tends to be regarded as a manic trait (see **manic–depressive psychosis**), and pessimism, in the sense of over-estimating obstacles, as a depressive trait (see **depression**).

Oral Appertaining to the mouth. Hence:

Oral character **Character** displayed by persons with **fixations** at the oral stage (see below). Typical oral character traits are **optimism and pessimism**, generosity, moodiness, **depression**, **elation**, talkativeness, greed, and the tendency to engage in wishful thinking.

Oral erotism Sensuous pleasure derived from the mouth.

Oral sadism Pleasure in hurting by biting. Pleasure in **phantasies** of biting and eating destructively (cannibalism). According to Abraham (1927), there is an oral-sadistic phase of **infantile libidinal development** which follows dentition.

Oral stage In **classical theory**, the first stage of both **libidinal development** and **ego development**, in which the mouth is the main source of pleasure and hence the centre of experience. According to Abraham, the oral stage can be divided into two sub-stages, those of *oral sucking* and *oral biting*. The stage begins at birth, though it is not clear whether it ends with weaning or at whatever age it would be natural for the infant to wish to be weaned. Persons who are fixated at the *oral level* not only tend to retain the mouth as their primary (usually unconscious) **erotogenic zone** and to be **mother**-fixated (**breast**-fixated) but also to be prone to manic and depressive **mood**-swings (see **manic-depressive psychosis** and **depression**) and to *identify* with others rather than to relate to them as others. The reason for this is that the unconscious **dependence** on the breast is associated with survival of primary **identification** with it, as a result of which satisfying experiences are reacted to as though they confirmed the **phantasy** of fusion with the mother (manic swing) and disappointments are reacted to as though they were loss of the mother (depressive swing). See Abraham (1927) for the seminal papers on the oral stage and its importance in the **psychopathology** of mania and depression. See Lewin (1951) for a more recent exposition of the effects of the oral stage.

For historical reasons, **object theory** still uses the term oral stage to refer to the time at which 'the breast' and 'the mother' are the infant's primary object.

Oral triad Term used by Lewin (1946) for the conjoined wishes to be suckled by, **sleep** with, and be devoured by the **breast**, wishes which, in his view, underlie the **psychopathology** of **mania**. See **elation**; **dream screen**.

Orectic Adj. of desire or appetite. Occasionally used as an antonym of *cognitive*.

Organic *Either* relating to an organism, to a living, dynamic structure, *or*, as in *organic illness*, *organic symptom*, *organic origin*, to the bodily as opposed to the psychological. This latter usage is, strictly speaking, medical and not psychoanalytical. In *organic psychosis*, the differentiation is from *functional psychosis* and refers to the fact that the **psychosis** is the result of disease of the brain.

Organ neurosis Term used in **classical theory** for what is now more usually called **psychosomatic** illness.

Orgasm The culminating-point in sexual intercourse; the moment at which **tension-affects** are replaced by **discharge-affects**.

See **affects**; **fore-pleasure**; **end-pleasure**. The word is occasionally used to refer to an equivalent moment in **pre-genital** acts, hence *gastro-intestinal orgasm* for satiation of the **oral** instinct; and, by still further extension, *pharmacotoxic orgasm* (Rado, 1933) for the response to addictive drugs.

Over- Since many psychiatric symptoms are the occurrence at a high degree of either intensity or frequency of experiences common to mankind, the prefix 'over-' is frequently used to designate behaviour which is considered pathological solely on account of its excessive frequency or intensity. Hence the *over-anxiety* of **phobics**, the *over-conscientiousness* of **obsessionals**, the *over-protectiveness* of **mothers** who overwhelm their children with smother-love, etc. The concept implies that it is possible to establish a normal level of **anxiety**, conscientiousness, etc.

Over-determination A symptom, **dream**-image, or any other item of behaviour is said to be over-determined if it has more than one **meaning** or expresses drives and conflicts derived from more than one level or aspect of the personality; or, alternatively, and perhaps preferably, if it provides a 'final common pathway' to a number of convergent tendencies. Since **psychoanalysis** assumes the presence of a residuum of wishes dating from the past and that the various stages of **development** are superimposed on one another in layers, all behaviour is regarded as over-determined in the sense that it is possible to interpret it as the result of simultaneous activity at several levels.

Paedophilia Lit. love of children, but in practice reserved for the tendency to commit sexual offences against them. See **child sexual abuse**.

Pain According to context, 'pain' refers *either* to the familiar physical sensation *or* to distress associated with instinctual **tension**, the latter being, according to the **pleasure–pain principle**, the condition which instinctual action attempts to relieve. In Freud's writings, physical pain is *Schmerz* and mental pain due to tension is *Unlust* which Strachey translates as '**unpleasure**'. Other translations, however, use 'pain' for both German words.

Parameter Term borrowed from mathematics to describe those aspects of psychoanalytical technique which can (arguably) be modified to meet the needs of particular classes of patients. Frequency of attendance, length of sessions, degree of management of, and interference in, the patient's life, insistence or not on the use of the couch, are all parameters which may be varied to meet the clinical needs of adolescents, **psychotics**, children, or other patients who do not belong to the categories for which **classical analytical technique** was designed. See also **active technique**.

Paranoia Functional **psychosis** characterized by **delusions** of grandeur and persecution, but without intellectual deterioration. In classic cases of paranoia, the delusions are organized into a coherent, internally consistent delusional system on which the patient is prepared to act. This consistency differentiates from *paranoid schizophrenia*. See **schizophrenia**.

Paranoid **1.** Relating to **paranoia** (see above). **2.** Tending to use projective mechanisms (see **projection**). **3.** Loosely: touchy, suspicious. The contemporary tendency to use 'paranoid' to describe persons who use projection as a **defence** arises from two sources:

(a) Freud's **interpretation** of delusions of persecution (see under **delusion**) as projections of unconscious **homosexual** wishes; and (b) Melanie Klein's concept of the **paranoid-schizoid position**, during which, in her view, the infant deals with his innate destructiveness by attributing it to (projecting it on) the **breast** by which it feels persecuted (see also **Kleinian**).

Paranoid anxiety Dread of being attacked by 'bad' objects, either internal, projected internal (see **projection**), or external. When used in its strict, **Kleinian** sense it refers to **anxiety** inferred to be the result of the patient projecting on to objects his own denied (self-)destructive **impulses**. See **paranoid-schizoid position**.

Paranoid-schizoid position Psychic configuration postulated by Melanie Klein in which the individual deals with his innate destructive impulses by (a) **splitting** both his **ego** and his **object-representations** into **good** and **bad** parts, and (b) projecting (see **projection**) his destructive impulses on to the bad object by whom he feels persecuted. According to Klein, the paranoid-schizoid position constitutes the infant's first attempt to master its **death instinct** and precedes the **depressive position**. Failure to leave the paranoid-schizoid position (i.e. to reach the depressive position) is responsible, in Klein's view, not only for many **schizoid** and **paranoid** disorders, but also for obsessional difficulties (see **obsessional neurosis**) in which the 'persecuting bad object' is introjected (see **introjection**), forming the core of the **super-ego**. See Segal (1964).

Paranoid technique One of the four **techniques** described by Fairbairn in his *A Revised Psychopathology of the Psychoses and Psychoneuroses* (see **Fairbairn's revised psychopathology**). These techniques are used by the subject to effect the transition from **infantile** to mature **dependence** (see also **mature and immature**). According to Fairbairn, the infant constructs two images of the **mother** (**breast**) on whom he is originally dependent, one being that of her as a **good**, satisfying **object**, the other being that of her as a **bad**, frustrating object, and the four techniques differ in where the subject locates these two objects. In the paranoid technique he locates the good object inside himself and the bad one outside himself – in Fairbairn's terminology, he internalizes the accepted object and externalizes the rejected object (see **internalization** and **externalization**) – identifying with the good object (see **identification**) but conceiving himself to be subject to **persecution** by objects external to himself. By use of this manoeuvre, the subject achieves 'quasi-independence' of the mother at the price of being subject to paranoid anxiety. Since this technique, like the other three, can be regarded as a **defence** against **separation anxiety**, it tends to be called the *paranoid defence*, but it is clear from Fairbairn's own text that he regarded it as a normal developmental process. See Fairbairn (1952). See **instinct theory and object theory**.

Paranosic This is encountered only in the phrase *paranosic* gain, which is synonymous with 'primary gain'. See **gain, primary and secondary**.

Parapraxis A faulty action due to the interference of some **unconscious** wish, **conflict**, or train of thought. Slips of the tongue and pen are the classic parapraxes. See Freud's *The Psychopathology of Everyday Life* (1901), where he uses parapraxes to demonstrate the existence of unconscious mental processes in the healthy.

Parricide Murder of one's **father**. In the analytical literature it occurs in connection with either the individual's **Oedipus complex** and the resulting death wishes towards the father or the murder of the primal father in the primal horde. See also **totem**.

Part instinct See **instinct, component**.

Part object See **object; whole and part objects**.

Passive 'Suffering action, acted upon' – *C.O.D.* When applied to a person: unwilling to initiate action, prone to become dependent (see **dependence**) on someone else, seeking relationships in which he can become *passive-receptive* or *passive-dependent*. When applied to sexual behaviour: either those roles which are contingent on the activity of the other, e.g. passive **homosexuality** or female **heterosexuality**, or those roles which can be interpreted as **reversals** of the subject's own active instincts, e.g. **masochism** and **exhibitionism**, both of which are, according to **classical theory**, passive forms of the subject's own **sadism** and **voyeurism**. See **active and passive** for the use made by classical analysis of the concepts active and passive.

Pathobiography Psychoanalytical study of a historical character based on the available biographical evidence and not on direct clinical observation. This genre, of which Freud's *Leonardo da Vinci* (1910) is a good example and Freud and Bullitt's study of Wilson (1967) a bad one, suffers from the grave limitation that one of the clinical criteria of correct **interpretation**, the patient's (ultimate) agreement with it, is not forthcoming.

Pathology See **psychopathology**. See also **aetiology and pathology**.

Pathoneurosis **Neurosis**, the symptoms of which are localized in a part of the body previously affected by **organic** disease.

Penis and phallus Strictly speaking, the *penis* is an anatomical term referring to the male generative organ, the *phallus* an anthropological and theological term referring to the idea or image of the male generative organ, i.e. the penis is an organ with biological functions, the phallus is an idea venerated in various religions as a **symbol** of the power of nature. Hence Jung's (probably apocryphal) remark that the penis is only a phallic symbol. The psychoanalytical literature uses both 'the penis' and 'the phallus' to refer to the idea (mental **representation**) of the penis, but prefers the adjectival 'phallic' to 'penile'. For instance, boys are said to go through a **phallic phase** during which they are not only preoccupied with their penis but also with the idea of potency, virility, manliness, and strength and power generally.

Penis awe Term used by Phyllis Greenacre to describe the **emotion** evoked by the sight of the **penis** in certain patients, some of whom described it as being surrounded by a halo. See Greenacre (1953).

Penis envy Envy of the **penis** occurring either in women in respect of men generally or in boys in respect of adult males. According to Freud, penis envy is universal in women, is responsible for their **castration complex**, and occupies a central position in the psychology of women. Freud's tendency to interpret the psychology of women negatively as a response to the discovery of not having a penis, i.e. to regard them as *hommes manqués*, was stigmatized by Jones as '**phallo–centric**'. Jones himself interpreted the girl's wish to have a penis as itself a **defence** against **anxiety** concerning *feminine* wishes towards the **father**. See also **active and passive**.

Perception The process of organizing sensations into meaningful structures, into images or percepts. Perception is creative in as much as what is perceived is a function of the needs, interests, preoccupations, and prior experiences of the subject, while **sensation** is passive, since it is the result of the impact of the **environment** on the sense-organs. Once **self-awareness** has arisen, the individual's own mental images become perceptible, and a distinction can be made between external and internal perception, the former being the ordering and interpreting of **sensations**, the latter being the ordering and interpreting of mental images. Hence a perceptive person is one who takes cognizance of his own and others' mental activity.

The psychoanalytical theory of **defence** involves the assumption of **unconscious** perception in respect of both internal and external perceptions, since it asserts that defences are instituted to prevent **impulses**, **memories**, etc., becoming conscious. This implies that the mental agency initiating defence must perceive the threatening percept before it becomes perceptible to consciousness. This is one of the reasons which led Freud to replace 'the Conscious' by 'the **ego**'. Prior to this change in terminology, it had been necessary to assert that the Conscious was unconsciously conscious of some forbidden impulse. The Ego, however, is defined as being partly unconscious and is held capable of making automatic, unconscious adjustments to changes in internal **tension**. It is, however, not difficult to find analytical writings which fall into the trap of asserting that a patient was unconsciously conscious (or aware) of something.

Persecution Delusions of being persecuted occur in **paranoia** and paranoid **schizophrenia**. *Persecutory ideas* are suspicions of being persecuted not amounting to fixed beliefs. *Persecutory anxiety* is synonymous with **paranoid anxiety**. *Persecution mania* is an obsolete term for paranoia.

Persona Jungian term for 'the demeanour which correspond(s) with the requirements of the individual's everyday life'. See Bennet (1966). The word literally means a mask.

Personality disorder See **borderline personality disorder**; **narcissistic personality disorder**.

Personality types For Jung's and Eysenck's views on personality types, see **extraversion and introversion**. The psychoanalytical literature discusses personality typing under the heading of **character** and uses two systems of classifying it, clinical and developmental. Clinical character types are labelled by reference to the psychiatric condition to which they are inferred to be analogous or which they most resemble, hence **hysterical**, **obsessional**, **phobic**, **schizoid**, **depressive**, **manic** characters. Developmental character types are labelled by reference to the stage of **libidinal development** from which the characteristics are inferred to derive; hence **oral**, **anal**, **phallic**, **genital** characters.

Personology Term borrowed by Marjorie Brierley (1951) from General Smuts to describe the study of the personality 'not as an abstraction or bundle of psychological abstractions, but rather as a vital organism, as the organic psychic whole which *par excellence* it is' (Smuts), and used by her to distinguish the science of personality from **metapsychology**, the two differing in that the former retains the person and his experience while the latter conceives of it as the result of the interaction of impersonal structures. See also **holism**.

Perversion, sexual Any form of adult sexual behaviour in which **heterosexual** intercourse is not the preferred goal. The psychoanalytical literature prefers 'perversion' to 'deviation' or 'anomaly' on the ground that such behaviour is the result of perversion and distortion of both **libidinal** and **ego development**, i.e. on the ground that they are perversions of **development**. As a result, **psychoanalysis** holds that the sexual perversions have a defensive function (see **defence**) and enable the **subject** to avoid or master **anxiety**, the source of the anxiety varying from one perversion to another. According to Freud (1916), the perversions are the negative of the **neuroses**, in as much as the pervert enacts impulses which the **neurotic** represses (see **repression**). An alternative formulation is that the pervert regresses to **infantile sexuality** (see **regression**), whereas the neurotic uses other defences either instead of or after regression, both formulations implying that perverse behaviour in adult life is a revival of one or other of the component instincts (see **instincts, component**) which comprise infantile sexuality and out of which the adult heterosexual instinct develops. Another way of putting this is the formulation that the infant is polymorphously perverse (see **polymorphous perversity**) and that the perversions represent regressions to one or other of the perverse propensities of infantile sexuality. See Freud (1905, 1916). Despite these and other formulations of the difference between neurosis and perversion, no satisfactory account exists as to why some individuals become perverts while others develop neuroses, or, in particular, while some 'capitalize', as Fairbairn (1952) puts it, precisely those propensities which others strive hardest to repress. Male **homosexuality** is the only perversion for which constitutional factors have been seriously adduced as an explanation.

Contemporary **psychiatry** classifies the perversions as **behaviour disorders** on the grounds that the 'symptoms' are behaviour which the patient claims to enjoy rather than disabilities which themselves cause him suffering. The claim to enjoy behaviour which **psychopathology** considers defensive raises problems as to the authenticity of perverse behaviour and relationships (see **authentic and inauthentic**). For the specific perversions, see **exhibitionism**; **fetishism**; **homosexuality**; **masochism**; **narcissism**; **paedophilia**; **sadism**; **voyeurism**.

Pessimism See **optimism**.

Petrification Term used by Laing (1960) to describe one of the processes by which persons who lack **primary ontological security** defend themselves against threats to their **identity**. He uses the term to include *both* depersonalizing oneself (turning oneself to stone) to prevent oneself being overpowered by the other, and depersonalizing the other to prevent him affecting one. The term has relations to the psychiatric terms **depersonalization** and **derealization**.

Phallic See **penis and phallus**. Hence:

Phallic character Person who displays **compulsive** character traits referable to the **phallic phase** (see below); more specifically, a person who conceives of sexual behaviour as a display of potency, in contrast to the **genital character**, who conceives of it as participation in a relationship.

Phallic phase Stage of infantile **libidinal development** (see also **infantile**) in which the child is preoccupied with his **penis**, its functions, and the idea of potency generally. It succeeds the **anal** and precedes the **oedipal** phases.

Phallic woman 1. The idea of woman with phallic attributes, usually either an **infantile** conception of the **mother** during the **pre-oedipal** phases of **libidinal development**, or a **neurotic** conception of woman found in men with an aversion to women or with a masochistic, submissive attitude towards them (see **masochism**, **submission**). The concept is also encountered in primitive religions, mythology, and folklore. 2. A woman who is conceived by others, or by herself, to be the incarnation of such an idea. In both usages it is unclear whether the woman should be regarded as masculine or hermaphroditic.

Phallo-centric Term used by Jones to describe the tendency of **classical theory** to attach excessive importance to the **penis** and, in particular, to explain the psychology of women as a reaction to their discovery that they lack a penis. See **active and passive**; **castration**; **envy**; **penis envy**.

Phantasy The psychoanalytical concept of phantasy shares the ambiguities inherent in the everyday use of the word. In one sense, phantasy refers to imagining, daydreaming, fancying, as contrasted with adaptive thought and behaviour (see **adaptation**). In this sense it is synonymous with **neurotic** daydreaming. In another sense it refers to the imaginative activity which underlies all thought and feeling. In theoretical writing the latter sense is usually intended; hence the spelling 'phantasy' adopted by English but not by American writers. (See **fantasy**.) All schools agree that conscious mental activity is accompanied, supported, maintained, enlivened, and affected by **unconscious** phantasy, which begins in childhood, is primarily (originally) concerned with biological processes and relations, and undergoes symbolic elaboration (see **symbol**). There is, however, considerable difference of opinion as to the practical value of making **interpretations** in terms of unconscious phantasy, **Kleinians** holding that such interpretations are alone effective, the ego psychologists (see **ego psychology**) believing that they are likely to be 'wild' (i.e. to be dramatic statements about, say, wishing to attack the **breast** or **penis**, which make little sense to the adult patient's **ego**). Kleinian theory uses 'unconscious phantasy' as a bridge concept between **instinct** and thought. 'On the views here developed: (a) Phantasies are the primary content of unconscious mental processes. (b) Unconscious phantasies are primarily about bodies, and represent instinctual aims towards **objects**. (c) These phantasies are, in the first instance, the psychic representatives of *libidinal* and destructive instincts . . . (j) **Adaptation** to **reality** and reality-thinking require the support of concurrent unconscious phantasies . . .' – Susan Isaacs (1952). **Classical theory** makes much the same point by locating phantasy in the **id**.

Phantasies may be **deep** or **superficial**, **oral**, **anal**, **phallic**, **genital**, **conscious** or **unconscious**, **libidinal** or aggressive (see **aggression**), **infantile** or adult, sadistic or masochistic (see **sadism** and **masochism**), **creative** or neurotic, **hysterical**, **obsessional**, **depressive**, **schizoid**, **paranoid**, etc. See also **imagination**; **symbolism**.

Phenomenology The study of experience. Phenomenological studies (a) confine themselves to conscious experiences without postulating that they are the effect of underlying processes, without explaining them as the manifestations of noumena, essences, principles, etc., of which the senses have no knowledge; (b) formulate their data from the **subject**'s point of view.

Psychotherapists and philosophers who take a phenomenological standpoint usually reject the idea of the **unconscious** and also those parts of psychoanalytical theory such as **metapsychology** which are formulated as though the **subject** can be observed from the outside, i.e. without the observer identifying with the subject (see **identification**). See also **essentialism**; **existentialism**; **ontology**; **personology**.

Phobia 1. The symptom of experiencing unnecessary or excessive

anxiety in some specific situation or in the presence of some specific object. Hence *agoraphobia*: anxiety in open spaces (see **agoraphobia**); *claustrophobia*: anxiety in an enclosed space (see **claustrophobia**); phobia of spiders, snakes, etc. **2. Neurosis** in which phobia in sense **1** is the predominant symptom. In this sense synonymous with *phobic illness* and **anxiety hysteria**. Hence:

Phobic anxiety Anxiety provoked by some external object or situation out of all proportion to its real dangerousness. See **phobic defence**.

Phobic character Person who habitually deals with situations that are likely to cause **anxiety** and **conflict** by avoiding them, typically by restricting his life and refusing to be parted from an ideal, protecting parent or parent-figure. Hence *counter-phobic character*: person who adopts a *counter-phobic attitude* towards life, doing and taking pleasure in doing precisely those activities which are dangerous and arouse anxiety in 'normal' persons. The counter-phobic attitude is usually regarded as a form of **manic defence**, the satisfactions of it deriving from the sense of triumph and **omnipotence** evoked by successful mastery of anxiety.

Phobic defence The defensive manoeuvre (see **defence**) of avoiding those objects and situations which give rise to phobic anxiety. All schools agree that the *phobic object* (situation) arouses anxiety not on its own account but because it has become a **symbol** of something else, i.e. because it represents some impulse, wish, **internal object**, or part of the **self** which the patient has been unable to face. **Classical theory** regards phobic illness as a form of **hysteria**, hence its synonym, 'anxiety hysteria', but contemporary psychiatric textbooks usually link it with **obsessional neurosis**. Behaviour therapists (see **behaviour therapy**) regard it as a suitable condition for treatment by deconditioning, on the ground that the symptom is an isolated phenomenon which can be treated without reference to the patient's personality.

Phobic technique One of the four techniques described in **Fairbairn's revised psychopathology**. These techniques are used by the **subject** to effect the transition from **infantile** to mature **dependence**. According to Fairbairn, the infant constructs two images of the **mother** (**breast**) on whom he is originally totally dependent, one being that of her as a **good**, satisfying **object**, the other that of her as a **bad**, frustrating object, and the four techniques differ in *where* the subject locates these two objects. In the phobic technique he locates both outside himself – in Fairbairn's terminology he **externalizes** both the accepted and the rejected object – imagining himself to be protected by the good object but at a risk from attacks by (the) bad object(s). As a result, he achieves a sense of security at the cost of **phobic anxiety**. **Conflict** between this technique and the progressive urge to maturity leads to oscillation between wishes to escape from the suffocating protection of the good object (**claustrophobia**) and wishes to return to it to escape from a world imagined to be peopled with bad objects (**agoraphobia**). See Fairbairn (1952). See also **instinct theory and object theory**.

Phylogenetic Relating to the evolution of the species. See **ontogeny and phylogeny**.

Play Activity engaged in for its own sake, for the pleasure it gives without reference to serious aims and ends, typically contrasted with **work** or the performance of other socially or biologically necessary acts. Play is of interest to psychoanalysts on several counts. It is an activity which engages simultaneously functions which theory tends to oppose, since (a) the subject is simultaneously expressing **phantasy** and adapting to the external **world** (see **adaptation**), and (b) the **subject**'s individual, private **imagination** (phantasy) is engaged in communal activity (or at least, in the case of solitary play, activity which is observable by others). Being an activity which in some senses doesn't count (being 'pretend' or 'pretend real'), and in which the actions are 'acting' and not actual, censorship, **inhibition**, and **guilt** are in partial abeyance; as a result, play affords evidence of wishes, **anxieties**, etc., which are otherwise repressed (see **repression**). It is therefore used by child analysts (see **child analysis**) as a substitute for **free association**, the games the child makes up with the toys given it by the analyst being used as evidence for inferring the nature of its unconscious phantasies. Even the **psychoanalysis** of adults has resemblances to play in as much as the clinical situation is set apart from the rest of life, the patient's utterances are not acted upon by the analyst, and free association allows free play for the imagination. *Play therapy* usually refers to non-interpretative therapy of children. *Sexual play* is either a euphemism for petting or a description of pre-pubertal or childhood sexual behaviour. See Winnicott (1971).

Pleasure principle According to Freud (1911, 1917), the **psyche** is initially actuated solely by the pleasure or *pleasure–pain principle*, which leads it to avoid **pain** or **unpleasure** aroused by increases in instinctual **tension** and to do so by hallucinating (see **hallucination**) the **satisfaction** necessary to reduce the tension. Only later, after the **ego** has developed, is the pleasure principle modified by the **reality principle**, which leads the individual to replace hallucinatory **wish-fulfilment** by adaptive behaviour (see **adaptation**).

Its usual, shortened form, 'pleasure principle', is misleading since the concept does not imply that pleasure is positively pursued but that unpleasure is avoided. The concept can be regarded as analogous to Cannon's **homeostasis**, since it postulates a built-in tendency to keep instinctual tension at an optimal or minimal level. (Freud sometimes wrote as though he meant 'minimal', but 'optimal' corresponds to most contemporary interpretations of the concept.)

For a summary of the difficulties involved in assuming that the pleasure and reality principles are always opposed to one another, or that the pleasure principle alone is operative in infancy, see Rycroft (1962).

Polymorphous perversity According to **classical theory**, the human infant is *polymorphously perverse*, i.e. his **infantile** sexual wishes are not canalized in any one direction and he regards the various **erotogenic zones** as interchangeable. According to some versions of this concept, there is a specific polymorphously perverse stage of **libidinal development**, though it is not clear where this stage should be placed in the chronology of infantile development.

Position Term used by **Kleinian** theory to describe certain configurations of **object-relations** and **libido**-distribution through which the individual passes during **development**. The two positions which have become established in Kleinian theory are the **paranoid-schizoid** and **depressive**, though references to a **manic** position also occur. The concept has affinities with the classical concept of 'stage of **libidinal development**', but differs in that it refers to complex patterns of **phantasy** and object–relationship rather than to attachment to one particular object and **erotogenic zone**. Both positions occur in the first year of life, i.e. during the **oral** stage of **classical theory**.

Positive and negative These are usually synonyms for loving and hating, but *positive Oedipus complex* refers to love of the parent of the opposite sex and rivalry with the parent of the same sex, while the *negative Oedipus complex* refers to love of the parent of the same sex and rivalry with the parent of the opposite sex. See also **Oedipus complex**; **negative therapeutic reaction**; **negativism**.

Pre-conscious Adj. referring to thoughts which are **unconscious** at the particular moment in question, but which are not repressed (see **repression**) and are, therefore, capable of becoming **conscious** (available to recall).

Pre-genital Adj. referring to those phases of infantile **libidinal development** (see also **infantile**) which precede the **genital**, and to **impulses** and **phantasies** derived therefrom.

Pre-oedipal Adj. referring to those stages of **libidinal development** which precede the **oedipal**, and to the relationship to the **mother** during them.

Primacy In analytical writings, this means prepotence not pre-eminence. A person is said to have achieved *genital primacy* (see **genital**) if his capacity for heterosexual **object–relationships** (see also **heterosexual**) and for mental **autonomy** is sufficient to withstand any regressive (see **regression**) or **infantile** tendencies which may still be present, if his **pre-genital**, infantile component **instincts** have become subordinated to the genital sexual instinct, i.e. if they have been included in **fore-pleasure**, or repressed or sublimated (see **repression** and **sublimation**).

Primal Primitive, primeval, primordial. Often referring to ideas which have a legendary or mythopoieic quality. The *primal scene* is the patient's (child's) conception of his parents having intercourse regarded as an idea around which **phantasy** has been woven rather than as a recollection of something actually perceived. The *primal* *horde* is Freud's term for the type of community which Darwin surmised, on the basis of reports about the habits of apes, to have been the original structure of human society, viz. a group consisting of a dominant male, the *primal father*, a number of females whom he reserved for himself, and a number of males whom he kept in subjection. Freud used this hypothesis to explain (a) the origin of **exogamy** and the incest **taboo** – the primal **father** kept the women to himself and forced other potent males out of the group; (b) the origin of **guilt** – the sons combined, murdered the father, and divided the women among them, but felt and passed on to their descendants their guilt at having committed **parricide** and **incest**; and (c) totemism – the **totem** animal symbolizes (see **symbol**) the murdered father. See **ontogeny**.

Primary When used as part of a technical term, 'belonging to first stage of **development**'. The *primary processes* were so called by Freud because he believed that they were more primitive and manifested themselves at an earlier stage of development than the secondary processes. See **processes, primary and secondary**. *Primary* or *automatic anxiety* is that form of **anxiety** which is evoked by the experience of **separation** from a necessary object or by dissolution of the **ego** (from without, as in **trauma**, or from within, as in a true **nightmare**) and to prevent which the mechanism of **signal anxiety** develops later.

The *primary object* is that **object**, i.e. the **breast** or the **mother**, to which the infant initially relates. *Primary object-love* is the form of **love** experienced by the infant in relation to its primary object. *Primary identification* is the infant's feeling of oneness with the mother before it has discovered the otherness of objects; in contrast to secondary identification, which occurs after the infant has learnt to distinguish between the **self** and the other. *Primary narcissism* is that form of self-love which is present at birth; in contrast to secondary **narcissism**, which only occurs after **object–love** has developed. *Primary gain* is the relief from anxiety and **conflict** acquired by developing a **neurosis**; in contrast to secondary gain, the advantages which can be extracted from the fact of having a neurosis.

Processes, primary and secondary Two types of mental functioning, the former being characteristic of **unconscious** mental activity, the latter being characteristic of **conscious** thinking. *Primary process thinking* displays **condensation** and **displacement**, i.e. images tend to become fused and can readily replace and symbolize one another (see **symbol**), uses mobile **energy**, ignores the categories of space and **time**, and is governed by the **pleasure principle**, i.e. reduces the unpleasure of instinctual **tension** by hallucinatory **wish-fulfilment** (see also **hallucination**). In **topographical** formulations it is the mode of **thinking** operative in the **id**. *Secondary process thinking* obeys the laws of grammar and formal logic, uses bound energy, and is governed by the **reality principle**, i.e. reduces the **unpleasure** of instinctual tension by adaptive behaviour (see **adaptation**). Freud believed the primary processes to be ontogenetically (see **ontogeny**) and phylogenetically earlier than the secondary processes – hence the terminology – and regarded them as inherently maladaptive, all **ego development** being secondary to their **repression**. The secondary processes, in his view, developed *pari passu* with the **ego** and with adaptation to the external **world** and have an intimate connection with verbal thinking. The primary processes are exemplified in dreaming (see **dreams**), the secondary processes by thought. Day-dreaming, imaginative and creative activity (see **imagination** and **creativity**) and emotional thinking contain an admixture of the two processes. The two processes resemble the discursive and non-discursive symbolism described by Susanne Langer (1951).

For a summary of some of the objections to the view that the primary and secondary processes are mutually antagonistic, and that the primary processes are maladaptive, see Rycroft (1962).

See Freud (1900, 1911, 1917) for his own accounts of the two processes. See also **verbalization**; **word-presentation**.

Process theory Statements that **psychoanalysis** is, or should be recognized as, a process theory are usually protests against **topographical** and **structural** formulations which tend to imply that the **mind** is a thing with parts, e.g. a **psychical apparatus** consisting of three bits, an **id**, an **ego**, and a **super-ego**, and pleas that psychoanalysis should be formulated in terms of mental processes and their organization. See **personology**.

Prognosis Prognostication; forecast of the course of an illness. Prognoses are of two kinds: estimates as to how a disease will run with and without treatment. **Psychoanalysis** assumes that the **neuroses** have a bad prognosis, i.e. that they are chronic illnesses that are unlikely to lead to spontaneous recovery, their origin in childhood being adduced as the theoretical reason for this assumption. Facts bearing on this assumption are, however, remarkably hard to come by and the issue is in any case bedevilled by the fact that psychiatric follow-ups (see **psychiatry**) record the course of symptoms while psychoanalysts think in terms of the patient's total personality. Loss of symptoms which psychiatric statistics record as recovery may be assessed by a psychoanalyst as the result of an insignificant shift in the patient's **psychopathology**. See Eysenck (1965), Malan (1963).

Projection Lit. throwing in front of oneself. Hence its use in **psychiatry** and **psychoanalysis** to mean 'viewing a mental image as objective **reality**'. In psychoanalysis two sub-meanings can be distinguished: (a) the general misinterpretation of mental activity as events occurring to one, as in **dreams** and **hallucinations**; and (b) the process by which specific **impulses**, wishes, aspects of the **self**, or **internal** objects are imagined to be located in some **object** external to oneself. Projection of aspects of oneself is preceded by **denial**, i.e. one denies that one feels such and such an emotion, has such and such a wish, but asserts that someone else does. Sometimes the projected wish or emotion remains directed at its original object – 'I don't love (hate) X, but Y does'; but, perhaps more frequently it is accompanied by **reversal** – 'I don't love (hate) X, but X loves (hates) me'. Projection of internal objects consists in attributing to someone in one's environment feelings towards oneself which derive historically from some past external object whom one has introjected (see **introjection**), e.g. imagining that X loves (hates) one the way one imagined Y did in the past. Since introjected objects may themselves be the depositories of projection, projection of internal objects may lead to endowing the recipient with aspects not only of one's past objects but also of one's past self.

Projection was first described in connection with **delusions** of **persecution**, which Freud (1911) interpreted as being the result of denial, projection, and reversal, his hypothesis being that the **paranoid** patient denied his **homosexual** feelings, projecting them on to someone else and then doubly reversing them, thereby transforming and disguising the homosexual impulse into the delusion that he was hated, i.e. he denied that he loved the male X, but asserted instead that X hated him. Of recent years, largely owing to the influence of Melanie Klein (see **Kleinian**), projection has been accepted as a normal developmental process (see **development**) and most accounts of **infantile** development assume that the infant regularly attributes to its objects impulses that are in fact its own and then introjects objects distorted by these projections, thereby acquiring internal objects possessing its own qualities. According to Klein, indeed, all fear of the **mother** in infancy and all paranoid ideas in later life ultimately stem not from any actual experience of being hated, rejected, or maltreated, but from projection on to the **breast** of the infant's own self-destructive **death instinct**. See **paranoid-schizoid position**.

Projective tests (or projection tests) Psychological tests which attempt to ascertain personality traits by inviting the subject to interpret pictures or indeterminate shapes such as ink-blots in the light of his imagination.

Proto-conversation Term coined by Mary Catherine Bateson (1979) to describe non-verbal interactions between **mothers** and infants which are inferred to be preparatory to verbal conversation. Proto-conversation includes smiling, gurgling, gesturing, and playful manipulations and attunements of 'vocalizations'. The significance of the concept arises from the fact that the observations on which it is based demonstrate that infants are active participants in establishing **object-relations** and attachment behaviour (see **attachment theory**). See also **infantile**.

Pseudo- False or misleading. Hence:

Pseudocyesis False pregnancy. Condition in which the patient believes herself to be pregnant, shows some of the signs of pregnancy, typically amenorrhoea and enlargement of the abdomen, but in fact is not pregnant.

Pseudologia fantastica Condition in which the **subject** habitually tells circumstantial lies of a kind likely to enchance his own importance and interest to others.

Pseudo-mutuality Phenomenon displayed by married couples and families in which the members are united by their capacity to satisfy each others' **neurotic** needs. See Wynne (1958).

Psyche The mind. The psychoanalytical literature, following Freud, uses psyche and **mind** (*Seele*) synonymously. Its two adjectives, *psychical* and *psychic*, are also synonymous with 'mental' (neither having any connection with '**psychical research**', in the sense of investigation into paranormal phenomena, extra-sensory perception, etc.). However, whereas 'mind' tends to be used in contrast to 'body', 'psyche' is usually contrasted with '**soma**'.

Psychesoma Since psychoanalytical writings conform to the convention of assuming that persons consist of two parts, a body (**soma**) and a mind (**psyche**), *psychesoma* is sometimes used when it is necessary to assert the unity of the organism. See **psychosomatic**.

Psychiatrist A medical practitioner who specializes in **psychiatry**. A **psychoanalyst** may or may not be a psychiatrist. **Lay analysts** are not psychiatrists, since they are not medically qualified. A medically qualified analyst is unlikely to claim also to be a psychiatrist unless he has also had experience in general psychiatry, i.e. in the treatment of forms of **mental illness** for which **psychoanalysis** is not indicated.

Psychiatry That branch of medicine which is concerned with patients whose presenting symptoms are mental (see **mental illness**), regardless of whether the symptoms are of physical or mental origin. The popular equation of psychiatry with **psychoanalysis** is unfounded for several reasons: (a) Psychiatric practice includes the treatment of a number of illnesses known to be of physical origin, e.g. general paralysis of the insane, senile **dementia**, the organic **psychoses**, mental deficiency. (b) Its repertoire of treatments includes a number of techniques which are neither psychoanalytical nor psychotherapeutic, e.g. electroconvulsive therapy and the use of tranquillizers, anti-depressants, and sedatives. (c) Many psychiatrists are actively opposed to psychoanalysis and never recommend it even for those types of illness for which psychoanalysts consider it suitable. (d) The nature of the functional psychoses, **schizophrenia** and **manic-depressive psychosis**, which between them are responsible for the bulk of admissions to mental hospitals, remains problematical, the *organic school* claiming that they are due to as yet undiscovered physical causes, the *dynamically-orientated school* claiming that they are **psychogenic** (without, however, usually claiming that they are treatable by existing techniques of psychoanalysis or **psychotherapy**). (e) In this country at least, only a small proportion of psychiatrists have had any training in psychoanalysis.

Psychic, psychical See **psyche**; **mind**.

Psychic(al) apparatus This is the central concept of Freudian **metapsychology**. 'We assume that mental life is the function of an apparatus to which we ascribe the characteristics of being extended in space and of being made up of several portions [viz. the **id, ego**, and **super-ego**]' – Freud (1940). Formulations which locate mental activity in some part of the apparatus are termed **topographical**, those which define it in terms of the interaction of its portions or in changes in its shape are **structural**, while those which postulate the movement of **energy** within it are termed **economic. Psychoanalysts** differ sharply in their attitude towards the psychic apparatus, some taking joy in it, others finding it an embarrassment. The former regard it as the concept which justifies the claim of **psychoanalysis** to be an objective, impersonal **science** as exact and precise in its formulations as longer- and better-established disciplines; the latter feeling that it eliminates the person and therefore achieves objectivity at the price of ignoring its own subject-matter. **Classical theory** and **ego psychology** use the concept; **object theory** rejects it while attempting to salvage many ideas classically formulated in terms of it; **existentialism** uses it as the starting-point of its criticisms of psychoanalysis. For Freud's own formulations, see Freud (1900, 1917, 1940). For sophisticated handling of the concept, see Rapaport (1951). For benevolent criticism of it, see Brierley (1951). For out and out rejection of it, see Guntrip (1961). It should perhaps be added that Freud was consistently clear that the concept is a **fiction**. See **instinct theory and object theory**; **ontology**; **personology**; **phenomenology**; **process theory**.

Psychical research Parapsychology; the study of paranormal phenomena (extra-sensory perception, psychokinesis). See Jones's biography, vol. 3 (1957), for an account of Freud's life-long interest in psychical research and the occult and his **ambivalence** towards them. 'The wish to believe fought hard with the warning to disbelieve.'

Psychoanalysis **1.** The form of treatment of the **neuroses** invented by Freud in the 1890s and elaborated since then by himself, his disciples and followers. The key defining concepts are (a) **free association**, which replaced **hypnosis**; (b) **interpretation**, which replaced suggestion; and (c) **transference**. *Psychoanalytical technique* consists essentially in instructing and helping the patient to associate freely, in interpreting both his associations and the obstacles he encounters in trying to associate, and in interpreting his feelings and attitudes towards the analyst. Forms of **psychotherapy** which use Freudian theory in combination with other techniques are, strictly speaking, *psychoanalytically orientated psychotherapy* and not psychoanalysis. **2.** The psychological theories of the origin of the neuroses and (later) of general mental **development** formulated by Freud, his disciples and followers concurrently with the invention and elaboration of psychoanalytical treatment. The key defining concepts are (a) the **unconscious**, the idea that there exists mental activity of which the subject is unaware but which none the less exerts a dynamic effect on his behaviour; (b) **resistance**, the idea that **consciousness** resists the emergence of **unconscious** tendencies into consciousness and does so by the use of **defences**; (c) **transference**, the idea that the relationship of the subject to his present objects is unconsciously influenced by his relationship to past objects and that, in particular, the relationship of the patient to his analyst recapitulates his childhood relationships with his parents. **3.** Although **1** and **2** define psychoanalysis in terms that are (I hope) acceptable to Freudian analysts of all schools, the laity use the term in a much wider sense to include the theories and therapies of all **psychotherapists** who follow Freud, Jung, and Adler, this despite the fact that the **Jungians** call themselves *analytical psychologists* and their theory analytical psychology and the **Adlerians** call themselves *individual psychologists*. For *existential psychoanalysis*, see **existentialism**.

Psychoanalyst Any person who has received a training in

psychoanalysis at a recognized psychoanalytical institute and who practises psychoanalytical treatment.

Psychobiological 1. Relating to psychological problems in biology or to problems which require both psychological and biological consideration. 2. Relating specifically to the psychobiological school of psychiatry founded in America by Adolf Meyer.

Psychodrama Form of **psychotherapy** in which the patient is required to act a part in some drama constructed with special reference to his symptoms or problems, the other parts being taken by members of the therapeutic team.

Psychodynamics *Either* 1. the study of mental processes from a **dynamic** point of view. *Or* 2. the theoretical formulation of the workings (dynamics) of some specific person's mind, without implying that the processes are abnormal.

Psychogenesis The origin and development of mental processes.

Psychogenic Qualifier of illnesses and symptoms assumed to be of mental origin.

Psychologist Any person trained in or practising any form of **psychology**.

Psychology Traditionally defined as 'the science of mind', but of recent years, and increasingly, 'the science of behaviour'. This latter definition bypasses philosophical problems about the nature of **mind** but makes it necessary to regard **thinking** as a form of behaviour. Qualifiers of 'psychology' refer either to specialized branches of the subject – *abnormal, normal, animal, human, child, genetic* (developmental), *industrial, social, clinical, academic, educational* – or to different systems of thought – *behaviouristic, Gestalt, psychoanalytical, Freudian, Jungian, Adlerian, cognitive*. **Freudian** psychology is *psychoanalysis*; **Jungian** psychology is *analytical psychology*; **Adlerian** psychology is *individual psychology*. See **depth psychology**; **ego psychology**.

Psychomotor acceleration Psychiatric term for the speeding-up of thought and action occurring in **mania**.

Psychomotor retardation Psychiatric term for gross slowing-down of both mental and physical processes occurring in deep **depression**. Often regarded as evidence that the depression is **endogenous**, i.e. of constitutional not **psychogenic** origin.

Psychoneurosis Technical psychoanalytical term for one group of the **neuroses**, viz. those in which the symptoms are interpretable as manifestations of **conflict** between **ego** and **id**. Psychoneurosis differs from **psychosis** in that **reality-testing** is unimpaired, i.e. the patient has **insight** into the fact that he is ill and that his symptoms are invalid; from the **perversions** in that the symptoms are in themselves distressing and that the ego is intact; from **character** neurosis in that the conflict has produced symptoms and not character traits; and from **actual neurosis** in that the conflict dates from the past. The three subdivisions of psychoneurosis are *conversion hysteria*, *anxiety hysteria* (**phobia**), and *obsessional neurosis*. They have in common not only the characteristics cited above but also that they are accessible to psychoanalytical treatment. (See **anxiety hysteria**; **conversion hysteria**; **obsessional neurosis**.)

Psychopath Person whose behaviour makes him liable to the psychiatric diagnosis of **psychopathy**.

Psychopathology *Either* **1.** the study of abnormal mental functioning. *Or* **2.** the theoretical formulation of the abnormal workings of some particular person's mind. Often used loosely to include **psychodynamics**.

Psychopathy Psychiatric and medico-legal term for what used to be called moral imbecility. It is defined by the Mental Health Act, 1959, as 'a persistent disorder or disability of mind (whether or not including subnormality of intelligence) which results in abnormally aggressive or seriously irresponsible conduct on the part of the patient, and requires or is susceptible to medical treatment'. 'Promiscuity or other immoral conduct' is specifically excluded from the forms of conduct which make a patient liable to the diagnosis. The concept is a logical hybrid since it combines medical and legal criteria, but it fulfils the useful function of enabling offenders to be treated in special hospitals. The concept is not recognized by Scottish law. Psychiatrically the condition is listed as one of the **behaviour disorders**.

Psychosexual Relating to the mental aspects of **sexual** phenomena. The literature frequently uses 'sexual' when 'psychosexual' is intended.

Psychosis Both **psychiatry** and **psychoanalysis** use this term to describe those mental illnesses which are liable to render their victims *non compos mentis*; in contrast to **neurosis** for those in which the patient's sanity is never in doubt. Psychiatric definitions are usually in terms of the patient's lack of **insight** into the fact that he is ill; psychoanalytical definitions usually include a reference to failure in **reality-testing**. Psychiatry distinguishes between the *organic psychoses*, which are due to demonstrable organic disease, usually of the brain, and the *functional psychoses*, in which no organic lesion is demonstrable. Controversy exists as to whether the functional psychoses are due to as yet undiscovered physical and constitutional causes or whether they are **psychogenic** illnesses, differing from the neuroses only in their greater severity; this controversy is one of the issues which divide the **organic** and **psychodynamic** schools of psychiatry. Both psychiatry and psychoanalysis recognize three functional psychoses: **schizophrenia**, **manic-depressive psychosis**, and **paranoia** (though the last is sometimes regarded as a variety of the first).

According to **classical theory**, the psychoses, even if **psychogenic** in origin, are inaccessible to psychoanalytical treatment, the reason advanced being that they are narcissistic disorders (see **narcissism**) in which the patient is incapable of forming a **transference**. The small but heroic band of analysts who do attempt to analyse psychotics maintain, however, that they do form transferences, but that these transferences differ qualitatively from neurotic transference; instead of regarding the analyst as an **object** (and, to some measure, a **good** object), the psychotic regards him as a part of himself or as an enemy (identificatory and persecutory transference (see **identification** and **persecution**)). Of recent years the theoretical distinction between psychosis and neurosis has become confused by the idea that psychotic processes form part of the **psychopathology** of the neuroses and even that the normal infant passes through psychotic developmental stages. This idea, which forms an essential part of the **Kleinian** system of thought, derives in the first instance from the work of Abraham, who postulated that both **schizophrenia** and **manic–depressive psychosis** were **regressions** to the **oral** stage of **libidinal** and **ego development**. See **paranoid-schizoid position; depressive position**.

Psychosomatic Illnesses and symptoms are designated 'psychosomatic' if (a) the symptoms are accompanied by demonstrable physiological disturbances of function, and (b) the symptoms and the illness as a whole can be interpreted as a manifestation of the patient's personality, conflicts, life–history, etc. Condition (a) distinguishes from **neurosis**, particularly **conversion hysteria**. Condition (b) distinguishes from **organic** disease pure and simple. Delimitation of the field of psychosomatic illness is bedevilled by two factors: the ease with which condition (b) can be fulfilled by enthusiastic speculation and the possibility that constitutional factors may predispose to specific types of both mental and physical illness. Much of the literature on psychosomatic illness consists of demonstrations that patients suffering from a particular physical illness share common features of personality. See also **soma**.

Psychotherapist: *Either* **1.** any person who practises **psychotherapy** of whatever kind regardless of whether he is **lay** or medical or to which school he belongs. *Or* **2.** any person who practises psychotherapy but who is not a **psychoanalyst**. The latter illogical usage derives from two sources: (a) the existence of persons who practise psychotherapy, but who for whatever reason wish to make it clear that they are not psychoanalysts, and (b) the claim made by **psychoanalysis** (and largely accepted) that it is a deeper, more intensive and thorough form of treatment than other forms of psychotherapy and is therefore in a class of its own. A *psychoanalytically orientated psychotherapist* is a person who claims to use psychoanalytical theories and techniques without making any claim to have been trained by a psychoanalytic institute.

Psychotherapy Any form of 'talking cure' (in all forms of psychotherapy one or other party talks and in most forms both). Psychotherapy may be either *individual* or **group**, superficial or deep (see

deep and superficial), interpretative (see **interpretation**), support-
ive, or suggestive, the latter three differing in the intention underlying the therapist's utterances. *Intensive* refers either to the frequency
of the patient's attendances or to the zeal displayed by the therapist.
The term always differentiates from physical treatment, but, according to context, either includes or excludes **psychoanalysis** (see
psychotherapist above), despite the fact that psychoanalysis can
correctly be described as long-term, intensive, interpretative psychotherapy. See also **focal therapy**.

Psychotic anxiety Term used mostly by **Kleinian** analysts to refer
to **depressive** and **paranoid** (persecutory) **anxiety**. These two
forms are deemed 'psychotic' on two grounds: (a) they are held to
stem from levels of the personality and stages of **development** at
which the **psychoses** originate, i.e. the **depressive position** and
paranoid–schizoid position; and (b) the dread is of total annihila-
tion. Non-Kleinians using the phrase are likely to be referring to
dread of loss of **identity**.

Puerperium, puerperal (The weeks immediately) following
childbirth. Hence as in *puerperal psychosis*, *puerperal depression*, for
psychosis and **depression** following and, by inference, caused
or precipitated by childbirth.

Q, quantity In his *Project for a Scientific Psychology*, which was written in 1895 but only published posthumously in 1950, Freud used 'Q' to represent whatever it is that distinguishes activity from rest in the nervous system and which is capable of being quantified. Q was conceived as being attached to **neurones** and of being capable of passing from one neurone to another. It forms the forerunner of Freud's later concept of psychic **energy** and is of interest in showing that this concept was originally conceived in neurological terms. See **energy**; **cathexis**.

Quantum Lit. an amount, but usually, as in *quantum physics*, the discrete unit into which a quantifiable entity is divisible. (The quantum theory of physics asserts that in radiation the energy of electrons is discharged not continuously but in discrete quanta.) **Classical theory** postulates the existence of quanta of psychic **energy**, which are generated in the **id**, which are capable of being discharged in action, and of being bound (attached) to those mental structures which constitute the **ego**. References to quanta of **libido** and **affect** are also encountered in the literature. Since **psycho-analysis** has no means of measuring psychic energy, the idea that it consists of discrete quanta is a purely speculative notion – nor do analytical users of the word 'quantum' always wish to imply such a hypothesis. See also **Q**.

Quasi-independence The second of Fairbairn's three stages of development (see **Fairbairn's revised psychopathology**). It succeeds **infantile dependence**, in which the infant is objectively dependent on the actual **breast**, and precedes mature dependence, in which the **mature** adult relates genitally (see **genital character**) to a person (a whole **object**). During the stage of quasi-independence the child achieves partial independence of the breast by means of one or other of the transitional **techniques** which enable him to relate to an idea of the breast located either inside himself (**paranoid technique** and **obsessional technique**) or outside himself (**hysterical technique** and **phobic technique**). This schema of development differs from that of **classical theory** in that (a) the stages of development are defined in terms of the relation to an object and not in terms of **erotogenic zones**, and (b) the various **neuroses** are regarded not as **regressions** to different levels of **libidinal development**, but as alternative solutions to the problem of achieving detachment from the breast.

Rage Rage in the sense of a fit of **anger** is, with one important exception, rarely mentioned in the analytical literature. (The entry for it in the index of the Standard Edition of Freud merely reads 'See Aggressiveness'.) The exception is in the work of **Kohut** (1972), who uses the phrase *narcissistic rage* to describe the reactions of persons with **narcissistic personality disorders** to injuries to their self-esteem. He includes within rage everything from irritation at minor slights to acts of premeditated vengeance carried out in cold blood. See also **humiliation**.

Rapport 'That mysterious affective contact' between analyst and patient, without which psychoanalytical treatment is impossible. It is perhaps characteristic of the intellectualist bias of **psychoanalysis** that rapport should appear to it to be mysterious. The concept implies that the natural attitude of one human being to another is to observe him with detachment as though he were a thing and that some mysterious extra process has to take place if they are to communicate (see **communication**). But perhaps it is really the other way round and rapport occurs naturally unless it is inhibited (see **inhibition**) by such factors as the absence of shared **symbols**, suspicion on the part of one or both parties, or lack of **imagination** on the part of the therapist. See **affect**; **empathy**.

Rationalization The process by which a course of action is given *ex post facto* reasons which not only justify it but also conceal its true motivation.

'Rat Man' Nickname given in the analytical literature to the patient described by Freud (1909b) in his paper *Notes Upon a Case of Obsessional Neurosis*. He was plagued by images of a rat gnawing at his lady friend's and deceased father's anuses.

Reaction-formation Defensive process (**defence** mechanism) by which an unacceptable **impulse** is mastered by exaggeration (hypertrophy) of the opposing tendency. Solicitude may be a reaction-formation against cruelty, cleanliness against **coprophilia**, etc. Reaction-formation is regarded in **classical theory** as an **obsessional defence** and it is usually assumed that the **unconscious**, rejected impulse survives in its original, **infantile** form. Sometimes, however, the possibility is envisaged of reaction-formation forming the basis of **sublimation** (in which case the infantile impulse is no longer repressed (see **repression**) but transformed).

Real, reality Psychoanalysis combines allegiance to the common-sense or natural scientific view that a distinction can be made between external phenomena which are 'real' or 'really there' and mental phenomena which are subjective images, with the conviction that mental phenomena are of dynamic consequence and, therefore, in some other sense also real. As a result it uses 'real' to mean either objectively present or subjectively significant. It also assumes that all objective phenomena occupy a space external to the subject which is called *external reality* (or less frequently *objective reality*), and that images, thoughts, **phantasies**, feelings, etc., occupy a space inside the subject which is called *internal reality* or *psychical reality* – internal and external reality both being realms in which things are and processes occur. The assumption of an inner realm of reality is a **fiction** since mental processes can in no sense be considered spatially related to one another – their connections are all temporal. Although the use of this fiction corresponds to general usage – we all locate our thoughts and feelings inside ourselves – it enables psychoanalysis to bypass problems of meaning by equating 'significant' and 'real' and to ignore the differences between man-created thoughts and external phenomena by treating them *both* as objects existing in space – a procedure which enables psychoanalysis to claim that it is a natural and not a moral **science**.

Psychoanalysis, then, postulates two realms of reality: external (objective) reality and internal (psychical, subjective) reality. In the terms *reality-testing*, *reality-adaptation*, and *reality principle*, 'reality' means 'external reality'; *derealization*, however, refers to psychical reality, since patients with this symptom complain that, although they perceive the external world correctly, it no longer means anything to them, it seems 'unreal' (see **derealization**).

The processes of **internalization**, **introjection**, and **incorporation** are usually defined in a way that implies that objects can be transferred from external to internal reality, while **projection** and **externalization** are defined in terms of movement of objects in the opposite direction, although in fact these terms refer to shifts in the amount of significance with which external objects (**percepts**) and mental images (**concepts**) are endowed.

See **objective and subjective**; **internal**; **meaning**; **neurology**; **adaptation**; and immediately below.

Reality-adaptation The process of becoming adapted to the external **environment**. For the edge put on this concept by the assumption in **classical theory** that the infant is totally maladapted and obeys the **pleasure principle** without reference to external **reality**, see **adaptation**.

Reality principle According to Freud, mental activity is governed by two principles: the **pleasure principle** and the reality principle, the former leading to relief of instinctual **tension** by hallucinatory **wish-fulfilment** (see also **hallucination**), the latter to instinctual gratification by accommodation to the facts of, and the objects existing within, the external **world**. According to Freud's original formulations, the reality principle is acquired and learned during **development**, whereas the pleasure principle is innate and primitive.

Reality-testing The capacity to distinguish between mental images and external **percepts**, between **phantasy** and external **reality**, to correct subjective impressions by reference to external facts. According to **classical theory**, the infant lacks any capacity for reality-testing. **Delusions** and **hallucinations** occurring in **psychosis** are defined as failures in reality-testing. See **pleasure principle**.

Reference, ideas of The symptom, often **psychotic**, of interpreting indifferent phenomena as though they had reference to oneself.

Regression In general, reversion to an earlier state or mode of functioning. Specifically, defensive process (see **defence**) by which the **subject** avoids (or seeks to avoid) **anxiety** by (partial or total) return to an earlier stage of **libidinal** and **ego development**, the stage to which the regression occurs being determined by the existence of **fixation points**. The theory of regression presupposes that, except in ideal cases, **infantile** stages of development are not entirely outgrown, so that the earlier patterns of behaviour remain available as alternative modes of functioning. It is, however, not maintained that regression is often a viable or efficient defensive process; on the contrary, it is usually a question of out of the frying-pan into the fire, since regression compels the individual to re-experience anxiety appropriate to the stage to which he had regressed. For instance, regression from the **phallic** or **oedipal** level to the **oral** level, undertaken as a defence against **castration anxiety**, lays the patient open to re-experiencing **separation anxiety**. As a result, regression tends to be followed by further defensive measures designed to protect the **ego** from its effects.

Sublimations may also undergo regression, i.e. they may revert to their infantile precursors, painting becoming smearing, intellectual curiosity becoming **voyeurism** or greed.

Controversy exists as to the value of *therapeutic regressions*, i.e. regressive behaviour occurring during treatment and in relation to it, typically with increased **dependence** on the analyst. On the one hand, so it is argued, it may enable the analyst to gain access to early phases and levels of development and facilitate reorganization of the personality on a new pattern; on the other it may, it is also argued, create irreversible dependence on the analyst and militate against **verbalization** and sublimation of infantile tendencies. According to **classical theory**, the relaxed position on the analytical couch and the opportunities provided for **free association** provide as much regression as is necessary for the treatment of the **psycho-neuroses**. See Balint (1952) and Winnicott (1958) for the case in favour of therapeutic regression in the treatment of **character** disorders and **borderline** patients. (See **basic fault**; **new beginning**; **true and false self**.)

'Regression' is also used in a rather specialized sense in the theory of **dreams** to provide an explanation of the fact that they are hallucinatory phenomena. The theory states that the **energy** which in waking life would go to the musculature and be discharged in action is compelled by the **inhibitions** operative in **sleep** to 'regress' to the sense-organs, provoking **hallucinations**. The underlying assumption here is that the **psyche** is constructed like a reflex arc with psychic impulses 'normally' moving from the sensory to the motor ends and only in sleep compelled to move in the opposite, regressive, direction.

Reification The process of treating **concepts** as though they were things (abstract nouns as though they were concrete nouns). Metapsychological **structural** concepts (see **metapsychology**) lend themselves to reification by the unsuspecting, since it is easy to forget that the **super-ego**, **ego**, and **id** are concepts designed to explain processes and to discuss their physical attributes and spatial relations. Similarly, in **object theory**, concepts like 'the good **mother**' (see also **good**) or 'the bad **breast**' (see also **bad**) may be discussed as though they were objects or persons inhabiting the subject. See **fiction**; **mind**; **personology**; **phenomenology**; **process theory**.

Relation For *object-relation*, see **object**. For *interpersonal relations*, see **interpersonal**. The *analytical relation(ship)* refers to the interpersonal relationship *between* patient and analyst in contrast to the patient's **transference** on the analyst or the analyst's **counter-transference**. In *doctor–patient relation*, *mother–child relation*, etc., the relation refers to the transactions between the two parties and not to status or kinship relations, i.e. the word is being used psychologically and not sociologically.

Religion For Freud's view that religious ideas are 'illusions, fulfilments of the oldest, strongest, and most urgent wishes of mankind', see his *The Future of an Illusion* (1927), where he interprets belief in God as a response to recognition of human helplessness: '. . . the terrifying impression of helplessness in childhood aroused the need for protection – for protection through love – which was provided by the father; and the recognition that this helplessness lasts throughout life made it necessary to cling to the existence of a father, but this time a more powerful one.' For his view that religious emotions are **regressions** 'to an early phase of **ego**-feeling', see his *Civilization and Its Discontents* (1930); also **oceanic feeling**. For a Protestant psychoanalyst-pastor's views of Freud's attitude to religion, see

Psycho-Analysis and Faith (1963) (the letters of Sigmund Freud and Oskar Pfister). Since Freud's time, psychoanalysis has become increasingly **mother**-orientated and the new theologians have been busy eliminating the idea of God 'out there'; as a result, it is difficult to assess the relevance of Freud's writings to the contemporary religious scene.

For the parallels between religious and obsessional **rituals** (see also **obsession**), see Freud's *Obsessive Actions and Religious Practices* (1907), where he wrote: 'In view of these similarities and analogies one might venture to regard obsessional neurosis as a pathological counterpart of the formation of a religion, and to describe that neurosis as an individual religiosity and religion as a universal obsessional neurosis.' See **obsessional neurosis**.

Reparation The process (**defence** mechanism) of reducing **guilt** by action designed to make good the harm imagined to have been done to an ambivalently invested **object** (see **ambivalence**); the process of re-creating an internal object which has in **phantasy** been destroyed. In **Kleinian** writings there is a tendency to regard all creative activity (see **creativity**) as reparative, and to consider reparation one of the normal processes by which the individual resolves his inherent ambivalence towards objects. See **depressive position**.

Repetition-compulsion Term used by Freud to describe what he believed to be an innate tendency to revert to earlier conditions. The concept was used by him in support of the **death instinct**. Since the animate develops out of the inanimate, there is, he believed, an innate drive, the death instinct, to return to the inanimate. The concept was also used to explain the general phenomenon of **resistance** to therapeutic change. According to Freud (1926), the compulsion to repeat operates as a 'resistance of the **unconscious**' which necessitates a period of '**working through**', even after the patient has acquired insight into the nature and functions of his **defences** and has decided to relinquish them. In this context the concept means little more than mental sluggishness. Nowadays working through tends to be regarded as analogous to **mourning**, in as much as all change involves abandoning attachments to objects, e.g. parental figures, and familiar patterns of behaviour.

Representation That which enables the mind to present to itself the image of something not actually present. A *mental representation* is a relatively permanent image of anything that has previously been perceived (see **perception**), or alternatively the process by which such images are constructed (acquired). It is synonymous with 'mental image', 'memory image', 'mnemic image', and with some usages of '**internalization**'. An *object-representation* is the mental representation of any person who constitutes an **object** for the **subject**, i.e. to whom he is psychologically related. Strictly speaking all 'objects' are 'object-representations'. *Symbolic representation* is the process by which the mental image of one object comes to stand for (the mental image of) another one, the former becoming a **symbol** of the latter.

Repression The process (**defence** mechanism) by which an unacceptable **impulse** or idea is rendered **unconscious**. Freud dististinguished between *primary repression*, by which the initial emergence of an instinctual impulse is prevented, and *secondary repression*, by which derivatives and disguised manifestations of the impulse are kept unconscious. '*The return of the repressed*' consists in the involuntary irruption into consciousness of unacceptable derivatives of the primary impulse, not the dissolution of the primary repression. According to Freud, all **ego development** and **adaptation** to the **environment** are dependent on primary repression, in the absence of which impulses are discharged immediately by hallucinatory **wish-fulfilment** (see also **hallucination**). On the other hand, excessive secondary repression leads to defective ego development and the emergence of **symptoms** not **sublimations**. Repression presupposes a repressing agency, either the **ego** or the **super-ego**, and a **stimulus**, which is **anxiety**, and it leads to division of the personality into two parts. In Freud's early writings the **unconscious** is sometimes called 'the repressed'. Repression differs from **inhibition** in that it presupposes the opposition of two **quanta** of **energy**: that invested in the repressed impulse and striving for release, and that invested in the repressing agency (the **counter-cathexis**) striving to maintain the repression, i.e. repression resembles a dam holding back the flow of a river, whereas inhibition resembles switching off an electric light.

Resistance When used as a technical term, the opposition encountered during psychoanalytical treatment to the process of making **unconscious** processes **conscious**. Patients are said to be in a state of resistance if they oppose the analyst's **interpretations** and to have weak or strong resistances according to whether they find it easy or difficult to allow their analyst to understand them. Resistance is a manifestation of **defence**, with the possible exception of 'the resistance of the unconscious', **repetition-compulsion**.

Restitution *Either* 1. the defensive process (see **defence**) of reducing **guilt** by making amends to an ambivalently (see **ambivalence**) invested **object**. (See **reparation**.) *Or* 2. the process by which a **schizophrenic** or **paranoid** patient constructs **delusions** which restore to him a sense of significance. According to Freud (1911), the paranoid experiences an internal catastrophe, often symbolized (see **symbol**) by the idea of a **world-catastrophe**, as a result of which everything becomes indifferent and irrelevant to him. He then constructs delusions which restore meaning to the world. 'The delusional formation, which we take to be the pathological product, is in reality an attempt at recovery, a process of reconstruction.'

Retardation Symptom of **depression** in which the patient's thought-processes and physical movements are greatly slowed down. Sometimes used to differentiate **endogenous** and **exogenous** depression, it being claimed that retardation is evidence that the depression has a physiological cause. See **mania**; **manic-depressive psychosis**; **psychomotor acceleration**.

Reverie 'A fit of abstracted musing . . . a "brown study" or daydream' – *S.O.E.D.* Used by Bion to describe that state of mind of the **mother** which enables the infant to make sense of and tolerate states of **anxiety**. See **alpha function**. The concept presumably has affinities with the **Winnicottian** *primary maternal preoccupation*.

Reversal 1. An instinctual vicissitude. According to **classical theory**, instincts are capable of undergoing reversal so that **sadism** can change into **masochism**, **voyeurism** into **exhibitionism**, etc., the reversal being usually, though not always, from **active** to **passive**. 2. **Defence** mechanism which exploits the possibility of reversal 1. According to Anna Freud, **reaction-formation** is a defence in which 'the ego avails itself of the instinct's capacity for reversal' – A. Freud (1937).   .

Ritual Originally a religious or magical ceremony or procedure; borrowed by both **psychiatry** and **psychoanalysis** to describe a form of behaviour displayed by patients suffering from **obsessional neurosis**, in which the patient attempts to reduce **anxiety** by carrying out a more or less complex and stereotyped series of actions. Obsessional rituals can be regarded as a privately constructed system of counter-**magic** by which the patient attempts to ward off fantastic fears by equally fantastic actions, the logic of both being animistic and dependent on **primary process** thinking. In *washing rituals*, patients feel compelled to wash themselves according to a rigidly prescribed and complex routine in order to allay a dread of being infected or of infecting others, the fear of infection being one which their own intelligence does *not* endorse. In this respect, obsessional rituals differ sharply from the rituals of the ignorant, superstitious, and religious. They also differ from religious rituals in being private and solitary. See **religion**.

Role diffusion See **identity *v*. role diffusion**.

Rorschach test Probably the most sophisticated **projective test**, in which the subject is invited to describe what he can see into a series of symmetrical ink-blots, some of which are coloured, his answers being used as evidence of his **phantasy** life, personality structure, psychiatric diagnosis, and even intelligence. Designed in the 1920s by Rorschach, a Swiss psychoanalyst.

Saboteur, internal Term used by Fairbairn (see **Fairbairn's revised psychopathology**) to describe what he also calls the anti-libidinal **ego**, one of the three part-egos into which the original unitary ego becomes split (see **splitting**), the other two being the central ego (the self) and the **libidinal** ego. According to Fairbairn, the inevitable disturbance of the infant's original solely libidinal attitude towards the **mother** leads first to **ambivalence** towards her and then the splitting off from his ego of two parts: one libidinal, which is attached to a **good** or 'accepting' image of the **breast**, the other aggressive (anti-libidinal, see also **aggression**), which is attached to a **bad** or 'rejecting' image of the breast. Fairbairn's libidinal ego corresponds to Freud's **id**, while the Internal Saboteur contributes to the formation of the **super-ego**. See **paranoid-schizoid position; schizoid position**.

Sadism 1. Sexual **perversion** in which the subject claims to get erotic pleasure from inflicting pain on his object. 2. Pleasure in cruelty. 3. *Oral sadism*: pleasure in biting (see also **oral**). 4. *Anal sadism*: pleasure in cruelty of a kind theoretically associated with the **anal** phase of **libidinal development**. It is unclear whether sadism is an infantile component instinct (see **instinct, component**) pure and simple, or whether it is a fusion of libidinal and aggressive impulses (see **aggression**); or whether, if the latter, the aggressive element in it is a manifestation of innate aggressive or destructive tendencies or a response to **frustration** and/or **humiliation**. It is also unclear whether the 'pleasure' derived from sadistic activity resides in the sight of the other's pain or in the sense of power in being able to inflict pain.

According to Freud prior to 1920, sadism is capable of **reversal** into **masochism**, but later he used masochism as evidence in favour of the **death instinct** and held that masochism was the primary tendency and that it underwent reversal into sadism. See **active and passive**.

Sadness A quiet mood, resembling **sorrow** and **grief**, provoked either by acceptance that some **loss** has occurred or by recognition of the transience of all sources of satisfaction. It differs from **depression** in that **conflict** forms no part of it.

Sado-masochism See **sadism**; **masochism**.

Sanity and insanity These are popular and medico-legal terms, which **psychiatrists** and **psychoanalysts** only use when they have dealings with the law, a sane person being someone who is *compos mentis* and fit to plead in a court of law, an insane person someone who is unfit to plead. There is, however, a tendency to equate insanity and **psychosis**.

Satisfaction The **emotion** accompanying the achievement of a goal. *Instinctual satisfaction*: the emotion accompanying **discharge** of an instinctual **impulse**. Classical **instinct theory** (see also **classical theory**) is compelled by its adherence to the **pleasure principle** to define satisfaction in terms of diminution of instinctual **tension**. See **instinct**; **fore-pleasure and end-pleasure**.

Schizoid Adj. **1.** Originally, referring to persons in whom there is a divorce between the emotional and intellectual functions. The usage derives from Bleuler (1911), who held that this divorce was the essential disturbance in **schizophrenia** and in schizoid types of personality. **2.** By extension, referring to anyone whose character suggests comparison with schizophrenia or who (if he did become **psychotic**) would be more likely to develop schizophrenia than **manic-depressive psychosis**. **3.** Hence, by further extension, withdrawn, suspicious, tending to have a vivid **phantasy** life. **4.** Referring to persons whose **psychopathology** includes the use of **defences** such as **splitting**, **denial**, **introjection**, and **projection**, which enable **guilt** and **depression** to be denied. **5.** Used to describe these defences and to describe the position in infancy from which the use of these defences derives.

Usages **4** and **5** derive from an assumption made by **object**

theory that everyone is either schizoid or **depressive**, the difference being determined by vicissitudes of development occurring during the **paranoid–schizoid** (Klein, see **Kleinian**) or schizoid (Fairbairn, see **Fairbairn's revised psychopathology**) and **depressive positions**. Hence:

Schizoid character Either **1.** a person who is detached, withdrawn, or whose intellectual and emotional functions seem divorced. *Or* **2.** a person whose introjections of **good** objects and projections of **bad** objects (see also **object**) and parts of the self render him relatively independent of others and free of guilt at the price of distrust of others and over-estimation of himself.

Schizoid defences This term refers to the combined use of introjection of good objects and denial, splitting, and projection of bad aspects of the self as a defence against guilt, **anxiety**, and depression.

Schizoid position Term used by Fairbairn to describe the situation occurring in early infancy in which the infant interprets rejection and **frustration** as evidence that his love is destructive and responds by splitting of the **ego** into three parts – the central ego (self), the libidinal ego, which is attached to a good 'accepting' image of the **breast**, and the anti-libidinal ego (**internal saboteur**), which is attached to a bad 'rejecting' image of the breast. The concept resembles Klein's paranoid-schizoid position, but makes no use of the idea of a **death instinct**.

The difficulties surrounding the concept of 'schizoid' derive from two sources: (a) it is used in both descriptive and psychopathological senses; (b) the psychopathological usage is confused because it derives from two different versions of object theory: those of Klein and Fairbairn, which agree in thinking it legitimate to correlate **infantile** developmental stages (see also **libidinal development**) and psychotic processes but differ in their basic assumptions about the nature of **instinct**, Klein using Freud's theory of a **life instinct** and a death instinct, Fairbairn conceiving of **aggression** as a response to frustration and rejection.

Schizophrenia Term invented by Eugen Bleuler to describe the mental illness previously known as **dementia praecox** and now used generally by **psychiatry** to describe functional **psychoses** in which the symptoms are withdrawal and poverty of affect (in contrast to both the capacity for **rapport** displayed by the healthy and **neurotic**, and the **depression** or **elation** displayed by the **manic-depressive**), **delusions**, **hallucinations**, confusion, **autistic** and schizophrenic **thinking** (in which syntax is disrupted) and disturbances in the sense of **identity**. For Bleuler, the essence of schizophrenia was divorce between the intellectual and emotional functions, as exemplified by the phenomenon known as 'incongruity of **affect**', in which the idea expressed and the emotion accompanying it are incompatible. Descriptive psychiatry distinguishes three varieties of schizophrenia: **hebephrenia**, **catatonia**, and **paranoid** schizophrenia.

For the attitude of both **classical theory** and **object theory** to the problem of schizophrenia, see **psychosis**. For the theory that schizophrenia is the result of disturbed **interpersonal** relations within the family, see **double bind**. For detailed accounts of the psychoanalysis of schizophrenia, see Searles (1965), which includes an exhaustive bibliography.

Schizophrenogenic Adj. applied usually to parent, typically **mother**, whose personality and behaviour is held (by user) capable of inducing **schizophrenia** in her children. Also applied to families and situations. See **double bind**.

Schreber case The reference is to a paper by Freud (1911b) in which he discussed and interpreted the **delusions** of persecution suffered by Daniel Paul Schreber, a German judge, and described by him in his *Memoirs of My Nervous Illness* (1903). Schreber was in fact never one of Freud's cases – they never even met – but the paper is seminal, since it contains Freud's definitive statements of his views on **projection**, **paranoia**, and homosexuality (see **homosexual**). Since (a) Freud's views on paranoia and homosexuality and their connection with one another are questionable, and (b) Freud made no attempt to inform himself about Schreber's childhood, the 'case' has been the subject of controversy. See Niederland (1984), Schatzman (1973), Shengold (1989), Lothane (1992).

Science Since critics of **psychoanalysis** (e.g. Eysenck, 1965) often dismiss it on the ground that it is unscientific, and since an occasional psychoanalyst (e.g. Home, 1966) argues that psychoanalysis is not a science but a humanity, it needs to be pointed out that the proposition 'psychoanalysis is not a science' can be made true or untrue by choosing the appropriate definition of science. If one defines science in a way that makes knowledge derived from experiment and measurement an essential part of the definition, psychoanalysis fairly obviously is not one. If one defines it in terms of the attempt to establish causal relationships between events, the question hinges on whether one believes that the laws of **causality (determinism)** can be applied to living organisms capable of **consciousness** – as Freud did and Home does not. If one defines it as, for instance, the *C.O.D.* does, as 'systematic and formulated knowledge', psychoanalysis is a science, and the issue becomes one of deciding to what branch of science it belongs, i.e. whether it is a natural, biological, or moral science. See Rycroft (1966) for the idea that psychoanalysis constitutes a bridge between the biological sciences and the humanities, and Szasz (1961) for the view that it is a moral science.

Scopophilia Pleasure in looking. Listed by **classical theory** as one of the infantile component instincts (see **instincts, component**). The spelling 'scop*t*ophilia' dates from a mistake made by Freud's first translators. See **voyeurism**.

Scotomization Defensive process (see **defence**) by which the subject fails (consciously) to perceive (see **perception**) circumscribed areas either of his environmental situation (see **environment**) or of himself. (Derived from *scotoma*: a blank area in the visual field.) See **denial**.

Screen memory A childhood memory which is in itself trivial but which can be treated as a **dream**, **interpretation** of its **manifest** content revealing a significant **latent** content. Its aptness for symbolizing the patient's childhood situation is presumably responsible for it having been remembered and for it recurring sufficiently frequently in the patient's **free associations** to attract attention.

Secondary elaboration The process by which a **dream** is modified by the dreamer's need to give it greater coherence and internal consistency. It represents the contribution of the secondary processes to the text of a dream. See **processes, primary and secondary**.

Secondary gain See **gain, primary and secondary**.

Secondary processes See **processes, primary and secondary**.

Seduction theory A misnomer, referring to the idea briefly held by Freud (1896) that *all* **neuroses** are the result of sexual violation and abuse in childhood by adult males, usually the **father**. The discovery of the **Oedipus complex** and the significance of sexual **phantasies** in childhood are usually attributed to Freud's disillusion in his own theory.

Since Masson's (1984) attack on Freud for having, in his view, dishonestly abandoned the seduction theory for fear of professional isolation, discussion has raged as to the frequency of **child sexual abuse** and the extent to which **psychoanalysis** has ignored it as a cause of neurosis. It seems it is *not* true to say that Freud ever asserted that child abuse never occurred, but it seems that it *is* true to say that, until Masson, most analysts underestimated its frequency and were predisposed to assume that patients' accounts of having been sexually abused in childhood were **Phantasies**. See Rycroft (1991).

Self That 'which in a person is really and intrinsically he' – *S.O.E.D.* A 'permanent subject of successive and varying states of consciousness' – *S.O.E.D.* When used by itself: the **subject** regarded as an **agent**, as being aware of his own **identity** and of his role as subject and agent. When used as part of a hyphenated word: the subject regarded as the **object** of his own activity.

The self differs from the **ego** in that it refers to the subject as he experiences himself, while the ego refers to his personality as a structure about which impersonal generalizations can be made. One of the existentialist criticisms (see **existentialism**) of **psychoanalysis** is that its theory, particularly its **metapsychology**, leaves no room for the self.

There seem to be two competing theories of the development of the self. According to one, infants at birth lack any sense of self but acquire one by **introjection** of parental objects (Freud, Klein). According to the other, infants are born with a core self which goes through a series of developmental stages, a process which is either facilitated or impeded by the **environment** (Fairbairn, Winnicott,

Stern). Observation of **mother**–infant interactions suggests that infants and mothers engage in **proto-conversations** in which the infant is an active, initiating participant from the beginning. See Trevarthen (1993).

Hence:

Self-analysis The process of analysing oneself. The main obstacle is the **counter-transference**.

Self-awareness Awareness of oneself as the **object** of one's own experience.

Self-consciousness Self-awareness, but also: awareness of the possibility that someone else is aware of oneself. When accompanied by embarrassment, this implies a defect in self-awareness. Either one fears that the other will perceive oneself in a way that is incompatible with one's image of oneself, or one fears that one's presentation of oneself is inadequate to the situation one is in. See **identity**; **shame**.

Self-disorder See **narcissistic personality disorder**.

Self-esteem See **narcissism**.

Self-love See **narcissism**.

Self-objects Objects 'which we experience as parts of our self' – Kohut (1978).

Self-observation Listed by Freud as a **super-ego** function on the ground that it arises by **introjection** of the experience of being observed by parental figures and is, in the first instance, moralistic. See **introspection**.

Self-preservation Prior to the 1920s, Freud's theory of **instincts** ran parallel with contemporary biological views, his **ego instincts** corresponding to the self-preservative instinct, and his **sexual** to the reproductive.

Self-psychology Theory propounded by **Kohut** to explain *self-disorders* (**narcissistic personality disorders**). See Kohut (1978).

Self-punishment See **masochism**.

Self-reproaches Self-reproaches and self-accusations occur in **depression** and the **depressive** phase of **manic-depressive psychosis**, often in delusional and bizarre forms.

Self, true and false Winnicott (1958) distinguished between a true and false self, the latter being a defensive structure, a 'false' **adaptation** to an **environment** which has not met his 'true' self during the formative months of infancy. In the **Winnicottian** view, patients with a false self must **regress** to a state of **dependence** on the analyst, during which the latter can respond to the emergent true self. For a rather similar concept of Balint's, see **new beginning** and **basic fault**.

Semantic(s) Originally, that branch of philology which is concerned with the meaning of words. Nowadays, often, the study of **meaning** in general. According to Szasz (1961), Home (1966), Rycroft (1966), **psychoanalysis**, or at least some parts of it, is a semantic theory since it shows that **dreams** and neurotic **symptoms** have meaning.

Sensation The irreducible elements of experience out of which **perceptions** and conceptions are constructed, e.g. light, sound, smell, touch, taste, pain, heat, cold. Sensations depend on the organ stimulated not on the object stimulating it.

Sensual and sensuous In non-analytical writings, *sensual* usually refers to taking an excessive or greedy pleasure in the senses, while *sensuous* lacks moral overtones. The psychoanalytical view that all pleasure is, in some sense, **sexual** confuses this distinction; this despite the fact that the theory of **sublimation** includes the idea that the pleasure derived from sublimated and unsublimated activities differ in quality.

Sentiment 'An organized system of emotional dispositions centred about the idea of some object' – McDougall (1908), according to whom there are three sentiments: love, hate, and self-regard. See **love**, **hate**, **affect**, and **emotion**, for some of the consequences of psychoanalytical theory's assumption that love and hate are **instincts** and not 'organized system(s) of emotional dispositions'.

Separation anxiety **Anxiety** at (the prospect of) being separated from someone believed to be necessary for one's survival. Separation anxiety may be objective, as in infancy or in adult invalids, or **neurotic**, when the presence of another person is used as a **defence** against some other form of anxiety. In both cases two factors are involved: dread of some unspecified danger, either from the outside or from mounting internal **tension**, and dread of losing the object believed capable of protecting or relieving one (see **object-loss**). **Instinct theory** tends to emphasize the connections between separation-anxiety and instinctual tension, **object theory** the dread of losing contact with objects.

Separation, mother–child Largely as a result of the work of Bowlby and Winnicott (see **Winnicottian**), the idea that much psychiatric illness is due to separation from the **mother** during infancy and childhood has achieved considerable currency. The hypothesis is not simply that separation causes distress at the time or even unhappiness later, but that it is the cause of specific **mental illnesses**, notably **psychopathy**, **phobia**, and **depression**. Explanations as to *how* separation produces these effects vary in sophistication and complexity, e.g. (a) it causes insecurity; (b) it increases hostility and **ambivalence**; (c) it interferes with introjective and identificatory processes (see **introjection** and **identification**) and thereby interferes with **ego development**; and (d) it institutes **mourning** processes at an age when the child is too immature to complete them, leaving him, as it were, 'stuck' in the phase of **despair** or **depression**. Hypothesis (d), which is Bowlby's, has the advantage that it is capable of subsuming the others.

The hypothesis is a rarity among psychoanalytical concepts in that it is capable of statistical handling, since the most obvious causes of gross mother–child separation – hospitalization of either mother or child, death of the mother, desertion by the mother – are ascertainable facts. It appears, however, that the statistical findings are not sufficiently clear-cut to command universal assent. (See 'Parental Deprivation and Mental Health', leader in the *Lancet*, 6 August 1966, for a review of the literature.) The concept of separation is less straightforward than it seems since (a) only gross separation can be clearly distinguished from maternal **deprivation**, which can, of course, occur without physical separation; and (b) it involves consideration of two variables: the age of the child at which separation occurs and the duration of the separation. See **separation anxiety**. See Bowlby (1951, 1961, 1973).

Sex, sexual 1. Biologically: all organisms, except the most simple and primitive, exist in two forms (sexes), one male, the other female, new members of the species arising by fusion of two sex cells, one produced by a male, the other by a female. Hence *sexual reproduction*, *sexual intercourse*, *sexual organs*, all referring to structures and functions necessary for the creation of new individuals. *Sexual characteristics* are those which enable sex to be identified; they are either *primary*, those directly related to reproduction, or *secondary*, those usually associated with one sex but not directly involved in reproduction. **2.** Psychologically: *sexual* refers to drives, behaviour patterns, emotions, and sensations observed or inferred to be intrinsically connected with reproductive activity (or with the use of the reproductive organs as a source of sensations). **3. Psychoanalysis** has upset traditional concepts of sex by asserting (a) that adult sexual behaviour has **infantile** precursors – **infantile sexuality**, **oral** and **anal** erotism (see **erotic**), **component instincts**, etc. – which play a part in the development of not only the adult sexual instinct but also of the personality as a whole; and (b) that infantile and adult sexual drives have effects on non-sexual behaviour, these effects being mediated by **symbolization** and **sublimation**. As a result, the psychoanalytical literature uses 'sex', 'sexual', and 'sexuality' to refer to phenomena which are manifestly non-sexual but are latently (or inferentially) derivatives or analogues of sexual phenomena (see **manifest and latent**). Ernest Jones recommended that the confusions created by this extension of the concept 'sex' should be guarded against by using 'sex' in its restricted, traditional sense and 'sexuality' for the wider range of phenomena.

Hence, according to context, 'sexual' means 'relating to the male–female differentiation'; 'relating to reproductive behaviour, instincts or organs'; 'erotic, pleasurable'. See also **gender**.

Sexual abuse See **child sexual abuse**; **seduction theory**.

Sexuality, infantile This term embraces not only manifestly **sexual** behaviour occurring in childhood, but also all pleasure derived from the **erotogenic zones** and all manifestations of the **component instincts**.

Shame Shame is the Cinderella of the unpleasant **emotions**, having received much less attention than **anxiety**, **guilt**, and **depression**. Freud (1896) interpreted it as fear of ridicule, while Piers (1953) interprets it as the response to failure to live up to one's **ego ideal** (i.e. whereas guilt occurs if we transgress an injunction derived from outside ourselves but represented in the **super-ego**, shame occurs if we fail to achieve an ideal of behaviour we have set ourselves). According to Lynd (1958), who is not a psychoanalyst, shame has a close connection with the sense of **identity** and with **insight**. It is provoked by experiences which call into question our preconceptions about ourselves and compel us to see ourselves through the eyes of others – and to recognize the discrepancy between their perception of us and our own oversimplified and egotistical conception of ourselves. If faced up to, shaming experiences increase insight and **self-awareness**; if denied, they provoke the development of a defensive carapace. See Rycroft (1968) for the suggestion that shame as a persistent neurotic symptom occurs in **schizoid** individuals who both overvalue (fancy) themselves and possess insight into the fact that their self-overevaluation is not shared by others.

Sociologists distinguish between guilt and shame cultures, Judaeo-Christian Western civilization being an example of the former, traditional Japanese culture and that of the European aristocratic-military classes being examples of the latter.

Shame differs from guilt in being more closely connected with bodily sensations, e.g. blushing, and in being, as Lynd points out, more readily evoked by failures to conform to non-codifiable social rules. Whereas transgressions of moral codes and laws produce guilt, tactlessness and errors in taste induce shame. See Wurmser (1981).

Shock 1. *Physiological shock*: state of collapse, pallor, depressed blood pressure, etc., occurring as (immediate) response to bodily trauma (injury, wound, major surgery, etc.). 2. *Psychological shock*: the response to a totally unexpected experience, for which one has not been prepared by **vigilance** or **anxiety**, and which compels one to reorientate oneself. Unpleasant shocks of sufficient severity to cause symptoms or, if occurring in childhood, to disturb **development** are known as **traumata**.

Sib, sibling Old English words for relatives or kin, revived by psychologists and sociologists to avoid the necessity for specifying the sex of the **subject**'s brothers and sisters. Hence *sibling-rivalry*:

rivalry with brothers and/or sisters. A *sibship* is a set of brothers and/or sisters.

Sign, symptom, and symbol A sign indicates the presence of some process or phenomenon. It requires differentiation from **symptom** and **symbol**. In medicine, a *sign* is a phenomenon observed by the examining physician which indicates to him the presence of some pathological process, which enables him to assert that the patient has (or has not) the signs of such-and-such a disease; whereas a *symptom* is a phenomenon which causes the patient distress and of which he asks to be relieved. A sign may or may not be perceptible to the patient, and if perceptible may or may not cause him distress. A symptom may or may not also be a sign. In **conversion hysteria**, the patient complains of physical symptoms but the physician fails to discover any signs of physical illness – but, if fortunate, he will discover signs of **neurotic** illness. A *pathognomonic sign* indicates by itself the presence of some particular illness.

In psychoanalytical theory, a sign indicates the presence of something, whereas a symbol refers to something other than itself and derives its significance from that something else. Inarticulate cries, unlearned gestures and expressions, and the physical manifestations of **anxiety** are signs of what the subject is experiencing, whereas **dream** images, neurotic **conversion** symptoms are symbols, since their referents can only be arrived at by **interpretation**. Signs reveal their meaning directly (to members of the same species), symbols require decoding. According to general usage, but not according to **classical theory**, which defines symbols in a special sense (see **symbolism**), **words**, national flags, and emblems are symbols since they derive their significance solely from the learned knowledge that they refer to something other than themselves.

Signal anxiety One of the two forms of **anxiety** described by Freud (1926) in his third and last theory of anxiety, the other being **primary** (or automatic) **anxiety**. In Freud's formulation it is the response of the **ego** to internal danger and the stimulus to the formation and use of **defence** mechanisms. In ordinary language it is that form of apprehensiveness which alerts one to internal changes which might disturb one's equanimity and which, for instance, normally wakes one up before a **dream** can develop into a **night-mare**. It can be regarded as an inturned form of **vigilance**, the scanning alertness which prevents one being taken by surprise by changes in one's **environment**.

Sleep Although Freud's own writings take sleep for granted, merely assuming that there is a physiological need for it and that the function of **dreams** is to prevent **unconscious**, repressed tendencies (see **repression**) from disturbing it, the work of Lewin and others suggests that it may itself have a **psychopathology** deriving from an unconscious equation of sleep with fusion with the **breast** (primary **identification** with the **mother**). As a result of this equation, excessive sleeping may be a manifestation of **regression** to the **oral** level and insomnia may be due either to **ambivalence** towards the (internal) mother and dread of fusing with her (it), or, as in **mania**, to the presence of a **phantasy** of being fused with the mother which renders sleep (psychologically) superfluous.

Recent physiological research has shown that there are two kinds of sleep: normal, or orthodox, and dreaming, or paradoxical; and also that dreaming only occurs in the latter form, which can be identified by, *inter alia*, movements of the eye (without opening of the lids) and slow voltage electroencephalic (brain) waves. It also seems likely that the function of dream-sleep is to enable the brain to process the intake of the previous day – the analogy is with a computer, the brain being programmed during the day. If this is correct, Freud's idea that we dream in order to preserve sleep needs reversing – we sleep in order to dream. His theory that **infantile** tendencies express themselves in dreams is reconcilable with these physiological ideas if one assumes that repressed wishes, phantasies, etc., constitute a backlog of material striving for processing – an assumption which is in line with Freud's own ideas on the role of **trauma**, traumatic experiences being ones which the **subject** is incapable of assimilating as they occur. See Oswald (1966).

Slips of the tongue See **parapraxes**.

Solipsism Correctly, philosophical theory that only the **self** is knowable or that the apparent external world consists of our own thoughts. Sometimes used, notably by Suttie (1935), to describe what **classical theory** calls the **narcissism** of the infant, i.e. the assumption that the external world exists solely to satisfy its wishes and its failure to appreciate that its objects are persons with *their* wishes and needs.

Soma, somatic The body, bodily. Usually, in contrast to the **psyche**, psychological; but very occasionally, all the cells of the body with the exception of the germ cells, i.e. that part of the body which constitutes the mortal individual, in contrast to that part which ensures the continuance of the species. *Somatic compliance* refers to some physical factor which determines the site of a **neurotic** symptom, e.g. the location of a **conversion symptom** in an organ previously affected by a physical illness. See also **psychosomatic**.

Sorrow According to McDougall (1908), sorrow is 'a derived **emotion**, one of the retrospective emotions of desire; [that], in short, it is a special form of regret, essentially a regret that springs from the sentiment of love, and therefore a tender regret.' See **sadness**; **grief**; **mourning**.

Sphincter Ring-shaped muscle controlling a bodily opening. References to the acquisition or loss of *sphincter control* are to the sphincters controlling defaecation and urination.

Splitting Process (**defence** mechanism) by which a mental structure loses its integrity and becomes replaced by two or more part-structures. Splitting of both **ego** and **object** is described. After splitting of the ego, typically only one resulting part-ego is experienced as '**self**', the other constituting a (usually) unconscious 'split-off part of the ego'. After splitting of an object, the emotional attitude towards the two part-structures is typically antithetical, one object being experienced as '**good**' (accepting, benevolent, etc.), the other as '**bad**' (rejecting, malevolent, etc.). Splitting of both ego and object tends to be linked with **denial** and **projection**, the trio constituting a **schizoid** defence by which parts of the self (and of **internal objects**) are disowned and attributed to objects in the environment. The phrase '*splitting of the ego*' is used in four confusingly different senses: (a) To describe gross splitting of the personality into two parts as in dual or multiple personality. In this sense it is synonymous with '**dissociation**'. (b) To describe the **ego** in the sexual **perversions**, particularly **fetishism**. According to Freud (1927b, 1938), the ego of the fetishist is split in as much as his attitude towards his object enables him to disavow **castration anxiety** which another part of his ego admits. (c) To describe reflective **self-awareness**. According to Sterba (1934), psychoanalytical treatment requires the patient to split his ego, one part identifying with the analyst (see **identification**) and observing and reflecting on the **free associations** produced by the other. In this sense, splitting, so far from being a pathological phenomenon, is a manifestation of self-awareness. (d) To describe the developmental and defensive process described above.

Stages of man According to Erikson (1963), there are eight stages of man, during each of which the individual displays (or fails to display) 'ego-qualities – criteria by which the individual demonstrates that his **ego**, at a given stage, is strong enough to integrate the timetable of the organism with the structure of social institutions'. The eight stages are: **trust v. basic mistrust**, corresponding to the **oral** phase of **classical theory**; **autonomy v. shame and doubt**, corresponding to the **anal** phase of classical theory; **initiative v. guilt**, corresponding to the **phallic** and **oedipal** phases of classical theory; **industry v. inferiority**, corresponding to the **latency period** of classical theory; **identity v. role diffusion**, corresponding to adolescence and early manhood; **intimacy v. isolation**, corresponding to 'the prime of life'; **generativity v. stagnation**, corresponding to middle age; and **ego integrity v. despair**, corresponding to old age.

Stereotype Sociological term for the popular or conventional idea of how any particular class of person behaves, looks, etc. The idea that all Jews are hook-nosed and avaricious and that all madmen are violent are obvious stereotypes; more subtle are the various preconceptions about kinds of behaviour appropriate to men and women, the young and old, etc., which imply that deviations from them are unnatural. See **active and passive**; **masculine**; **feminine**.

Stimulus That which evokes a response or reaction in living tissue. According to Freudian **metapsychology**, stimuli are either **in-**

ternal or external, the former being instinctual **impulses** coming from within the organism but impinging on the **psychic apparatus**, the latter being sensory impressions derived from the **environment**. Stimuli heighten **tension**, produce **unpleasure (pain)**, which is relieved by **discharge** according to either the **pleasure** or the **reality principles**. The *stimulus barrier* is that part of the psychic apparatus which protects the **ego** from excessive stimulation; it is directed against both internal and external stimuli. According to some accounts, traumatic experiences (see **trauma**) disrupt the stimulus barrier. *Stimulus hunger* is craving for stimulation; the assumption underlying the concept being that organisms require and seek an optimal quantity of stimulation. *Sign-stimulus* is an ethological term (see **ethology**); it refers to behaviour which acts as a stimulus to complementary behaviour in another member of the same species. Smiling and crying are sign-stimuli.

Strata Geological **metaphor** by which memories, phases of **development**, etc., are conceived to have been deposited one on another in such a way that earlier **memories** and phases are deeper down than later ones. The metaphor insinuates the idea that early '**material**' is more inaccessible than later, and that severe, intractable illnesses are earlier in origin than milder ones. When, as can happen, early 'material' turns out to be easily accessible, recourse can be taken to a further geological metaphor, that of 'faulting'.

Structural Structural formulations describe mental activity in terms of the interaction of psychic structures such as **ego**, **super-ego**, and **id**. '**Internal objects**' are also structures, since they are conceived of as relatively permanent parts of the mind. Structural concepts seem to be unavoidable in psychological theories which relate past and present experience and which take cognizance of **conflict**. See **psychic apparatus**; **concept**; **dynamic**.

Subconscious Synonym for **unconscious** never used in psychoanalytic writings.

Subject The person whose experience and behaviour are under consideration. All psychoanalytical writings, even the most abstract, are ultimately about some one person, who is the **subject**, all other persons who are mentioned being his **objects**. In theoretical writings, this one person is an abstraction, referred to as 'the subject', 'the individual', 'the patient', 'the infant', who is conceived of being related to, or as having impulses directed towards, various objects such as 'the **breast**', 'the **mother**', 'the parents', etc. The parallel with grammar is exact: the subject is the person whom the sentence, generalization, or theory is about; the verb (plus adverb) describes the nature of the **impulse** (**instinct**) or relationship under discussion; and the object is the person with whom the subject has (wishes to have) dealings.

Subjective Pertaining to the **subject**. See **objective and subjective**.

Sublimation Developmental process (see **development**) by which instinctual **energies** (see **instinct**) are discharged (see **discharge**) in non-instinctual forms of behaviour. The process involves (a) displacement of energy from activities and objects of primary (biological) interest on to those of lesser instinctual interest; (b) transformation of the quality of the **emotion** accompanying the activity such that it becomes 'desexualized' and 'deaggressified' (see **desexualization** and **deaggressification**); and (c) liberation of the activity from the dictates of instinctual **tension**. Some definitions include a social element, viz. that true sublimations are socially acceptable. Intellectual curiosity is regarded as a sublimation of **scopophilia** in so far as (a) it is directed towards non-sexual topics; (b) the pleasure accompanying it is not sexual; and (c) its variations in intensity are independent of instinctual tension. The concept seeks to explain the evolution of 'higher functions' from lower ones. The evidence on which it is based is of two kinds: first, the emergence of new interests and gifts during the course of psychoanalytical treatment; secondly, the emergence of 'regressive' symptoms (see **regression**) in persons having a neurotic breakdown. In the example of intellectual curiosity, sublimation means the increase in intellectual curiosity following analysis of childhood inhibitions of sexual curiosity.

All sublimations depend on **symbolization** and all **ego development** depends on sublimation. Most accounts of the concept assert that the instincts available for sublimation are the pre-genital component instincts (see **pre-genital** and **instincts, component**) rather than the adult sexual instincts. In other words, the concept is developmental and evolutionary. Anna Freud (1937) lists sublimation as a **defence** (but one 'which pertains rather to the study of the normal than to that of neurosis') on the ground that it provides a progressive solution of infantile **conflicts** (see also **infantile**) which might otherwise lead to **neurosis**. The concept is borrowed from chemistry and alchemy.

Submission, submissiveness The act of yielding to others. The analytical literature tends to subsume submissive behaviour under the headings of **passivity** and **masochism**. According to the ethologists (see **ethology**), submissive gestures automatically inhibit the aggressive threats (see **aggression**) of other members of the same species. See **active and passive**.

Suicide 1. Person who intentionally kills himself. 2. The act of so doing. According to Stengel (1964), 'on the average one third of the people who commit suicide have been suffering from a **neurosis** or **psychosis** or a severe **personality disorder**', **depressive** illness or **melancholia** being the mental disorder with the highest suicidal risk. He distinguishes between *suicide*, in which self-destruction is the only or main intention, and *attempted suicide*, into which other motives enter. 'Some warning of suicidal intention has almost invariably been given. Those who attempt suicide tend, in the suicidal act, to remain near or move towards other people. Suicidal attempts act as alarm signals and have the effect of an appeal for help, even though no such appeal may have been consciously intended.' It is estimated that attempted suicide is six to eight times commoner than successful suicide. Psychoanalytical theories of suicide interpret the urge to self-destruction either as an attack on an introjected object (see **depression**) or as a derivative of the **death instinct**. (See also **introjection**.)

Super-ego That part of the **ego** in which **self-observation**, self-criticism, and other reflective activities develop. That part of the ego in which parental introjects (see **introjection**) are located. Since Freud maintained that self-observation is dependent on **internalization** of the parents, these two definitions tally. The super-ego differs from the **conscience** in that (a) it belongs to a different frame of reference, i.e. **metapsychology** not ethics; (b) it includes **unconscious** elements; and (c) injunctions and inhibitions emanating from it derive from the subject's past and may be in **conflict** with his present values. It is not maintained that the super-ego is an accurate replica of the parental figures who have been introjected, since the relevant internalizations are held to occur early in childhood, when the infant endows his objects with his own characteristics. As a result, the severity or intolerance of the super-ego derives (in part at least) from the violence of the subject's own feelings in infancy. It is also assumed that the energies of the super-ego derive from the **id**, i.e. that the self-attacking tendency of the super-ego provides an outlet for the subject's own aggressive impulses (see **aggression**). This is an example of **turning against the self**. Although earlier formulations gave the **father** the central role in the formation of the super-ego, most contemporary accounts postulate precursors of the super-ego occurring in the **pre-oedipal** phases of **development**, these precursors being the 'Internal objects' of **object theory**. The concept first appears in Freud's *The Ego and the Id* (1923), and most descriptions of it are coloured by Freud's preoccupation with **obsessional neurosis** which permeates that book.

Some accounts of psychoanalytical treatment give as one of its aims modification of the super-ego in the direction of greater tolerance and realism, while others describe the transfer of its functions to the ego. This ambiguity derives from the fact that the concept includes disparate elements, the 'archaic' element of **infantile** introjects and the sophisticated element of reflective **self-awareness**. In other words, it is both a container of the past and a higher level of (ego) functioning.

Corruption of the super-ego refers to the attempt to diminish **guilt** by seducing or corrupting some figure identified (see **identification**) with one's super-ego, i.e. to reduce one's own sense of unworthiness by bringing a super-ego figure down to one's own level. *Super-ego lacunae* are gaps in a patient's moral sense.

Suppression Suppression usually refers to **conscious**, voluntary **inhibition** of activity in contrast to **repression**, which is **unconscious**, automatic, and instigated by **anxiety** not by an act of **will**.

Symbiosis In biology, 'permanent union between organisms each of which depends for its existence on the other' – *C.O.D.* Mahler's (1968) *symbiotic psychosis* occurs in children and is characterized by total and exclusive dependence on the **mother**; the implication of the name is that the mother needs the dependence as much as the child. The mother–infant relationship, particularly during the first few weeks, is sometimes described as symbiotic on the ground that the mother needs the infant as much as the infant needs the mother. Relationships displaying pseudo-mutuality (see under **pseudo-**) are sometimes described as symbiotic, though they are really cross-parasitic.

Symbol, symbol formation, symbolization, symbolism In general, a symbol is something that refers to or represents something else, in contrast to a **sign**, which indicates the presence of something. In this sense, **words**, emblems, badges are all symbols since they derive their significance from the fact that they refer to something else, their referent, the connection between them and their referents being based on association of ideas and, usually, established by convention. In all these instances, however, the connection between symbol and referent is **conscious**, whereas the psychoanalytical theory of symbolism concerns itself with the **unconscious** substitution of one image, idea, or activity for another. Jones (1916) distinguished between 'true' symbolism and 'symbolism in its widest sense', and wrote, 'If the word symbolism is taken in its widest sense, the subject is seen to comprise almost the whole development of civilization. For what is this other than a never-ending series of evolutionary substitutions, a ceaseless replacement of one idea, interest, capacity, or tendency by another?' True symbolism, on the other hand, 'arises as the result of intrapsychic **conflict** [see also **intrapsychic**] between the repressing tendencies [see **repression**] and the repressed . . . only what is repressed is symbolized; only what is repressed needs to be symbolized . . . The two cardinal characteristics of symbolism in this strict sense are (1) that the process is completely unconscious . . . and (2) that the affect investing the symbolized idea has not, in so far as the symbolism is concerned, proved capable of that modification in quality denoted by the term "**sublimation**".' According to this definition of symbolism, the substitutions involved in the creation of **dream** images and

symptoms are examples of symbol formation, while those involved in sublimation are not. 'True' or psychoanalytical symbolism, in fact, resembles dreaming and symptom formation in that they are private constructions, the meaning of which is discoverable only in terms of the individual experience of the subject and not by reference to dictionaries or social conventions. The apparent exceptions to this, the so-called *universal symbols*, encountered in dreams, mythology, and folklore, are explained by reference to 'the uniformity of the fundamental and perennial interests of mankind' and to the uniformity of the human capacity for seeing resemblances between objects.

Symbolization is usually listed as one of the **primary processes** governing unconscious **thinking** as exemplified in dreams and symptom formation, though not by Freud himself (see Freud, 1900, 1917, 1940), presumably on the ground that the processes involved in symbol formation are **displacement** and **condensation**. He would also, it seems, not have agreed with the idea that words are not 'true' symbols, since in his last work (1940) he wrote: 'Dreams make an unlimited use of linguistic symbols, the meaning of which is for the most part unknown to the dreamer. Our experience, however, enables us to establish their sense. They probably originate from earlier phases in the development of speech.' In his *Introductory Lectures* (1916) he also described symbolism as an 'ancient but obsolete mode of expression'. For the theoretical assumptions underlying both statements, see **ontogeny and phylogeny**. Jones's is, however, the 'classical' analytical theory (see **classical theory**) of symbolism. See Rycroft (1956), for an attempt to reconcile the analytical and non-analytical usages on the basis of primary and secondary process symbolism, and Segal (1957), for the distinction between symbols which represent instinctual processes and those which substitute for them. See also Rycroft (1991).

Psychoanalytical theory asserts that the object or activity symbolized is always one of basic, instinctual, or biological interest, the substitution or displacement always being away from the body, i.e. and e.g. knives, aeroplanes, guns can be interpreted as *phallic symbols*, but the **penis** could never be a knife symbol. Displacements in the opposite, centripetal direction are '**regressions**'. An exception is the *functional symbolism* of Silberer, which occurs when a fatigued or sleepy person sets out to think about abstractions and instead finds visual images coming to mind.

Symptom Any deviation from **health** of which a patient complains.

Symptom formation **Classical theory** regards **neurotic** symptom formation as analogous with dream-work (see under **dream**), the symptom effecting a **compromise** between the repressed wish (see **repression**) and the dictates of the repressing agency. See also **sign, symptom, and symbol**.

Syndrome A group of **signs** and **symptoms** known to occur together, but not in themselves constituting a disease, either because the connections between the items composing it are unknown or because it may be a manifestation of a variety of diseases. *Effort syndrome* is an obsolescent term for a variety of **neurosis** in which the patient complains of fatigue and breathlessness following exertion but has no physical signs to support his conviction that he suffers from heart disease.

Synthetic 'Synthesizing', not 'artificial', is always intended. The 'synthetic functions of the **ego**', described by Hartmann (1958), are all concerned with **integration**.

Taboo 1. Anthropological term for the setting apart of an object or person or for the absolute prohibition of some class of acts on the ground that it would be a violation of the culture's whole system of thought (**Weltanschauung**); i.e. an object is taboo if it is untouchable, an act is taboo if it is 'unthinkable' in terms of the culture's structure. 2. Hence, by extension, any action which is prohibited by authority or by social pressure can be described as 'taboo'. In the psychoanalytical literature, the taboos most frequently mentioned are those on **incest** and on killing the **totem** animal except on ceremonial occasions. See Freud's *Totem and Taboo* (1913), in which he speculated that the incest taboo arose as result of the need of the males of the **primal** horde to prevent fighting among themselves after they had murdered the primal **father**, who, prior to his murder, had kept all the females for himself. The theory assumes that the taboo prevented the sons from possessing precisely those females they had murdered the father to acquire. See **ontogeny and phylogeny** for the general biological theory which led Freud to believe such speculative theories were legitimate. See also **Oedipus complex**.

Technique This term used in a somewhat special sense by Fairbairn (1952) to describe processes very similar to **defences** but which he regarded as normal adaptive processes during his second stage of development, that of transition or **quasi-independence**. See **Fairbairn's revised psychopathology**; **hysteria**; **obsessional technique**; **paranoid technique**; **phobic technique**.

Tension For *Tension-affects*, see **affect**; **fore-pleasure**. *Tension state* is a psychiatric diagnostic term for a condition in which the patient is tense, under strain, etc., whether as a result of external stress or of internal **conflict**. Freud's conceptions of the **constancy** and **pleasure principles** make *instinctual tension* the prime mover of all behaviour. See also **instinct**.

Territoriality Ethological concept (see **ethology**) referring to the fact that in many species of animals, individuals establish areas which they defend against intruding members of their own species. This behaviour pattern presumably fulfils two functions: spreading of the species over the available **environment**, and reducing the occasions for fighting between members of the same species (control of intra-specific **aggression**). **Psychoanalysis** tends to interpret behaviour in human males which is (arguably) territorial as being **sexual** and **oedipal** in origin.

Thanatos Greek God of Death used by Freud to personify the **death instinct**. Cf. **Eros** and the **life instinct**.

'The' 'The **father**', 'the **mother**', usually, and 'the **breast**' and 'the **penis**' always refer to the ideas of these persons or organs existing in the **subject**'s mind and not to the actual, external **object**, i.e. they are '**internal** objects' which form part of the subject's psychic structure.

Therapeutic alliance The therapeutic alliance is that established between the analyst and the rational part of the patient's **ego**. It enables the patient to cooperate with the analyst and to understand **interpretations**. Theoretically, it implies a split in the patient's ego. See Sterba (1934).

Therapy The process of treating a patient. To be distinguished from *therapeutics*, that branch of medicine which is concerned with the theory of treatment, with the mode of action of agents and procedures used in treatment. Hence **psychotherapy**, physiotherapy, radiotherapy, occupational therapy, etc.

Thinking 1. Any form of mental activity in which ideas are involved. 2. More specifically, mental activity which is concerned with the solution of problems. **Psychoanalysis**'s main contribution to the **psychology** of thinking is Freud's (1900, 1911, 1917) distinction between the **primary and secondary processes**, the former being that form of thinking (mental functioning) characteristic of the **unconscious** (**id**), the latter being that characteristic of **consciousness** (the **ego**).

Autistic thinking is wish-fulfilling (see **wish-fulfilment**), ego-centric, and oblivious of the categories of space and **time**. *Obsessional* *thinking* (see **obsession**) is riddled by **ambivalence**, with resulting attempts to reconcile contradictory propositions and to avoid coming down firmly on one side of the fence; manifesting itself in speech and writing by a high incidence of 'buts' and 'ifs'. *Schizo-phrenic thinking* (see **schizophrenia**) shows gross interference of secondary process thinking by irruptions of primary process and autistic thinking, leading to frequent ellipses and neologisms, disrup-tion of syntax, and bizarre jumps in subject-matter – typically 'knight's moves', i.e. themes following one another in such a way that the listener senses that they are connected but is unable to see in what way. It seems probable that all the **neuroses** and **psychoses** show specific disturbances in thinking, these being revealed in characteristic grammatical and syntactical habits, but only the above-mentioned pathological types of thinking are generally recog-nized. See Lorenz and Cobb (1953), Lorenz (1953). See also **symbol**.

Threshold (or limen) In physiology and psychology, that intensity of stimulation which just evokes a response, gives rise to a **sensa-tion**; lower intensities being *subliminal*, higher intensities being *supra-liminal*. Psychoanalytical theories of **instinct**, **anxiety**, **frustra-tion**, etc., imply (usually without stating it) the idea of threshold, e.g. instinctual **tension** causes **unpleasure**, leading to **discharge** according to either the **pleasure** or **reality principle** only if the tension has passed a certain threshold. Frustration only causes anxiety or **aggression** if it is above a certain intensity or lasts longer than a certain length of time. Only anxiety beyond a certain threshold of intensity leads to the activation of **defence** mechanisms.

Time Time, and the philosophical puzzles associated with it, im-pinges on psychoanalytical theory at three specific points: (a) The distinction between the **primary** and **secondary processes** is made partly on the basis that the former disregards the category of time whereas the latter takes cognizance of it. Since, according to some theories of the origin of the sense of time, it arises as a result of experiencing delay between desire and **satisfaction**, the wish-fulfilling propensities (see **wish-fulfilment**) of the primary pro-cesses deny time, whereas the adaptive propensities (see **adaptation**) of the secondary processes lead to the discovery of time. (b) Freud's theory of **memory** assumes that all past experiences are represented in the present and are capable of exerting an effect on the present. (c) All definitions of the **self** and of the sense of **identity** inevitably include a reference to time.

Topographical Adj. for concepts and formulations which utilize the **fiction** of a **psychic apparatus** extended in space, i.e. describable by a diagram on which mental processes can be located. See **metapsychology**.

Totem Anthropological term for animal, plant, or other object which is venerated by a particular tribe or community and which it treats as a **symbol** of itself or as its protector. See Freud's *Totem and Taboo* (1913) for his speculative theory that the totem symbolizes the primal **father** who was murdered when his sons rebelled against his mastery of the **primal** horde. See also **Oedipus complex**.

Training analysis The psychoanalytical treatment of persons training to become **psychoanalysts**, as opposed to the therapeutic analysis of patients.

Trance State of **dissociation** occurring in patients under **hypnosis** and in mediums when they are purporting to be in touch with the spirit world. Trance-like states occur in **hysteria**, though these are usually called spells, seizures, or **dream**-states; and in childhood, in the form of sleep-walking. The feature common to all these is that some part of the **ego** (or **self**) is out of action, so that the subject either surrenders his **will** to another or acts on wishes and **phantasies** that are otherwise inhibited (see **inhibition**).

Transference 1. The process by which a patient displaces on to his analyst feelings, ideas, etc., which derive from previous figures in his life (see **displacement**); by which he relates to his analyst as though he were some former object in his life; by which he projects on to his analyst **object-representations** acquired by earlier **introjections** (see **projection**); by which he endows the analyst with the significance of another, usually prior, object. **2.** The state of mind produced by **1** in the patient. **3.** Loosely, the patient's emotional attitude towards his analyst.

In the early days of **psychoanalysis** transference was regarded as a regrettable phenomenon which interfered with the recovery of repressed memories and disturbed the patient's objectivity. By 1912, however, Freud had come to see it as an essential part of the therapeutic process: 'finally every conflict has to be fought out in the sphere of transference'. It is not, of course, assumed that the analyst is the only person on to whom individuals tend to transfer feelings derived from the past, but that the detachment of the analyst – his refusal to play along with the patient's preconceptions or to respond in accordance with his expectations – creates a novel situation in which it is possible to interpret to the patient that he is behaving *as though* the analyst were his father, mother, brother, sister, or whatever (see **interpretation**). Such explicit statements made by the analyst are *transference-interpretations*; the patient's emotional involvement with the analyst is the *transference-neurosis*. The patient's relationship to the analyst *qua* **father**, **mother**, etc., is the *transference-relationship*, as opposed to the *analytical relationship*, which is the totality of the relationship between analyst and patient, including the latter's recognition of the actual nature of the contract and transaction between them and of the analyst's actual personality. *Transference-resistance* is the use of transference as a **resistance** against either remembering the past or facing **anxiety** connected with the prospect of ending treatment and having to forego the (in fact largely illusory) sense of security provided by being in treatment. Transference may be paternal, maternal, **oedipal**, **pre-oedipal**, **passive**, **dependent**, **oral**, etc., according to the object transferred and the stage of **development** being recapitulated; **object** or **narcissistic** (identificatory, see **identification**), according to whether the patient conceives his analyst as an external person on whom he is dependent, whom he hates, etc., or as a part of himself; *positive* or *negative*, according to whether he conceives the analyst as a benign or malevolent figure.

Most accounts of transference include the idea that early **object-relationships** which the patient cannot possibly remember as such can none the less be reconstructed from the patient's transference-reactions. Instead of remembering his infancy and his relationship to the **breast**, the patient re-enacts it 'in the transference'. The work of Fairbairn, Klein, and Winnicott is inexplicable unless one realizes that they believe(d) that their patients' responses to themselves are valid evidence on which to base theories about the origin of object-relations in infancy (see **Fairbairn's revised psychopathology**; **Kleinian**; **Winnicottian**). Most accounts also assume that the therapeutic effects of analysis are largely due to the opportunity provided by it to resolve 'within the transference' conflicts dating from childhood and infancy, and attach little importance to novel aspects of the analytical relationship, such as the encounter with a person who combines interest with non-possessiveness and whose insight into the patient is probably more articulate and possibly actually greater than that of the actual parents.

Transitional object See **object, transitional**.

Transvestism Sexual **perversion** in which the subject claims to get sexual pleasure from dressing up in the clothes of the opposite sex. The operative word in this definition is *sexual*; simply enjoying dressing up in or preferring to wear clothes of the opposite sex is not included in the term. It is virtually confined to men, is not in itself an indication of **homosexuality**, and is compatible with **heterosexual** activity. According to Fenichel (1954), the transvestite believes (unconsciously) that putting on women's clothes enhances his virility by enabling him to identify with a **phallic woman**.

Trauma, traumata **1.** In general medicine, structural damage to the body caused by the impact of some object or substance. The term includes wounds, fractures, burns, etc. **2.** In **psychiatry** and **psychoanalysis**, any totally unexpected experience which the subject is unable to assimilate. The immediate response to a psychological trauma is **shock**; the later effects are either spontaneous recovery (which is analogous to spontaneous healing of physical traumata) or the development of a **traumatic neurosis**. **3.** In psychoanalysis, by extension, any experience which is mastered by use of **defences**. Trauma, in this sense, produces **anxiety**, which is followed either by spontaneous recovery or the development of a **psychoneurosis**. Traumatic theories of the origin of neurosis usually have the third, not the second, kind of trauma in mind. **4.** Loosely, inaccurately, but frequently, any distressing or upsetting experience, regardless of whether it has lasting effects or not.

An *infantile trauma* is one which occurred in infancy or childhood and is inferred to have played a causative role in the development of the **neurosis** under discussion. Infantile traumata may be either of type **2** or **3**, and the term has come to include not only single, isolated experiences, such as sexual assaults, surgical operations without psychological preparation, or the sudden death or disappearance of a parent, but also long-term situations such as oral **deprivation** (see also **oral**), **separation** from parents, severe house-training, or even abnormal family relationships in childhood. The concept of trauma is a strictly causal one (see **causality**). To label an event traumatic is to assert that it happened to the subject, without his in any way willing it or colluding in its occurrence (see **will**), and that its effects are causally determined consequences. As a result, proof that the neuroses are the result of traumata would justify Freud's assumption of the principle of psychic **determinism**.

According to Freud (1940), all neurotic illnesses are the result of infantile traumata: 'In every case the subsequent neurotic illness has this prelude in childhood as its point of departure . . . We can easily account for this preference for the first period of childhood. Neuroses are, as we know, disorders of the **ego**; and it is not to be wondered at that the ego, while it is weak, immature, and incapable of resistance, should fail in dealing with problems which it could later manage with the utmost ease . . .' But, he goes on, 'No human individual is spared such traumatic experiences; none escapes the **repressions** to which they give rise.' In the same passage, he also refers to instinctual demands from within as 'traumas', especially if they are met half-way by 'certain dispositions'. In other words, his theory of the traumatic origin of neurosis only holds if one assumes (a) that everyone is neurotic and (b) that the susceptibility to being traumatized is affected by 'dispositions'. 'It is easy, as we can see, for a barbarian to be healthy: for a civilized man the task is a hard one' – Freud (1940). See also **meaning**; **agent**.

Trauma, cumulative According to Khan (1963), **mothers** who fail to be '**good** enough mothers' to their children in infancy, or to provide a protective shield throughout childhood and adolescence, inflict on their children a **trauma** that is cumulative in its effects.

Traumatic neurosis Psychiatric illness, the symptoms of which (a) develop shortly after some unexpected, shocking experience (see **shock**), (b) are not explicable as the physical result of injury to the brain or any other part of the body, and (c) include either stereotyped actions or 'spells' in which parts of the traumatic event are repeated and/or stereotyped **dreams** repeating the experience. Traumatic **neurosis** differs from the other neuroses in that its symptoms, including the traumatic dreams, are not amenable to **interpretation**. In other words, traumatic neurosis has no unconscious **meaning** (see also **unconscious**). However, it has a function, viz. that of enabling the patient to assimilate retrospectively an unexpected experience by, as it were, getting in front of it again and **working through** it. Traumatic neuroses either recover spontaneously, become chronic, or become transformed into **psychoneuroses**. The last is only likely to occur if the symptoms prove advantageous, e.g. by making the patient eligible for a pension or, if a soldier, unfit for active service.

Traumatophilic Term sometimes used to describe patients who seem to have a knack for collecting traumatic experiences (see **trauma**).

Trust v. basic mistrust The first of Erikson's eight **stages of man**. It corresponds to the **oral** stage of **classical theory**. During it the infant either learns to feel at home in the world and to believe in the existence of goodness in both others and himself, or develops a 'sense of evil and malevolence'. 'Mothers, I think, create a sense of trust in their children by that kind of administration which in its quality combines sensitive care of the baby's individual needs and a firm sense of personal trustworthiness within the trusted framework of their culture's style' – Erikson (1953).

Turning against the self One of the four instinctual (see **instinct**) vicissitudes described by Freud (1915b), the other three being **reversal** into its opposite, **repression**, and **sublimation**, listed by Anna Freud (1937) as one of the mechanisms of **defence**. The concept seems to be used only to explain **moral masochism**, the phenomenon observed most clearly in **obsessional neurosis** in which the patient directs his **sadism** against himself. 'The desire to torture has turned into self-torture and self-punishment' – Freud (1915b).

Unconscious 1. Adj. referring to mental processes of which the **subject** is not aware. 'It is generally agreed [that] conscious processes do not form unbroken series which are complete in themselves' – Freud (1940); and **psychoanalysis** assumes that those processes which fill in the gaps can be designated 'mental', in contrast to those theories which maintain that the idea of unconscious mental processes is self-contradictory and that the intervening 'completing' processes are physical ones only. In other words, it assumes that mental processes can differ in quality, some being **conscious**, others unconscious. It also assumes that unconscious processes are of two kinds: those which become conscious easily, and those which are subject to **repression**. The former are *descriptively unconscious* or *pre-conscious* (see **pre-conscious**), the latter are *dynamically unconscious*. **Memories**, information, skills, etc., which can be recalled when needed are descriptively unconscious; memories, **phantasies**, wishes, etc., the existence of which can only be inferred, or which only become conscious after the removal of some **resistance**, are dynamically unconscious. Dynamically unconscious processes conform to the primary processes of thought, while pre-conscious and conscious processes conform to the secondary processes (see **processes, primary and secondary**).

2. N. The *Unconscious* or the *System Unconscious* is that part of the mind in which mental processes are dynamically unconscious; in contrast to the **conscious**. In the 1920s Freud renamed the Unconscious the **id**, and the Conscious, the **ego**. When used loosely, the unconscious is a metaphorical, almost anthropomorphic concept, an entity influencing the **self** unbeknown to itself. When used precisely, it is a structure with specific characteristics. 'To sum up: exemption from mutual contradiction, primary process (mobility of cathexes), timelessness, and replacement of external by psychical **reality** – these are the characteristics which we expect to find in processes belonging to the System Unconscious' – Freud (1915b).

Although Freud's distinction between conscious and unconscious processes operating according to different laws, the primary and secondary processes, can be accounted one of his basic discoveries, it is one which lends itself to abuse in at least two ways. First, it can be and is used to obliterate a number of other distinctions, e.g. voluntary and involuntary, unwitting and deliberate, unself-conscious and self-aware. Secondly, it can be used to create states of sceptical confusion; if a person (patient) accepts the general proposition that he may have unconscious motives, he may then find himself unable to disagree with some particular statement made about himself, since the fact that it does not correspond to anything of which he is aware does not preclude the possibility that it correctly states something of which he is unaware. As a result he may formally agree to propositions (**interpretations**) without in fact assenting or subscribing to them. Patients with a speculative turn of mind may, if they have an unwary analyst, entertain an infinite number of hypotheses about their unconscious motives without having any idea how to decide which of them are true.

Unconscious, collective Jungian term for that part of the **unconscious** which contains **archetypes** and is therefore common to all men.

Undoing (Germ.: *ungeschehenmachen* – to make something 'unhappen') **Defence** mechanism by which the subject makes as though some prior thought or action had not occurred. 'It is, as it were, negative magic, and endeavours . . . to "blow away" not merely the *consequences* of some event (or experience or impression) but the event itself . . . In obsessional neurosis the technique . . . is first met with in the "diphasic" symptoms, in which one action is cancelled out by the second, so it is as though neither action had taken place, whereas, in reality, both have' – Freud (1926). Undoing occurs, typically, in obsessional rituals. See **obsessional neurosis**; **omnipotence**; **ritual**.

Unpleasure This word, which is not a neologism, since it was used by Coleridge in 1814, is used to translate the German *Unlust*, the **pain** or discomfort of instinctual **tension**, as opposed to

Schmerz, the sensation of pain. The **pleasure principle** is correctly the pleasure-unpleasure principle. See also **constancy principle**.

Unreality, feelings of See **derealization**; **depersonalization**.

Urethra The duct by which urine is voided from the bladder. Hence *urethral erotism*: pleasure associated with urination and **phantasies** derived therefrom.

Uterus The womb. Hence *uterine phantasy*: **phantasy** about what it was (would be) like in the womb. **Sleep** is not uncommonly regarded as a uterine **regression**. 'Our relation to the world, into which we have come so unwillingly, seems to involve our not being able to tolerate it uninterruptedly. Thus from time to time we withdraw into the premundane state, into existence in the womb' – Freud (1916).

Vagina (lit.: sheath) The female genital passage. No word exists bearing the same relation to vagina as phallus does to **penis**. Hence 'vagina' has to do for both the anatomical organ and the idea of it. Hence *vaginismus*: spasm of the vaginal muscles, usually a **neurotic** symptom.

Verbalization The process of putting into words. Usually gobblede-gook for talking or formulating, but occasionally used to refer specifically to the transformation of visual imagery into words or to the conversion of primary process '**dream**' thinking (see **processes, primary and secondary**) into the verbal thinking of **consciousness**. **Psychoanalysis** constitutes an attempt to verbalize the unverbaliz-able, since its subject-matter, **unconscious** mental activity, is intrins-ically non-verbal and is therefore distorted by verbal formulations. See **word-presentation**.

Vigilance Neurological (see **neurology**) and physiological term for the sustained state of alertness which enables organisms to notice changes in their **environment**. A sentinel 'scanning' function which alerts the organism to the presence of danger or opportunities and prepares it for appropriate action. Vigilance can vary in intensity but is never totally in abeyance, even in sleep. **Signal-anxiety** can be regarded as an in-turned form of vigilance, by which the **subject** is alerted to changes in his inner state. **Phobic** anxiety can be regarded as a perversion of vigilance, in as much as the patient reacts to his phobic object as though it were dangerous and then takes the avoiding action which would be appropriate if it were. See Rycroft (1968) for a discussion of the relation of apprehensive-ness, concern, and expectancy to vigilance.

Voyeurism Sexual **perversion** in which the **subject**'s preferred form of sexual activity is looking at the sexual parts or activities of others. According to **classical theory**, voyeurism is a derivative of infantile **scopophilia**, one of the infantile **component instincts** (see also **infantile**). It also regards voyeurism and **exhibitionism** as paired opposites, the former being the **active** version of the latter, and the latter the **passive** version of the former. **Object theory** would emphasize the **phantasy** of control over the object viewed and the denial of exclusion from the relationship being spied on.

Weltanschauung (Germ.) World outlook; conception of reality; philosophy of life.

Whole and part objects A whole **object** is a person to whom the **subject** relates in a way that takes cognizance of the fact that he (the object) is a person. A part object is either a bodily organ to whom the subject relates as though it existed solely to satisfy his needs, or a person whom he treats as though he were an organ existing solely to satisfy the subject's needs. 'The **breast**' is the part object *par excellence*.

Will Although Freud's early writings contain references to will and counter-will, particularly in connection with **hysteria**, the concept of will forms no part of psychoanalytical theory, being incompatible with the assumption of psychic **determinism**, and with the idea that **mental illnesses** are caused by unconscious processes to which the notion of will is obviously inapplicable. None the less **prognoses** are often made on an assessment of the *will to recovery*, though this fact is often covered up by the use of phrases such as 'high motivation'. The usual psychiatric and psychoanalytic attitude towards will is summed up in the saying: 'The patient says he can't, his relatives say he won't, but the psychiatrist says he can't will.'

The notion of will is however too basic to human experience to be eliminated entirely, and it raises its head at at least three points in psychoanalytical theory: (a) The concept of **negativism** is used to describe *wilfulness*, i.e. the assertion of willpower by refusal to follow the lead of others or to co-operate with others, even to the point of 'cutting off one's nose to spite one's face'. Negativistic behaviour can be regarded as the mode of expressing will, which arises in persons who experience agreement and co-operation with others as threats to their **identity**. (b) The term '**active**' is used to describe not merely the ability to perform actions, but also the willingness to initiate action, while '**passive**' is used to describe not merely inactivity but also the willingness to be subject to the will of another. When Freud (1937) mentioned the ability to accept, when appropriate, a passive position as a criterion of health in men, he was referring to the ability to surrender one's will to another without feeling that one's identity is threatened. (c) The concept of motivation (see **motive**) can be used to bridge the gap between the idea of will and that of drive (**instinct**). If a person is described as being highly motivated in some particular direction, this means he is prepared to expend time and energy in achieving his aim, but the formulation does not reveal whether this is because his instincts impel him strongly or because his willpower is great. See Leslie Farber's *The Ways of the Will* (1966) for a general discussion of the problem of will and for accounts of the pathology of will – and for the absurd consequences of trying to will sexual responsiveness. See **active and passive**.

Winnicottian Refers to ideas introduced or elaborated by D. W. Winnicott (1896–1971), for many years the most prominent member of the **Independent Group** in the British Psycho-Analytical Society, and as such in incomplete opposition to both **classical analysis** and **Kleinian** theory. The clearest statement of his ideas is his *Primitive Emotional Development* (1945; in Winnicott, 1958). See **adaptation**; **environment**; **illusion**; **mother**; **object theory**; **object, transitional**; **regression**; **self, true and false**.

Wish-fulfilment Freud's wish-fulfilment theory of **dreams** (Freud, 1900, 1902) asserts that dreams express wishes as fulfilled. 'A thought expressed in the optative has been replaced by a representation in the present tense.' The theory assumes (a) that dreams have psychological **meaning**, an assumption which was revolutionary in 1900; (b) that the hallucinatory quality of dreams (see **hallucination**) enables the dreamer to represent as fulfilled wishes which would otherwise have awakened him; and (c) that the wishes expressed are, in general, ones unacceptable to the sleeper's waking **self**, either because they are incompatible with his values (e.g. death wishes towards his nearest and dearest) or because they are **infantile** and are therefore stated in a disguised, distorted manner. Assumption (c) is necessary because only a minority of dreams are manifestly wish-fulfilling. **Nightmares** and **anxiety** dreams constitute failures in the dream-work which normally converts the unacceptable **latent** dream-wish into a 'harmless' **manifest** dream. Traumatic dreams (see **trauma**), in which the traumatic experience is simply repeated, are admitted exceptions to the theory.

Since manifestly wish-fulfilling dreams are a rarity (the usual examples given are children's dreams and 'dreams of convenience', i.e. those obviously provoked by sexual tension, a full bladder, or other physical discomfort), Freud's insistence on the theory is puzzling unless one realizes that his interest in dreams was not on their own account but because he believed that they exemplified a general psychic tendency towards wish-fulfilling thought. In other words, he held that there were two kinds of mental activity, the primary and secondary **processes** – the former being **unconscious** and wish-fulfilling, the latter **conscious** and realistic – and that dreams were a normal phenomenon familiar to everyone in which the primary processes manifested themselves. In fact, the distinction between primary, wish-fulfilling processes and secondary, realistic processes was based on the study of neurotic **symptoms** and only transferred later to the **interpretation** of dreams. Dreams, on this theory, resemble symptoms in being **compromise formations**, the wish-fulfilling elements coming from the repressed (see **repression**) and the distorting dream-work coming from the repressing parts of the mind.

In one respect, Freud's formulation is fairly certainly wrong. Recent physiological research suggests that we do not dream in order to preserve **sleep**, but that, on the contrary, we sleep in order to dream.

Wolf-man Soubriquet given in the analytical literature to a Russian patient analysed by Freud from 1910 to 1914. A childhood **nightmare** of his, in which he saw six or seven white wolves perched in a walnut tree outside his bedroom window, formed the subject of Freud's *From the History of an Infantile Neurosis* (1918). Freud interpreted the **dream** as a symbolic representation of an act of parental intercourse witnessed by the infant wolf-man at the age of one and a half.

After the First World War the wolf-man had further analysis

with Freud, and then with Ruth Mack Brunswick. After the Second World War he had **psychotherapy** from three other analysts. He died, aged ninety-three, in 1979. See Muriel Gardiner (ed., 1971), Karin Obholzer (1982), Rycroft (1985, in 1991).

Word-presentation The mental image of a word. According to Freud (1915, 1923) the essential difference between **unconscious** mental processes and those which are **pre-conscious** or **conscious** is that the latter have been brought into connection with word-presentations; that an unconscious idea is a representation of the object itself, a *thing-presentation*, whereas a conscious idea has attached to it a verbal image, this verbal image having been acquired (learned) from others. This notion is only explicable if one remembers that Freud believed that the human psyche starts as a structure-less **id**, part of which differentiates to form the **ego** as a result of the impact of the **environment**. 'The ego is that part of the id which has been modified by the direct influence of the external world.' The attachment of word-presentations to mental processes is evidence that they *have* been modified by the direct influence of the external world. It is not clear whether Freud believed that, when conscious, we always think with words, or whether he thought that non-verbal conscious thinking (as occurs in dreaming, daydreaming, reveries, etc.) is an irruption of the unconscious into consciousness.

Word-presentations play a part in Freud's views on schizophrenic **thinking**. He held that in **schizophrenia**, the patient withdraws **cathexis** from thing-representations (i.e. divests them of significance) and then treats word-representations as though they were things, constructing a delusional world on the basis of words not objects (see **delusion**). In schizophrenic thinking words are subject to primary **process** thinking, i.e. they are treated as normal people treat visual images in **dreams**.

Work Serious activity, usually contrasted either with **play** or **love**. In the early days of **psychoanalysis**, recovery of the capacity to love and work was regarded as the criterion of successful analytical treatment.

Working through Originally, the process by which a patient in analysis discovers piecemeal over an extended period of time the full implications of some **interpretation** or **insight**. Hence, by extension, the process of getting used to a new state of affairs or of getting over a loss or painful experience. In this extended sense, **mourning** is an example of working through, since it involves the piecemeal recognition that the lost **object** is no longer available in a host of contexts in which he was previously a familiar figure.

World When internal (inner) and external (outer) world are used antithetically, *internal world* is synonymous with internal **reality**, psychical reality, *external world* is synonymous with **environment**, external reality. *World-catastrophe* is the idea that the world has come to an end or has been destroyed, often a part of schizophrenic **delusions** (see **schizophrenia**).

YAVIS syndrome According to Schofield (1964), young male American psychiatrists tend to select for **psychotherapy** female patients who display the 'YAVIS' **syndrome**, being Young, Attractive, Verbally fluent, Intelligent and Successful, and having the same social background and aspirations as themselves. This ironic comment on the American psychiatric and psychoanalytic scene is part of a general attack on the tendency to expend professional time and skill on patients who are not ill in any clinical sense at the expense of research on the major psychiatric disorders.

Zoophilia Bestiality. Excessive love of animals.

BIBLIOGRAPHY

ABRAHAM, K., *Selected Papers*, Hogarth Press, London, 1927.

AINSWORTH, MARY, 'Object Relations, Dependency and Attachment: a Theoretical Review of the Infant–Mother Relationship', *Child Development* (1969), 40, pp. 969–1025.

ALEXANDER, F., 'The Neurotic Character', *Int. J. Psycho-Anal.* (1930), 11, pp. 292–311.

BALINT, M., *Primary Love and Psycho-Analytic Technique*, Hogarth Press, London, 1952.

BATESON, G., et al., 'Towards a Theory of Schizophrenia' (1956), repr. in *Steps to an Ecology of Mind*, Paladin, St Albans, 1973.

BATESON, MARY CATHERINE, 'The Epigenesis of Conversational Interaction: a Personal Account Research Development', in A. Bullowa (ed.), *Before Speech: The Beginning of Human Communication*, Cambridge University Press, 1979.

BENNET, E. A., *What Jung Really Said*, Macdonald, London, 1966.

BERES, D., 'Communication in Psychoanalysis and in the Creative Process: a Parallel', *J. Amer. Psychoanal. Ass.* (1957), 5, pp. 408–23.

BETTELHEIM, B., *The Empty Fortress*, Free Press of Glencoe, New York, 1967.

BETTELHEIM, B., *Freud and Man's Soul*, Chatto & Windus, London, 1983.

BION, W. R., *Learning from Experience*, Heinemann, London, 1962.

BION, W. R., *Elements of Psychoanalysis*, Heinemann, London, 1963.

BION, W. R., *Second Thoughts*, Heinemann, London, 1967.

BLEULER, E., *Dementia Praecox or the Group of Schizophrenias* (1911), trans. J. Zinkin, repr. International Universities Press, New York, 1950.

BOWIE, M., *Lacan*, Fontana, London, 1991.

BOWLBY, J., *Maternal Care and Mental Health*, 2nd edition, World Health Organization, Geneva, 1952.

Bibliography

BOWLBY, J., 'Processes of Mourning', *Int. J. Psycho-Anal.* (1961), 42, pp. 317–40.

BOWLBY, J., *Attachment and Loss*, 3 vols., Hogarth Press, London: vol. 1: *Attachment*, 1969; vol. 2: *Separation, Anxiety and Anger*, 1973; vol. 3: *Loss, Sadness and Depression*, 1980.

BOYER, L. B., 'A Hypothesis Regarding the Time of Appearance of the Dream Screen', *Int. J. Psycho-Anal.* (1960), 41, pp. 114–22.

BRANDT, L. W., 'Some Notes on English Freudian Terminology', *J. Amer. Psychoanal. Ass.* (1961), 9, pp. 331–9.

BRIERLEY, MARJORIE, *Trends in Psycho-Analysis*, Hogarth Press, London, 1951.

BROWN, J. A. C., *Freud and the Post-Freudians*, Penguin Books, Harmondsworth, 1961.

CANNON, W. B., *The Wisdom of the Body*, W. W. Norton, New York, 1932.

CARSTAIRS, G. M., *This Island Now*, Hogarth Press, London, 1963.

CLARK, R. W., *Freud: The Man and the Cause*, Jonathan Cape and Weidenfeld & Nicolson, London, 1980.

CRISP, A. J., '"Transference", "Symptom Emergence" and "Social Repercussion" in Behaviour Therapy', *Brit. J. Med. Psychol.* (1966), 39, pp. 179–96.

DEUTSCH, HELENE, *The Psychology of Women*, 2 vols., Research Books, London, 1946.

DEUTSCH, HELENE, 'Some Forms of Emotional Disturbance and Their Relationship to Schizophrenia', in *Neuroses and Character Types*, International Universities Press, New York, 1965.

EHRENZWEIG, A., *The Hidden Order of Art*, Weidenfeld & Nicolson, London, 1967.

ERIKSON, E., 'The Dream Specimen of Psychoanalysis', *J. Amer. Psychoanal. Ass.* (1954), 2, pp. 5–56.

ERIKSON, E., 'Reality and Actuality', *J. Amer. Psychoanal. Ass.* (1962), 10.

ERIKSON, E., *Childhood and Society*, 2nd edition, W. W. Norton, New York, 1963.

EVANS, W. N., 'The Passing of the Gentleman', *Psychoanal. Quart.* (1949), 18, pp. 19–43.

EYSENCK, H. J., *Fact and Fiction in Psychology*, Penguin Books, Harmondsworth, 1965.

EYSENCK, H. J., and RACHMAN, S., *The Causes and Cures of Neurosis*, Routledge & Kegan Paul, London, 1965.

FAIRBAIRN, W. R. D., 'A Revised Psychopathology of the Psychoses and Psychoneuroses' (1941), see Fairbairn (1952).

FAIRBAIRN, W. R. D., *Psychoanalytic Studies of the Personality*, Tavistock Publications, London, 1952.

FARBER, L. H., *The Ways of the Will*, Constable, London, 1966.

FEDERN, P., *Ego Psychology and the Psychoses*, Basic Books, New York, 1952.

FENICHEL, O., *Problems of Psychoanalytic Technique*, Psychoanalytic Quarterly Inc., New York, 1941.

FENICHEL, O., *Collected Papers* (First Series), Routledge & Kegan Paul, London, 1954.

FERENCZI, S., 'Introjection and Transference' (1909), repr. in *First Contributions to Psycho-Analysis*, Hogarth Press, London, 1952.

FERENCZI, S., and RANK, O., *The Development of Psychoanalysis*, 1924; repr. International Universities Press, Madison, Ct, 1986.

FONAGY, P., 'Thinking about Thinking', *Int. J. Psycho-Anal.* (1991), 72, pp. 439–654.

FOULKES, S. H., and ANTHONY, E. J., *Group Psychotherapy*, Penguin Books, Harmondsworth, 1957.

FREUD, ANNA, *The Ego and the Mechanisms of Defence*, Hogarth Press, London, 1937.

FREUD, ANNA, *The Psychoanalytical Treatment of Children*, Hogarth Press, London, 1959.

FREUD, S., *On the Grounds for Detaching a Particular Syndrome from Neurasthenia under the Description 'Anxiety Neurosis'* (1894): Standard Edition, vol. 3, Hogarth Press, London, 1962.

FREUD, S., *Project for a Scientific Psychology* (1895): Standard Edition, vol. 1, Hogarth Press, London, 1966.

FREUD, S., *Further Remarks on the Neuro-Psychoses of Defence* (1896): Standard Edition, vol. 3, Hogarth Press, London, 1962.

FREUD, S., *The Interpretation of Dreams* (1900): Standard Edition, vols. 4 and 5, Hogarth Press, London, 1953.

FREUD, S., *The Psychopathology of Everyday Life* (1901): Standard Edition, vol. 6, Hogarth Press, London, 1960.

FREUD, S., *On Dreams* (1902): Standard Edition, vol. 5, Hogarth Press, London, 1953.

Bibliography

FREUD, S., *Three Essays on the Theory of Sexuality* (1905): Standard Edition, vol. 7, Hogarth Press, London, 1953.

FREUD, S., *Obsessive Actions and Religious Practices* (1907): Standard Edition, vol. 9, Hogarth Press, London, 1959.

FREUD, S., *Creative Writers and Day-Dreaming* (1908): Standard Edition, vol. 9, Hogarth Press, London, 1959.

FREUD, S., *Analysis of a Phobia in a Five-year-old Boy* (1909a): Standard Edition, vol. 10, Hogarth Press, London, 1955.

FREUD, S., *Notes Upon a Case of Obsessional Neurosis* (1909b): Standard Edition, vol. 10, Hogarth Press, London, 1955.

FREUD, S., *Leonardo da Vinci and a Memory of his Childhood* (1910): Standard Edition, vol. 11, Hogarth Press, London, 1957.

FREUD, S., *Formulations on the Two Principles of Mental Functioning* (1911a): Standard Edition, vol. 12, Hogarth Press, London, 1958.

FREUD, S., *Psycho-Analytic Notes on an Autobiographical Account of a Case of Paranoia (Dementia Paranoides)* (1911b): Standard Edition, vol. 12, Hogarth Press, London, 1958.

FREUD, S., *Totem and Taboo* (1913): Standard Edition, vol. 13, Hogarth Press, London, 1955.

FREUD, S., *Fausse Reconnaissance (Déjà Raconté) in Psycho-Analytic Treatment* (1914a): Standard Edition, vol. 13, Hogarth Press, London, 1958.

FREUD, S., *On Narcissism* (1914b): Standard Edition, vol. 14, Hogarth Press, London, 1957.

FREUD, S., *Observations on Transference Love* (1915a): Standard Edition, vol. 12, Hogarth Press, London, 1958.

FREUD, S., *Papers on Metapsychology* (1915b): Standard Edition, vol. 14, Hogarth Press, London, 1957.

FREUD, S., *Introductory Lectures on Psycho-Analysis* (1916): Standard Edition, vols. 15 and 16, Hogarth Press, London, 1963.

FREUD, S., *Mourning and Melancholia* (1917): Standard Edition, vol. 14, Hogarth Press, London, 1957.

FREUD, S., *Lines of Advance in Psycho-Analytic Therapy* (1919): Standard Edition, vol. 17, Hogarth Press, London, 1955.

FREUD, S., *Beyond the Pleasure Principle* (1920): Standard Edition, vol. 18, Hogarth Press, London, 1955.

FREUD, S., *The Ego and the Id* (1923): Standard Edition, vol. 19, Hogarth Press, London, 1961.

FREUD, S., *Inhibitions, Symptoms and Anxiety* (1926): Standard Edition, vol. 20, Hogarth Press, London, 1959.

FREUD, S., *The Future of an Illusion* (1927a): Standard Edition, vol. 21, Hogarth Press, London, 1961.

FREUD, S., *Fetishism* (1927b): Standard Edition, vol. 21, Hogarth Press, London, 1961.

FREUD, S., *Civilization and Its Discontents* (1930): Standard Edition, vol. 21, Hogarth Press, London, 1961.

FREUD, S., *New Introductory Lectures on Psycho-Analysis* (1933): Standard Edition, vol. 22, Hogarth Press, London, 1964.

FREUD, S., *Analysis Terminable and Interminable* (1937): Standard Edition, vol. 23, Hogarth Press, London, 1964.

FREUD, S., *Splitting of the Ego in the Defensive Process* (1938): Standard Edition, vol. 23, Hogarth Press, London, 1964.

FREUD, S., *Moses and Monotheism* (1939): Standard Edition, vol. 23, Hogarth Press, London, 1964.

FREUD, S., *An Outline of Psycho-Analysis* (1940): Standard Edition, vol. 23, Hogarth Press, London, 1964.

FREUD, S., and BREUER, J., *Studies on Hysteria* (1893–5): Standard Edition, vol. 2, Hogarth Press, London, 1955.

FREUD, S., and BULLITT, W. C., *Thomas Woodrow Wilson*, Weidenfeld & Nicolson, London, 1967.

FREUD, S., and PFISTER, O., *Psycho-Analysis and Faith*, Hogarth Press, London, 1963.

FUCHS, S. H., 'On Introjection', *Int. J. Psycho-Anal.* (1937), 18, pp. 269–93.

FURNISS, T., *The Multiprofessional Handbook of Child Sexual Abuse*, Routledge, London, 1991.

GARDINER, MURIEL (ed.), *The Wolf-Man by the Wolf-Man*, Basic Books, New York, 1971.

GITELSON, M., 'The Emotional Position of the Analyst in the Psycho-Analytic Situation', *Int. J. Psycho-Anal.* (1952), 33, pp. 1–10.

GLOVER, E., *Psycho-Analysis*, Staples Press, London, 1939.

GLOVER, E., 'The Psycho-Analysis of Affects', *Int. J. Psycho-Anal.* (1939), 20, pp. 299–307.

GLOVER, E., 'Examination of the Klein System of Child Psychology', *Psychoanal. Study of the Child* (1945), 1, pp. 75–118.

Bibliography

GORER, G., 'Cultural Community and Cultural Diversity', in *The Danger of Equality*, Cresset Press, London, 1966.

GORER, G., 'Psychoanalysis in the World', in C. Rycroft (ed.), *Psychoanalysis Observed*, Constable, London, 1966.

GREENACRE, PHYLLIS, 'Penis Awe and its Relation to Penis Envy', in R. M. Loewenstein (ed.), *Drives, Affects and Behavior*, International Universities Press, New York, 1953.

GREENACRE, PHYLLIS, 'The Childhood of the Artist', *Psychoanal. Study of the Child* (1957), 12, pp. 47–72.

GREENBERG, J., and MITCHELL, S., *Object Relations in Psychoanalytic Theory*, Harvard University Press, 1983.

GREENSON, R. R., 'The Psychology of Apathy', *Psychoanal. Quart.* (1949), 18, pp. 290–302.

GRODDECK, G., *The Book of the It*, trans. M. E. Collins, Vision Press, New York, 1923; repr. Mentor Books, New York, 1961.

GROSSKURTH, PHYLLIS, *Melanie Klein: Her World and Her Work*, Hodder & Stoughton, London, 1986.

GROSSMAN, C. M. and S., *The Wild Analyst*, Barrie & Rockliff, London, 1965.

GUNTRIP, H., *Personality Structure and Human Interaction*, Hogarth Press, London, 1961.

HARTMANN, H., *Ego Psychology and the Problem of Adaptation*, Imago, London, 1958.

HARTMANN, H., *Essays on Ego Psychology*, Hogarth Press, London, 1964.

HEIMANN, P., 'On Counter-Transference', *Int. J. Psycho-Anal.* (1950), 31, pp. 81–4.

HERMANN, I., 'The Use of the Term "Active" in the Definition of Masculinity', *Int. J. Psycho-Anal.* (1935), 16, pp. 219–22.

HINSHELWOOD, R. D., *A Dictionary of Kleinian Thought*, Free Association Books, London, 1989.

HOCH, P., and ZUBIN, J. (eds.), *Anxiety*, Grune & Stratton, New York, 1950.

HOLMES, J., *John Bowlby and Attachment Theory*, Routledge, London, 1993.

HOME, H. J., 'The Concept of Mind', *Int. J. Psycho-Anal.* (1966), 47, pp. 43–9.

HORNEY, KAREN, 'The Flight from Womanhood', *Int. J. Psycho-Anal.* (1926), 7, pp. 324–39.

ISAKOWER, O., 'A Contribution to the Patho-Psychology of Phenomena Associated with Falling Asleep', *Int. J. Psycho-Anal.* (1938), 19, pp. 331–45.

ISRAËLS, H., *Schreber: Father and Son*, International Universities Press, Madison, Ct, 1989.

JONES, E., 'The Theory of Symbolism' (1916), in Jones (1948).

JONES, E., *The Nightmare*, Hogarth Press, London, 1931.

JONES, E., *Papers on Psycho-Analysis*, Baillière, Tindall & Cox, London, 1948.

JONES, E., *Sigmund Freud, Life and Work*, 3 vols., Hogarth Press, London: vol. 1: *The Young Freud, 1856–1900*, 1953; vol. 2: *Years of Maturity, 1901–1919*, 1955; vol. 3: *The Last Phase, 1919–1939*, 1957.

JUNG, C. G., *Psychological Types*, Kegan Paul, Trench, Trübner, London, 1923.

KERNBERG, O., *Object Relations Theory and Clinical Psychoanalysis*, Jason Aronson, New York, 1976.

KHAN, M. M. R., 'The Concept of Cumulative Trauma' (1963), repr. in *The Privacy of Self*, Hogarth Press, London, 1974.

KING, P. H. M., and STEINER, R., *The Freud/Klein Controversies in the British Psycho-Analytical Society 1941–5*, Routledge, London, 1990.

KLEIN, MELANIE, *The Psycho-Analysis of Children*, Hogarth Press, London, 1932.

KLEIN, MELANIE, *Contributions to Psycho-Analysis*, Hogarth Press, London, 1948.

KLEIN, MELANIE, 'Notes on Some Schizoid Mechanisms', in M. Klein et al. (eds.), *Developments in Psychoanalysis*, Hogarth Press, London, 1952.

KLEIN, MELANIE, *Envy and Gratitude*, Tavistock Publications, London, 1957.

KOFF, R. H., 'A Definition of Identification', *Int. J. Psycho-Anal.* (1961), 42, pp. 362–70.

KOHON, G. (ed.), *The British School of Psychoanalysis: The Independent Tradition*, Free Association Books, London, 1986.

KOHUT, H., 'Thoughts on Narcissism and Narcissistic Rage' (1972), repr. in H. Kohut, *The Search for the Self*, International Universities Press, New York, 1978.

KOHUT, H., and WOLF, E. S., 'The Disorders of the Self and Their Treatment: an Outline', *Int. J. Psycho-Anal.* (1978), 59, pp. 413–25.

KUBIE, L. S., *Neurotic Distortion of the Creative Process*, University of Kansas Press, 1958.

LAING, R. D., *The Divided Self*, Tavistock Publications, London, 1960.

LAING, R. D., *The Self and Others*, Tavistock Publications, London, 1961.

LAING, R. D., *The Politics of Experience*, Penguin Books, Harmondsworth, 1967.

LAKOFF, R. T., and COYNE, J. C., *Father Knows Best: The Use and Abuse of Power in Freud's Case of 'Dora'*, Teacher's College Press, 1993.

LANGER, SUSANNE K., *Philosophy in a New Key*, Harvard University Press, 1951.

LAPLANCHE, J., and PONTALIS, J.-B., *Vocabulaire de la Psychanalyse*, Presses Universitaires de Paris, 1967.

Larousse Encyclopedia of Mythology, Batchworth, London, 1959.

LEVEY, H. B., 'A Critique of the Theory of Sublimation', *Psychiatry* (1939), 2, pp. 239–70.

LEWIN, B. D., 'Sleep, the Mouth and the Dream Screen', *Psychoanal. Quart.* (1946), 15, pp. 419–34.

LEWIN, B. D., *The Psychoanalysis of Elation*, Hogarth Press, London, 1951.

LIDZ, T., *The Family and Human Adaptation*, Hogarth Press, London, 1964.

LITTLE, MARGARET, 'Counter-Transference and the Patient's Response to It', *Int. J. Psycho-Anal.* (1951), 32, pp. 32–40.

LORENZ, K., *On Aggression*, Methuen, London, 1966.

LORENZ, MARIA, 'Language as Expressive Behaviour', *Arch. Neurol. Psychiat.* (1953), 70, pp. 277–85.

LORENZ, MARIA, and COBB, S., 'Language Behaviour in Psychoneurotic Patients', *Arch. Neurol. Psychiat.* (1953), 69, pp. 684–94.

LOTHANE, Z., *In Defence of Schreber*, Analytic Press, Hillsdale, N.J., 1992.

LYND, HELEN MERRELL, *On Shame and the Search for Identity*, Routledge & Kegan Paul, London, 1958.

MCDOUGALL, W., *An Introduction to Social Psychology* (1908), 22nd edition, Methuen, London, 1931.

MAHLER, M. S., and FURER, M., *On Human Symbiosis and the Vicissitudes of Individuation*, International Universities Press, New York, 1968.

MAHLER, M. S., PINE, F., and BERGMAN, A., *The Psychological Birth of the Human Infant*, Basic Books, New York, 1975.

MALAN, D. H., *A Study of Brief Psychotherapy*, Tavistock Publications, London, 1963.

MASSON, J. M., *The Assault on Truth*, Farrar, Strauss & Giroux, New York, 1984.

MAY, R., *Psychology and the Human Dilemma*, Van Nostrand, Princeton, N.J., 1967.

MEAD, MARGARET, *Sex and Temperament in Three Primitive Societies*, Routledge & Kegan Paul, London, 1935.

MEAD, MARGARET, *Male and Female*, Gollancz, London, 1950.

'MEDICA' [JOAN MALLESON], *Any Wife or Any Husband*, 2nd edition, Heinemann, London, 1955.

NIEDERLAND, W. G., *The Schreber Case: Psychoanalytic Profile of a Paranoid Personality. An Expanded Edition*, Analytic Press, Hillsdale, N.J., 1984.

OBHOLZER, KARIN, *The Wolf-Man Sixty Years Later*, Routledge & Kegan Paul, London, 1982.

OSWALD, I., *Sleep*, Penguin Books, Harmondsworth, 1966.

Oxford English Dictionary, Clarendon Press, Oxford, 1933.

PAYNE, SYLVIA, 'A Conception of Femininity', *Brit. J. Med. Psych.* (1935), 15, pp. 18–33.

PIERS, G., and SINGER, M., *Shame and Guilt*, C. C. Thomas, Springfield, Ill., 1953.

RADO, S., 'The Psychoanalysis of Pharmacothymia', *Psychoanal. Quart.* (1933), 2, pp. 1–23.

RANK, O., *The Trauma of Birth* (1924), English trans., Kegan Paul, London, 1929.

RAPAPORT, D., *Organization and Pathology of Thought*, Columbia University Press, 1951.

RAPAPORT, D., 'On the Psycho-Analytic Theory of Affects', *Int. J. Psycho-Anal.* (1953), 34, pp. 177–98.

Bibliography

RAYNER, E., *The Independent Mind in British Psychoanlaysis*, Free Association Books, London, 1990.

RIVIERE, JOAN, 'The Unconscious Phantasy of an Inner World Reflected in Examples from Literature', in M. Klein et al., *New Directions in Psychoanalysis*, Tavistock Publications, London, 1955.

ROSENBERG, ELIZABETH, 'Anxiety and the Capacity to Bear It', *Int. J. Psycho-Anal.* (1949), 30, pp. 1–12.

RUDNYTSKY, P. L., *The Psychoanalytic Vocation*, Yale University Press, 1991.

RYCROFT, C., 'A Contribution to the Study of the Dream Screen' (1951), in *Imagination and Reality*, Hogarth Press, London, 1968; repr. Karnac, London, 1987.

RYCROFT, C., 'On Idealization, Illusion and Catastrophic Disillusion' (1955), in *Imagination and Reality*, Hogarth Press, London, 1968; repr. Karnac, London, 1987.

RYCROFT, C., 'Symbolism and Its Relation to the Primary and Secondary Processes' (1956), in *Imagination and Reality*, Hogarth Press, London, 1968; repr. Karnac, London, 1987.

RYCROFT, C., 'The Function of Words in the Psychoanalytical Situation' (1958), in *Imagination and Reality*, Hogarth Press, London, 1968; repr. Karnac, London, 1987.

RYCROFT, C., 'Beyond the Reality Principle' (1962), in *Imagination and Reality*, Hogarth Press, London, 1968; repr. Karnac, London, 1987.

RYCROFT, C., 'Causes and Meaning' (1966), in *Psychoanalysis and Beyond*, Hogarth Press, London, 1985; repr. 1991.

RYCROFT, C., *Anxiety and Neurosis*, Allen Lane The Penguin Press, London, 1968; repr. Karnac, London, 1988.

RYCROFT, C., 'Not So Much a Treatment, More a Way of Life' (1971), in *Psychoanalysis and Beyond*, Hogarth Press, London, 1985; repr. 1991.

RYCROFT, C., 'Masson's Assault on Freud' (1984), in *Viewpoints*, Hogarth Press, London, 1991.

RYCROFT, C., 'The Wound and the Bow' (1989), in *Viewpoints*, Hogarth Press, London, 1991.

RYCROFT, C., *The Innocence of Dreams*, Hogarth Press, London, 1991.

SAMUELS, A., SHORTER, B., and PLAUT, F., *A Critical Dictionary of Jungian Analysis*, Routledge & Kegan Paul, London, 1986.

SARTRE, J.-P., *Being and Nothingness*, Philosophical Library, New York, 1956.

SCHAFER, R., *A New Language for Psychoanalysis*, Yale University Press, 1976.

SCHATZMAN, M., *Soul Murder: Persecution in the Family*, Allen Lane The Penguin Press, London, 1973.

SCHOFIELD, W., *Psychotherapy: The Purchase of Friendship*, Prentice-Hall, Englewood Cliffs, N.J., 1964.

SCHUR, M., 'Some Additional "Day Residues" of the "Dream Specimen of Psychoanalysis"', in R. M. Lowenstein et al. (eds.), *Psychoanalysis – A General Psychology*, International Universities Press, New York, 1966.

SCHUR, M., *Freud: Living and Dying*, International Universities Press, New York, 1972.

SEARLES, H., *The Non-Human Environment in Schizophrenia*, International Universities Press, New York, 1960.

SEARLES, H., *Collected Papers on Schizophrenia*, Hogarth Press, London, 1965.

SEGAL, HANNA, 'Notes on Symbol Formation', *Int. J. Psycho-Anal.* (1957), 38, pp. 391–7.

SEGAL, HANNA, *Introduction to the Work of Melanie Klein*, Heinemann Medical Books, London, 1964.

SHARPE, ELLA, *Dream Analysis*, Hogarth Press, London, 1937.

SHARPE, ELLA, *Collected Papers on Psycho-Analysis*, Hogarth Press, London, 1950.

SHENGOLD, L., *Soul Murder: The Effects of Childhood Abuse and Deprivation*, Yale University Press, 1989.

SLAVIN, M. O., and KRIEGMAN, D., *The Adaptive Design of the Human Psyche*, Guilford Press, New York and London, 1992.

SPITZ, R., 'Anaclitic Depression', *Psychoanal. Study of the Child* (1946), 2, pp. 313–42.

SPITZ, R., *A Genetic Field Theory of Ego Formation*, International Universities Press, New York, 1959.

STEELE, R.S., *Freud and Jung: Conflicts of Interpretation*, Routledge & Kegan Paul, London, 1982.

STENGEL, E., *Suicide and Attempted Suicide*, Penguin Books, Harmondsworth, 1964.

Bibliography

STERBA, R., 'The Fate of the Ego in Analytic Therapy', *Int. J. Psycho-Anal.* (1934), 15, pp. 117–26.

STERN, D., *The Interpersonal World of the Infant*, Basic Books, New York, 1985.

STOLLER, R. J., *Presentations of Gender*, Yale University Press, 1985.

STORR, A., *The Integrity of the Personality*, Heinemann, London, 1960; repr. Oxford University Press, 1992.

STORR, A., *Jung*, Fontana Modern Masters, London, 1973.

STORR, A. (ed.), *Jung: Selected Writings*, Fontana, London, 1983.

STRACHEY, J., 'The Nature of the Therapeutic Action of Psycho-Analysis', *Int. J. Psycho-Anal.* (1934), 15, pp. 127–59.

SUTTIE, I. D., *The Origins of Love and Hate* (1935), Penguin Books, Harmondsworth, 1960.

SZASZ, T., *The Myth of Mental Illness*, Secker & Warburg, London, 1962.

TREVARTHEN, C., 'Playing into Reality: Conversations with the Infant Communicator', *Winnicott Studies* (1993), No. 7, pp. 67–84.

TUSTIN, FRANCES, *Autism and Childhood Psychosis*, Hogarth Press, London, 1972.

VEITH, ILZA, *Hysteria: The History of a Disease*, University of Chicago Press, 1965.

WHEELIS, A., *The Quest for Identity*, Gollancz, London, 1959; W. W. Norton, New York, 1958.

WINNICOTT, D. W., *Collected Papers*, Tavistock Publications, London, 1958.

WINNICOTT, D. W., *Playing and Reality*, Tavistock Publications, London, 1971.

WISDOM, J. O., 'A Methodological Approach to the Problem of Hysteria', *Int. J. Psycho-Anal.* (1961), 43, pp. 224–37.

WURMSER, L., *The Mask of Shame*, Johns Hopkins University Press, 1981.

WYNNE, L. C., et al., 'Pseudo-Mutuality in the Family Relations of Schizophrenics', *Psychiatry* (1958), 21, pp. 205–20.

YERUSHALMI, Y. H., *Freud's Moses: Judaism Terminable and Interminable*, Yale University Press, 1991.

READ MORE IN PENGUIN

In every corner of the world, on every subject under the sun, Penguin represents quality and variety – the very best in publishing today.

For complete information about books available from Penguin – including Puffins, Penguin Classics and Arkana – and how to order them, write to us at the appropriate address below. Please note that for copyright reasons the selection of books varies from country to country.

In the United Kingdom: Please write to *Dept. EP, Penguin Books Ltd, Bath Road, Harmondsworth, West Drayton, Middlesex UB7 0DA*

In the United States: Please write to *Consumer Sales, Penguin USA, P.O. Box 999, Dept. 17109, Bergenfield, New Jersey 07621-0120*. VISA and MasterCard holders call 1-800-253-6476 to order Penguin titles

In Canada: Please write to *Penguin Books Canada Ltd, 10 Alcorn Avenue, Suite 300, Toronto, Ontario M4V 3B2*

In Australia: Please write to *Penguin Books Australia Ltd, P.O. Box 257, Ringwood, Victoria 3134*

In New Zealand: Please write to *Penguin Books (NZ) Ltd, Private Bag 102902, North Shore Mail Centre, Auckland 10*

In India: Please write to *Penguin Books India Pvt Ltd, 706 Eros Apartments, 56 Nehru Place, New Delhi 110 019*

In the Netherlands: Please write to *Penguin Books Netherlands bv, Postbus 3507, NL-1001 AH Amsterdam*

In Germany: Please write to *Penguin Books Deutschland GmbH, Metzlerstrasse 26, 60594 Frankfurt am Main*

In Spain: Please write to *Penguin Books S. A., Bravo Murillo 19, 1° B, 28015 Madrid*

In Italy: Please write to *Penguin Italia s.r.l., Via Felice Casati 20, I–20124 Milano*

In France: Please write to *Penguin France S. A., 17 rue Lejeune, F–31000 Toulouse*

In Japan: Please write to *Penguin Books Japan, Ishikiribashi Building, 2–5–4, Suido, Bunkyo-ku, Tokyo 112*

In South Africa: Please write to *Longman Penguin Southern Africa (Pty) Ltd, Private Bag X08, Bertsham 2013*

READ MORE IN PENGUIN

POLITICS AND SOCIAL SCIENCES

Accountable to None Simon Jenkins

'An important book, because it brings together, with an insider's authority and anecdotage, both a narrative of domestic Thatcherism and a polemic against its pretensions ... an indispensable guide to the corruptions of power and language which have sustained the illusion that Thatcherism was an attack on "government"' – *Guardian*

The Feminine Mystique Betty Friedan

'A brilliantly researched, passionately argued book – a time bomb flung into the Mom-and-Apple-Pie image ... Out of the debris of that shattered ideal, the Women's Liberation Movement was born' – Ann Leslie

The New Untouchables Nigel Harris

Misrepresented in politics and in the media, immigration is seen as a serious problem by the vast majority of people. In this ground-breaking book, Nigel Harris draws on a mass of evidence to challenge existing assumptions and examines migration as a response to changes in the world economy.

Political Ideas Edited by David Thomson

From Machiavelli to Marx – a stimulating and informative introduction to the last 500 years of European political thinkers and political thought.

Structural Anthropology Volumes 1–2 Claude Lévi-Strauss

'That the complex ensemble of Lévi-Strauss's achievement ... is one of the most original and intellectually exciting of the present age seems undeniable. No one seriously interested in language or literature, in sociology or psychology, can afford to ignore it' – George Steiner

Invitation to Sociology Peter L. Berger

Without belittling its scientific procedures Professor Berger stresses the humanistic affinity of sociology with history and philosophy. It is a discipline which encourages a fuller awareness of the human world ... with the purpose of bettering it.

READ MORE IN PENGUIN

POLITICS AND SOCIAL SCIENCES

Conservatism   Ted Honderich

'It offers a powerful critique of the major beliefs of modern con-
servatism, and shows how much a rigorous philosopher can contribute to
understanding the fashionable but deeply ruinous absurdities of his times'
– *New Statesman & Society*

Ruling Britannia   Andrew Marr

'This book will be resented by many of Marr's professional colleagues, for
he goes where none of us has dared. He lifts his eyes, and ours ...
Everyone with a serious interest in how we might be governed should read
it' – *Sunday Telegraph*

Bricks of Shame: Britain's Prisons   Vivien Stern

'Her well-researched book presents a chillingly realistic picture of the
British sytstem and lucid argument for changes which could and should be
made before a degrading and explosive situation deteriorates still further'
– *Sunday Times*

Killing Rage: Ending Racism   bell hooks

Addressing race and racism in American society from a black and a
feminist standpoint, bell hooks covers a broad spectrum of issues. In the
title essay she writes about the 'killing rage' – the intense anger caused
by everyday instances of racism – finding in that rage a positive inner
strength to create productive change.

'Just like a Girl'   Sue Sharpe
How Girls Learn to be Women

Sue Sharpe's unprecedented research and analysis of the attitudes and
hopes of teenage girls from four London schools has become a classic of
its kind. This new edition focuses on girls in the nineties – some of whom
could even be the daughters of the teenagers she interviewed in the
seventies – and represents their views and ideas on education, work,
marriage, gender roles, feminism and women's rights.

READ MORE IN PENGUIN

PHILOSOPHY

Values of Art   Malcolm Budd

'Budd is a first-rate thinker ... He brings to aesthetics formidable gifts of precision, far-sightedness and argument, together with a wide philosophical knowledge and a sincere belief in the importance of art' – *The Times*

Montaigne and Melancholy   M. A. Screech

'A sensitive probe into how Montaigne resolved for himself the age-old ambiguities of melancholia and, in doing so, spoke of what he called the "human condition"' – *London Review of Books*

Labyrinths of Reason   William Poundstone

'The world and what is in it, even what people say to you, will not seem the same after plunging into *Labyrinths of Reason* ... He holds up the deepest philosophical questions for scrutiny and examines their relation to reality in a way that irresistibly sweeps readers on' – *New Scientist*

Metaphysics as a Guide to Morals   Iris Murdoch

'This is philosophy dragged from the cloister, dusted down and made freshly relevant to suffering and egoism, death and religious ecstasy ... and how we feel compassion for others' – *Guardian*

The Penguin Dictionary of Philosophy   Edited by Thomas Mautner

This new dictionary encompasses all aspects of Western philosophy from 600 BC to the present day. With contributions from over a hundred leading philosophers, and including cross-references and unique usage notes, this dictionary will prove the ideal reference for any student or teacher of philosophy as well as for all those with a general interest in the subject.

Russian Thinkers   Isaiah Berlin

As one of the most outstanding liberal intellects of this century, the author brings to his portraits of Russian thinkers a unique perception of the social and political circumstances that produced men such as Herzen, Bakunin, Turgenev, Belinsky and Tolstoy.

READ MORE IN PENGUIN

LANGUAGE/LINGUISTICS

Sociolinguistics Peter Trudgill

Women speak 'better' English than men. The Eskimo language has several words for snow. 1001 factors influence the way we speak. Professor Trudgill draws on languages from Afrikaans to Yiddish to illuminate this fascinating topic and provide a painless introduction to sociolinguistics.

Bad Language Lars-Gunnar Andersson and Peter Trudgill

As this witty and incisive book makes clear, the prophets of gloom who claim that our language is getting worse are guided by emotion far more than by hard facts. The real truth, as Andersson and Trudgill illuminate in fascinating detail, is that change has always been inherent in language.

Multilingualism John Edwards

This superb survey explores all the contentious topics about language: links between gender and speech styles, and the attitudes, aptitudes and brains of bilinguals. In its wit, scholarship and rich supply of unusual facts, *Multilingualism* is a book of compelling interest to anyone who cares about the role of language in society.

Grammar Frank Palmer

In modern linguistics grammar means far more than cases, tenses and declensions – it means precise and scientific description of the structure of language. This concise guide takes the reader simply and clearly through the concepts of traditional grammar, morphology, sentence structure and transformational-generative grammar.

Longman Guide to English Usage
Sidney Greenbaum and Janet Whitcut

Containing 5000 entries compiled by leading authorities on modern English, this invaluable reference work clarifies every kind of usage problem, giving expert advice on points of grammar, meaning, style, spelling, pronunciation and punctuation.

READ MORE IN PENGUIN

READ MORE IN PENGUIN

PSYCHOLOGY

Private Myths: Dreams and Dreaming   Anthony Stevens

'Its case for dreaming as something more universally significant than a tour across our personal playgrounds of guilt and misery is eloquently persuasive ... [a] hugely absorbing study – its surface crisscrossed with innumerable avenues into science, anthropology and religion' – *Spectator*

Child Care and the Growth of Love   John Bowlby

His classic 'summary of evidence of the effects upon children of lack of personal attention ... presents to administrators, social workers, teachers and doctors a reminder of the significance of the family' – *The Times*

Recollections and Reflections   Bruno Bettelheim

'A powerful thread runs through Bettelheim's message: his profound belief in the dignity of man, and the importance of seeing and judging other people from their own point of view' – *Independent*. 'These memoirs of a wise old child, candid, evocative, heart-warming, suggest there is hope yet for humanity' – *Evening Standard*

Female Perversions   Louise J. Kaplan

'If you can't have love, what do you get? Perversion, be it mild or severe: shopping, seduction, anorexia or self-mutilation. Kaplan charts both Madame Bovary's "perverse performance" and the more general paths to female self-destruction with a grace, determination and intellectual firmness rare in the self-discovery trade. A most remarkable book' – Fay Weldon

The Social Psychology of Leisure   Michael Argyle

Michael Argyle explores our motivation in our leisure activities, examines the influence of age, class and gender and considers where we are most likely to find health, happiness, a sense of achievement and other such benefits. His conclusions challenge much received wisdom about human nature and illuminate the sources of our deepest pleasures.

READ MORE IN PENGUIN

PSYCHOLOGY

Psychoanalysis and Feminism   Juliet Mitchell

'Juliet Mitchell has risked accusations of apostasy from her fellow feminists. Her book not only challenges orthodox feminism, however; it defies the conventions of social thought in the English-speaking countries ... a brave and important book' – *New York Review of Books*

The Divided Self   R. D. Laing

'A study that makes all other works I have read on schizophrenia seem fragmentary ... The author brings, through his vision and perception, that particular touch of genius which causes one to say, "Yes, I have always known that, why have I never thought of it before?"' – *Journal of Analytical Psychology*

Teach Yourself to Think   Edward de Bono

Edward de Bono's masterly book offers a structure that broadens our ability to respond to and cope with a vast range of situations. *Teach Yourself to Think* is software for the brain, turning it into a successful thinking mechanism, and, as such, will prove of immense value to us all.

Cultivating Intuition   Peter Lomas

Psychoanalytic psychotherapy is a particular kind of conversation, a shared project and process in which both participants can express their individuality and negotiate their rights. Here Peter Lomas explores the aims and qualities of that conversation between therapist and patient.

The Care of the Self   Michel Foucault
The History of Sexuality Volume 3

Foucault examines the transformation of sexual discourse from the Hellenistic to the Roman world in an inquiry which 'bristles with provocative insights into the tangled liaison of sex and self' – *The Times Higher Education Supplement*

Mothering Psychoanalysis   Janet Sayers

'An important book ... records the immense contribution to psychoanalysis made by its founding mothers' – *Sunday Times*